Obote

Obote

A political biography

Kenneth Ingham

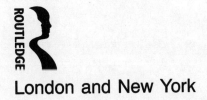

London and New York

First published 1994
by Routledge
11 New Fetter Lane, London EC4P 4EE

Simultaneously published in the USA and Canada
by Routledge
29 West 35th Street, New York, NY 10001

© 1994 Kenneth Ingham

Typeset in Baskerville by Intype, London

Printed and bound in Great Britain by T. J. Press (Padstow) Ltd, Padstow, Cornwall

Printed on acid free paper

British Library Cataloguing in Publication Data

A catalogue record for this book is available from the British Library

Library of Congress Cataloging in Publication Data has been applied for

ISBN 0–415–05342–0

Contents

Preface

I first encountered Milton Obote in 1958 when he became a member of the Uganda Legislative Council. I was not immediately impressed by him. His manner seemed to be deliberately abrasive although his early speeches seemed merely to echo what had already been said more effectively by other African elected members. Only later did I realize that his apparent aggressiveness was due to an intense mixture of sincerity and nervousness.

It was when we travelled round Uganda as members of a constitutional committee charged with making recommendations which might lead to self-government that I began to appreciate Obote's clear insight into the problems facing his country and his calm appraisal of the possible ways forward. This was all the more impressive since most other prominent Ugandan politicians were in a state of considerable tension because of the friction that had developed between the kingdom of Buganda and the Protectorate administration, friction which appeared to be frustrating unnecessarily the move towards self-determination. It was as a result of the conversations I had with Obote and other leading Africans during that period that I joined the Uganda Peoples' Congress. This was a party that had been recently formed by the amalgamation of a part of the older Uganda National Congress and the leaders of what was essentially a parliamentary party comprising most of the elected African members of the legislative council from outside the kingdom of Buganda. I was the first European to take that step and I was never an active member of the party. My joining it was intended mainly as an indication of my support for what seemed to me to be the most constructive effort being made at that time to unite Uganda in preparation for independence.

I left Uganda just before the country became independent. The difficulties that would have to be overcome could not be concealed by the widespread euphoria which followed hard on the heels of the departing colonial administration. But Obote's awareness of and sympathy for the differences of opinion that persisted in Uganda, and his willingness to try to negotiate a way through them, seemed to offer at least the possibility of success, given a happily buoyant economy.

I never lost my interest in nor my affection for Uganda. I watched with satisfaction the growing material prosperity of the country, but was increasingly worried by the undercurrent of political animosity that was threatening to erode its foundations. The conflict between the king-dom of Buganda and the Ugandan Government, the breakup of the kingdom, followed by the overthrow of the Ugandan Government, seemed to have put an end to all the high hopes there had been of Uganda's becoming a prosperous, democratic nation.

I spent a few months in Uganda during President Amin's period of office and was horrified by the damage that was being done to the economy and, even more important, to the morale of the people. Every-where there was fear and uncertainty about the future. There was an intense desire to return to the days of Obote, even among many of those who had rejoiced at his overthrow. Yet, when he did return, ostensibly at least with the hope of establishing new and friendly relations with those he had previously alienated, criticism soon built up again. Violent accu-sations were made against him and after a long and increasingly bitter civil war he was overthrown by another military coup.

Such an ending to a career that had been founded upon a desire for understanding among the diverse peoples of Uganda seemed to justify some investigation and I was anxious to undertake it. It was not an easy task. Feelings still run high. Opinions are easier to come by than hard evidence. Many are willing to express a view or to give their account of events. Few wish to have those views attributed to them if they happen to be critical of the present regime. This is understandable, given the sufferings to which Ugandans have been subjected, but it does not make for a heavily footnoted story, and anything one writes is open to accu-sations of bias or of special pleading. I am conscious of that, yet I think the effort worthwhile. The longer one waits before an attempt is made to write the story of Uganda's first quarter-century of independence, the more the myths and legends will accumulate, rendering any interpretation of those years increasingly tentative.

I am extremely grateful to the many people who have talked with me about this book, and I must express my deep appreciation of the financial assistance given by the British Academy, which enabled me to hold lengthy conversations with Dr. Obote and to meet others in East Africa who vouchsafed both useful information and opinions. I would not have undertaken to write the book without the consent of Obote himself, and I was considerably moved by the frankness with which he responded to my questions, many of them arising from the criticisms levelled against him by his opponents and no less painful in consequence. But I alone am responsible for the views the book contains. I must also thank Simon

Godden of the Department of Geography in the University of Bristol for preparing the map of Uganda which I have included in the book, and the *Sunday Times* Picture Library for permission to reproduce its photograph of Obote.

Kenneth Ingham, 1993

Abbreviations

Democratic Party	DP
East African Community	EAC
General Service Unit	GSU
Kabaka Yekka (the 'Kabaka Alone' movement)	KY
National Consultative Council	NCC
Nairobi District African Congress	NDAC
National Resistance Army	NRA
National Resistance Movement	NRM
Organisation of African Unity	OAU
Uganda Freedom Movement	UFM
Uganda National Congress	UNC
Uganda National Liberation Army	UNLA
Uganda National Liberation Front	UNLF
Uganda National Movement	UNM
Uganda People's Congress	UPC
Uganda Patriotic Movement	UPM
Uganda People's Union	UPU

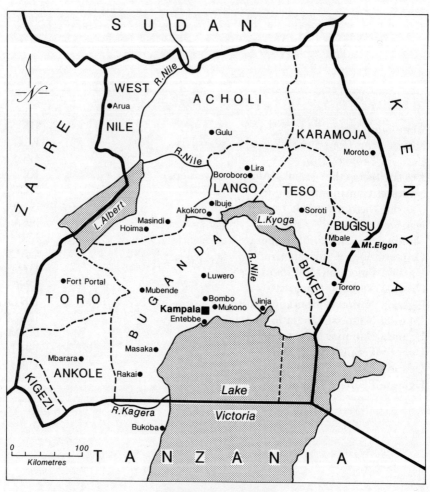

UGANDA 1962

Chapter 1

Introduction

In the *Independent* newspaper of 27 June 1992 a journalist who had recently visited Uganda wrote:

> The myth is that Idi Amin destroyed Uganda. He certainly began the slide and killed his personal enemies spectacularly, but for the ordinary people the Amin years were good years, the coffee price was high and the army was disciplined. ... Time and again on this visit people told me that the really bad times began with the Tanzanian invasion in 1979, which drove out Amin. The troops raped and looted and then restored Obote, beginning the years of genocide in which 300,000 people, mostly peasants, were systematically killed by Obote's army.

For more than a decade, this theme has been gradually developed by Obote's opponents. It appears to have gained credence outside Uganda, even among some who, if they were to cast back their minds to the 1970s, would recall the atrocities perpetrated by Amin's 'disciplined' army, the collapse of the country's hitherto buoyant economy, the 'quatermass' growth of a black market in every conceivable commodity, the flight of the intelligentsia – or such of them as escaped Amin's death squads – and the cloud of fear which hung over the 'ordinary people' who lived near enough to the roads to be at the mercy of Amin's armed predators. They might, too, if they looked up the newspapers of 1979, read that the Tanzanian invaders were greeted with joy and relief by the suffering people of Uganda, and that they did not 'restore Obote' but instead prepared the way for the presidency of Yusufu Lule, who took office in April 1979. Any raping or looting done by the invaders in the course of driving out Amin was performed before ever Obote returned to Uganda in May 1980. This was over thirteen months after Lule became president and eleven months after Amin's defeated rabble had crossed the borders into Kenya or the Sudan. As to the '300,000 people systematically killed by Obote's army' – a conservative estimate according to some sources – the figures are indeed an estimate, and the attribution of those deaths exclusively to Obote's army contradicts many of the newspaper reports of the time.

On what evidence was the journalist's report based? How extensively did he travel in Uganda before forming his opinions? From the information contained in his article he appears to have restricted his travels to the former kingdom of Buganda, less than a quarter of the total area of the country, and his informants all appear to have been natives of the former kingdom, less than a third of the total population. Without ascribing bias to those with whom he spoke, is it not rash to suggest that the views of one section of the people, located in one part of the country, reflect those of the whole population?

Misrepresentation, the bane of all but the most banal of politicians, beset Apolo Milton Obote to an unwonted degree throughout most of his public life. In the days before independence, his anti-colonialism, like that of most African leaders of that time, was believed by the colonial authorities to be a symptom of his communist sympathies. When, as president of Uganda in the late 1960s, he tried to assert a greater measure of control over the country's economy by imposing limited restraints upon foreign bankers and businessmen, he was deemed by the British government of the day to have dangerous, left-wing tendencies. That view was reinforced by his forceful criticism of the proposed sale of British arms to the South African government. During his second presidency, the accusations levelled against him grew rapidly in number and in virulence. With regard to one of them, it should be noted that 'Obote's army', upon which he was claimed to have relied for his authority and upon which has been heaped so much opprobrium, was recruited and officered during the time of his two predecessors as president, Lule and Godfrey Binaisa. Obote's main contributions to it were a training scheme under the direction of a commonwealth military team and later of a British army squad, and a not wholly effectual attempt to bring to trial any soldiers allegedly guilty of actions against the public.

Even his becoming president a second time was attributed to chicanery on the part of one of his supporters. The same *Independent* newspaper contained an obituary notice of Paulo Muwanga on 6 April 1991 in which it was stated that:

> As former head of state [of Uganda] in December 1980, Muwanga rigged the first post-Amin election, ensuring the defeat of the legitimate winners, the Catholic-backed Democratic Party, the victory of Milton Obote and the eruption of a bloody civil war.

This was written despite the report of a commonwealth observer team which, having noted a number of irregularities prior to the election, nevertheless stated that the overall conduct of the elections themselves had been fair and that the outcome probably represented the views of the people of Uganda. While it is also true that a bloody civil war was to follow, there was certainly no inevitability about it. Neither Obote nor the 'legitimate winner', the Democratic Party, initiated it, or initially wanted it, whatever role either may have played in it at a later date.

Why has Obote been subjected to such vilification by organs of opinion which, in general, are looked upon as trustworthy and restrained? Was opinion inside Uganda overwhelmingly against him? Was his removal from office by military force, on two occasions, in any way justified? Did he pursue divisive, tribalist policies as has been claimed? Did he undertake a campaign of genocide against the people of Buganda? Was his second presidency more oppressive than the regime of Idi Amin which preceded it? Why did what was regularly referred to in the 1930s as 'happy Uganda' become riddled with strife and corruption? Little in history is inevitable, but if one is to understand Uganda one must study its history. Obote has undoubtedly left his mark on that history, but his career was certainly the product of it.

The career of Apolo Milton Obote illustrates, with a number of idiosyncratic exceptions, the dilemma of African leaders who, since their countries achieved independence, have struggled to mould a diversity of peoples, casually linked together by the vagaries of colonial enterprise, into viable political and economic units. To date, his story falls into five parts: his boyhood and apprenticeship in politics, his first term of office as prime minister and then as president, his overthrow and his first period in exile, his return as president for a second term and now his second time in exile.

BOYHOOD AND POLITICAL APPRENTICESHIP

The circumstances of Obote's boyhood were similar to those of many other young people growing up in Uganda in the second quarter of the twentieth century. The grandson of a minor chief and son of a local government official he was exposed, like other future African leaders, both to the traditional claims of kinship and the problems of creating a new form of administration based upon practices to which his own people were unaccustomed. From an early age his loyalties, rooted in his extended family, were steadily widened to embrace the whole of Uganda. His education followed the same course. Beginning in the local primary school he moved, stage by stage, beyond the confines of his own district and province until he eventually reached the highest peak of the protectorate's educational system, extending his knowledge and his interests on the way. Both at home and in school and college he learned the virtues of tenacity and diplomacy in dealing with his fellows. He grew to appreciate the wider outlook provided by his people's association with a colonial power. He grew, too, to recognize the restrictions imposed by subordination to that same power and he personally endured the frustration of having the opportunity to study in England withdrawn by the Protectorate administration.

Obote's introduction to politics came, somewhat indirectly, from that same frustration. Although he never experienced life in prison, which seemed to guarantee rapid political advancement for a number of other future African leaders, the feeling of resentment against the Protectorate administration for having deprived him of the opportunity to study in England later expanded to embrace the restrictions which, he believed, were preventing the people of Uganda from taking responsibility for their own lives. It was this belief which made him a powerful critic of British administration, capable of playing an important role in leading his country to independence.

That, however, was ten years ahead. Forced, in the meantime, to seek work which was scarcely commensurate with his potential, Obote went to Kenya and there encountered revolt against the colonial power in a vivid form. The situation in Uganda was far less tense than in Kenya, but on his return to his own country after several years' absence he immediately came up against the brusque paternalism of British administration which, after his experience in Kenya, led him to respond by becoming a politician in order to publicize his feelings.

Elected by his own district to membership of the Uganda Legislative Council he was immediately brought into contact with the problem which, in the author's view, made the situation in Uganda fundamentally different from that in other African dependencies. Because of the historical development of the Protectorate there was, in its centre, a powerful society, distinct in culture and organization from the other peoples of the Protectorate, and one which believed itself superior to them, both from inner conviction and from its historical role as a vital partner of the British in extending the Protectorate over the rest of the country. Other colonial dependencies had their quota of differing cultures, of monarchical societies and of loosely-knit groups of clans. But none had so potent and preponderant a group at the very heart of the country, the focal point of the country's communications and the centre of its commercial life.

To incorporate such a society into a democratic, independent Uganda was a formidable task and one which, I argue, Obote alone of Uganda's future leaders attempted to tackle pragmatically, almost from the first days of his emergence on the political scene. But the problem created a situation which again was unique to Uganda. It meant that it was virtually impossible for any one person to be accepted as the undisputed leader of the country. It meant, too, that while other newly-independent African countries could experience a vicarious sense of unity through undivided allegiance to one charismatic champion, Uganda was divided from the outset, with the cracks papered over by an uneasy if well-intentioned alliance.

PRIME MINISTER AND PRESIDENT

Like many other African leaders, Obote had given little thought to what would happen after independence. This was not immediately a serious issue for him. Unlike many other former colonial dependencies Uganda's economy had always been sound. Food had been plentiful, and the British administrators had encouraged the growth of export crops which provided foreign exchange and the capital for a range of development programmes. Those benefits were carried over and even increased in the first years after independence. The same commercial superstructure remained. Indians and a handful of Europeans were primarily responsible for the country's trade. Obote, as prime minister, was content to leave things like that because he had more pressing political problems to deal with.

These were not of an ideological character. Although he admired Nkrumah and hoped for co-operation between African states, he believed that to get Uganda's affairs in working order was a sufficient task for the foreseable future. He was prepared for some form of closer relationship with his East African neighbours and would even have welcomed it, but there was little support for such a move within Uganda itself. Nor was he wedded to any political dogma regarding the conduct of affairs in his own country. The problems that beset him were not essentially of his own making. They were the product of Uganda's history.

Although independence had been achieved and Obote himself had assumed office as a result of an agreement with the centrally located kingdom of Buganda, it almost immediately became clear that an authoritarian, monarchical system of government was an uneasy component of what set out to be a democratic country. Friction was inevitable, however well-intentioned either party might be. That friction led to open conflict and, as in most other African countries, the group that controlled the army triumphed. At that stage, the bulk of the army was loyal to Obote. With the monarchy overthrown the dismemberment of the kingdom followed, converting the hostility of the inhabitants of the kingdom into open animosity. The disturbed state of Buganda meant that the anticipated constitutional proceedings were disrupted. Elections, both to the legislature and the presidency, were repeatedly postponed and became the grounds for further accusations of authoritarianism against Obote. Yet he himself was anxious to demonstrate, through the ballot box, the strength of the following he was confident he retained in the country at large.

With all these problems, Obote still was able to play a significant role in African and commonwealth affairs. Although never a dominant figure like Nkrumah or Nyerere, his sound common sense won him the respect not only of other African leaders but also of a number of British prime ministers. On one prime minister, Edward Heath, he made a less satisfactory impression, mainly because he loyally stood by his friends, Nyerere and Kaunda, when they denounced Britain's proposal to sell arms to South Africa. That meant that when he faced his greatest moment of crisis he could hope for no support from Britain.

Having declared himself president and Uganda a republic, Obote turned his attention at last to the economy. Although never a doctrinaire socialist he had long believed that, in a country woefully lacking in indigenous industrial or commercial experience, some form of state intervention would be necessary if the economy were not to remain indefinitely in the hands of non-native Ugandans. He was in no great hurry to change the situation, but he believed a beginning should be made to transfer control into African hands. His Common Man's Charter was intended to achieve that end. Little of it was put into effect before Obote was overthrown, but it has given rise to a great deal of criticism, much of it conflicting. For some it was a violent swing to the left. For others it was an attempt to consolidate wealth and power in the hands of a fortunate few who happened to be in office at the right time. In sharp contrast to this latter view, some who were in office thought the charter posed a serious challenge to their hopes of acquiring wealth and power for themselves. Most of the criticism, from whatever standpoint, was in the nature of special pleading. The result was that Obote's popularity in some influential circles ebbed sharply, but for the vast majority of Ugandans, outside the former kingdom of Buganda, he was still the leader whom they most trusted.

EXILE

His downfall was not the result of widespread unpopularity. It was mainly due to the fears of one man. Obote had always trusted one senior military commander, Idi Amin, and Amin's loyalty to the government was, by his own criteria, unexceptionable. But Amin had become involved, along with the minister of defence, Felix Onama, in an Israeli plot to cause unrest in the southern Sudan. Defence funds had been illegally channelled into the enterprise and it was Obote's discovery of this and his demand for an explanation that led Amin, in panic, to stage a military coup with the assistance of Onama and part of the army. That the Baganda rejoiced at Obote's overthrow there is no doubt – so too did the Conservative government in Britain – but neither was directly responsible for it. Nor was it a military coup in the sense in which such actions had taken place in many other parts of Africa. This was not an attempt by a professional army, backed by popular opinion, to rid the country of a corrupt or autocratic government. Such an interpretation is simply an attempt to impose a retrospective view upon events. Nor was it true that Obote had laid by large sums of money for such an eventuality. Obote went into exile in Tanzania virtually penniless, and lived in Dar es Salaam through the generosity of the Tanzanian government.

In the first instance President Nyerere was prepared to assist Obote in any attempt to seize power once more. An ill-prepared invasion of Uganda having failed, however, Nyerere was forced to accept an agreement with Amin which precluded any further attempt being made. Nevertheless, the immediate delight with which Amin's coup had been received had quickly evaporated as a result of the cruelties arbitrarily perpetrated by the military government and of its wanton destruction of the economy. Obote now became the focus of Ugandans' hopes of a return to civilian government. Even those who had welcomed his overthrow began to accept that he was probably the only person capable of leading the country back to stability and prosperity. A handful of younger aspirants to leadership attempted to form a movement in exile aimed at bringing themselves to power but they had little following within Uganda itself.

For several years, while more and more people fled from Amin's tyranny or else succumbed to it, nothing could be done. It was only when, in an attempt to divert attention from the internal troubles of Uganda, Amin launched an attack upon Tanzania, Obote could again hope to make a come-back. He was cautious about claiming the presidency after such a lapse of time, but Nyerere had no doubts. It was, however, the intervention of a misinformed British foreign secretary that upset Nyerere's plan. Seeking logistical support from Britain for a counter-invasion of Uganda, Nyerere was told that assistance would only be given if Yusufu Lule, a former minister in the colonial government and subsequently an international civil servant, were to become head of state. A hurried meeting was called of Ugandans in exile and the new arrangement was foisted upon them. Amin was duly overthrown by the Tanzanian army, supported by a smaller body of men loyal to Obote, but it was Lule who became president.

Lule's government was divided from the outset and he himself lacked the toughness of character to hold it together. He was overthrown and replaced by a more determined person, Godfrey Binaisa, but Binaisa had little general support and the desire to see Obote back was growing rapidly stronger. Unfortunately, the lapse of time before his return permitted discontent and disillusionment with ineffectual civilian government to replace the euphoria which had greeted its revival. The universal corruption which it had been hoped would disappear with the flight of Amin had become worse than ever because little attempt had been made to revive the economy. Any effort in that direction was thwarted by a rapidly expanding armed force, with divided loyalties, which preyed upon the people it had supposedly been created to defend.

OBOTE'S SECOND TERM AS PRESIDENT

Obote's belated return to Uganda was not welcomed by those prominent Baganda who had hoped to find in Lule the man who might be acceptable to the whole country while, at the same time, promoting the interests of the former kingdom. In the time that had been allowed to elapse since Amin's overthrow, the leaders of the Democratic Party (DP), spurred on by the representatives of the Roman Catholic Church, had also begun to cherish hopes of seizing power themselves. In the troubled state of Uganda Obote would have preferred a government of national unity, but, in any case, he wanted elections to be held to legitimize whatever government now took office. As in so many other African countries, the elections that did take place were the subject of vociferous criticism. Charges of corruption, dishonest dealings, unfair pressures and falsified results became not only the commonplace of political rhetoric but also the justification for armed rebellion.

The criticisms levelled against the conduct and outcome of the elections are certainly open to challenge, but still more so is the claim that they in any way provided grounds for what followed. Once again, military action in the first instance lacked popular support. Again, too, it was not the work of a professional army but of one man, seeking power and backed by only a portion of the armed rabble which had accumulated in the wake of Amin's departure. The leader of the rebellion did not, initially, represent the wishes of the defeated Democratic Party or of the Bugandan leadership. Only one member of his own party had been successful in the elections. The support he later gained from the DP and some of the Baganda came only after a campaign of sabotage and subversion had led to reprisals by the ill-disciplined armed forces at the government's disposal. Resentment against those reprisals, enhanced by skilful propaganda, enabled Obote's opponents to represent him as a tyrant equal to, and perhaps even worse than, Amin himself.

Those charges can be challenged, although they gained widespread currency and astonishingly ready acceptance in circles where one might have expected a more critical appraisal of the claims made against the government. Nevertheless, the rebellion was slowly losing its impact under pressure from an army which Obote, against the odds, did his utmost to discipline and train. Moreover, despite threats by the rebels against coffee producers and marketers, the source of most of Uganda's foreign exchange, the country's economy was reviving steadily throughout the first half of the 1980s. Unfortunately, the benefits of the revival were often lost because of the insecurity created by gratuitous acts of violence by rebels in the very areas where a respite was most needed.

Obote's second overthrow was also the result of a military coup, this time by senior army leaders of the old school who were encouraged by opposition politicians to protect their positions, threatened by the rise of the new, better-educated officer class with which Obote was hoping gradually to supersede them. They were, however, as incapable of running the country as they had been of competently directing the armed forces, and this provided the opportunity for the rebel leader and some of the opposition politicians to seize power.

EXILE AGAIN

Once more Obote was forced to rely upon the generosity of his friends to provide him with asylum. On this occasion he felt he could not impose upon the kindness of the Tanzanian government. In any case, he believed he should remove himself further away from the Ugandan scene. His longtime friend, President Kenneth Kaunda, offered him a house in Lusaka and that he willingly accepted, having no money of his own to pay for accommodation or even subsistence. From that remote refuge he continued to read and hear with deep concern of the problems of Uganda – the renewed decline in the economy, the failure of the new government to win the hearts of the people of the north and east of the country, the banishment of democratic elections to the distant future. He learned, too, of the campaign of denigration vigorously conducted against him by his political opponents.

Reflecting upon Obote's career one might be tempted to conclude that only a military government, or a government backed by loyal and powerful armed forces, could hold Uganda together. After all, that had been the method used by the British authorities, albeit very discreetly, after the early years of conquest. Those, too, and more blatantly, have been the means employed by indigenous leaders in many other African countries. To try to unite the country, as Obote did, by negotiation might seem to have been a hopeless task. Yet a case can be argued for thinking that, after the excesses of the Amin regime, unity might have been possible if only Obote had been able to return to Uganda immediately after Amin's overthrow and before dissident opinions had been able to re-form. What the country needed at that time was a return to order and prosperity. The former might have proved too formidable a task, even at that moment of extreme relief. That Obote was capable of restoring economic prosperity there was no doubt, as his later actions proved. But, as in his first period of office, so again Obote was forced by circumstances to rely on the armed forces to curb the violence which sprang up in the very centre of the country, and his hope of peace was shattered.

In one important respect he met with considerable success. Throughout virtually the whole of his two periods of office there was a constitutional opposition which was free to criticize the government as vigorously as it wished in parliament. The press, too, was scarcely ever muzzled. There are few parallels to these achievements in other African countries. It is open to question whether a multi-party system of government is wholly appropriate to conditions in Africa, but at least it might ensure that voices other than the official voice had a right to be heard. That was something Obote always considered to be of prime importance, and it certainly throws doubt upon the accusations of tyranny levelled against him. He may have lacked the charisma of Kenyatta, or Nkrumah or Nyerere, yet there was about him an air of moderation and good sense which won him considerable respect, not only in Africa but in Britain and the USA. Although his formal education was curtailed, he read widely throughout his adult life and in so doing he absorbed some of the wisdom of great literary, political and philosophical figures. That wisdom he genuinely attempted to bring to bear upon the problems of governing his country.

Chapter 2

A Ugandan boyhood

Apolo Milton Obote was born on 28 December 1925 at Akokoro, in the south-western corner of Lira District, Northern Uganda, about two miles north of the River Nile as it flows westward from Lake Kyoga. His paternal grandfather, Bulaim Akaki, had been a considerable warrior in his younger days and was still nominally chief of Akokoro which, under the recently imposed British administration, had become a sub-county. The stories of his grandfather's early life thrilled the young Obote, who inherited some of Akaki's pugnacity. It was, however, from his father, Stanley Opeto Anyanga, third son of Akaki, that he inherited what was to be one of his most telling characteristics, his ability as a negotiator. When the British began to extend their administration into Lira in the second decade of the twentieth century Akaki resisted any encroachment on his powers. To avoid provoking an ugly confrontation, the British official taking charge of the district, J. H. Driberg, suggested to Akaki that he should nominate one of his sons to be trained by the British to succeed him as chief in due course. To the indignation of his eldest surviving son, Yeremia, Akaki named his second son, Yakobo, as trainee chief, thinking that the discipline imposed upon the young man by his instructors would curb his rebellious nature.

There seemed little likelihood that this would prove to be a satisfactory arrangement. In the first place, Akaki quickly recognized that it was Driberg's covert intention to bypass him as much as possible and to work through Yakobo. Yeremia, meanwhile, was deeply resentful of having been superseded by his younger brother. Thus there developed a triangular struggle for power between the old chief, his second son, Driberg's pro-tegé, and his disgruntled eldest son. The problem of Yeremia's role was soon resolved when he was despatched to Lira by Driberg after trying to kill his sibling rival. By a coincidence this was to save Obote's life some years later. The resolution of the more complicated issue of the relations between the traditionalist Akaki and his more adaptable son was accomplished by Stanley. Working closely with his father, he made an arrangement whereby Akaki retained the dignity of his office while most of the work was done by Yakobo. Yakobo was himself not without skill in handling other people and, as Driberg had recognized, he was receptive to new ideas. Consequently, he flourished under the regime proposed by Stanley, and he was sufficiently impressed by his younger brother's tactful management of his father's affairs to appoint him supervisor of works in the sub-county, a job which was far more demanding and wide-ranging than its title might suggest.

Stanley's first wife had already had two sons when Obote was born to his second wife, Priscilla Acen Eyer. The naming of a child had formerly been the prerogative of the older women present at the birth and it had been the intention to call the baby Akaki after his grandfather. Yakobo, however, declared that in future a new method of naming children would be adopted. Anyone could, on making a gift to the chief, suggest a name. All the suggestions would then, in accordance with a modern practice which Yakobo was proud to introduce, be written on separate slips of paper which were put in a basket. The mother of the child would draw out a slip and the child would be given the name on it. So it was that Obote was named after a brother of Akaki and was the first child to be named in this way. Since few people could write, it was not difficult for anyone sufficiently interested to ensure that all the slips bore the same name, although there is no suggestion that this was done in Obote's case.

Like other children of his time, Obote grew up in close contact with all the members of his family. His grandfather, Akaki, constantly urged him to be suspicious of the British who, he said, had come to rule over their clan and make them work for their new overlords. It was a lesson Obote learned thoroughly, and he was later to maintain that it was equally applicable to Britain's relations with the rest of Uganda. His maternal grandfather, Oceng Atyera, was a man of a very different character. Uninterested in politics, he was, in Obote's opinion, the kindest man he ever knew. He was a skilled potter and a keen hunter and fisherman. He had a particular skill in handling bees, both wild and domesticated, and was noted for his treatment of sick animals. He was also a distinguished member of a sect of rainmakers. While Obote listened to Akaki's tales of earlier days and learned from him about the problems and responsibilities of leadership, he acquired from Oceng some knowledge of the herbs with which to treat animals and of how to hunt birds, but he was never attracted by the surgical work carried out by his maternal grandfather.

Life was not without its darker moments. When Obote fell sick Oceng was so convinced that his indisposition was in some way related to the recovery from illness of his great grandmother, Oceng's mother, that he determined to kill the old woman to ensure his beloved grandson's survival. Fortunately, the boy recovered and the murder was never carried out. Again, a jealous woman tried to kill Obote and his sister by giving them poisoned food. The children had been told never to accept food from strangers and refused to eat. When their mother, having tried without success to get the woman to eat the food herself, gave it to a dog the animal died and the children escaped unscathed.

More prolonged misfortune came as a result of Obote's being sent to stay with his uncle, Isaka, Stanley's youngest brother, in Lira. Isaka promised to send Obote to school but never did so. Instead, Obote became the virtual slave of his aunt, Rebecca. He had to get up at six o'clock in the morning and go into the bush to collect firewood, returning to boil water for his uncle's bath. He was given no breakfast, but after Isaka had left for work he had to bath his two young cousins. His next task was to wash and scrub the utensils used for supper the previous evening and for breakfast. He then made several journeys to a stream half a mile away to fetch water in a large kettle before sweeping the house and courtyard. After that he collected more firewood. Isaka returned for lunch at one o'clock and Obote was given any food left over. This had also to serve as his evening meal, and if Isaka brought a number of friends to eat at midday there would be little left when they had finished. Rebecca and her two children ate separately. Obote's afternoons were spent, like the mornings, in washing kitchen utensils and fetching water, and then he had to boil water for his uncle's evening bath. On Saturdays he washed his own and the other children's clothes and bed linen.

When his duties were extended to include cooking and his aunt upbraided him for being unable to carry a four-gallon tin of water from the stream, Obote, in desperation, decided to escape by walking to Akokoro, 68 miles away. Unfortunately, he did not know in which direction his destination lay, and it took him some time to discover the route by making surreptitious inquiries. When he was confident he could find the road he set out early one morning and made his way through the bush. Accused by some men of having stolen mangoes from their trees, he was beaten and pushed into the road where he was almost run over by a passing lorry. By good fortune, his narrow escape was seen by the wife of his uncle Yeremia, who, recognizing him, rescued him from his attackers and took him to the home in Lira to which Yeremia had been banished. There he told his story, and Yeremia sent for Isaka who claimed to have been unaware of what had been going on. It was agreed, however, that Obote should return to his parents. His father was informed and sent a man to fetch him home. Isaka later divorced Rebecca, although not on account of her behaviour towards Obote, and he became Obote's favourite uncle, not least because of his lively sense of humour.

By this time Stanley had become one of the two deputy sub-county chiefs of Akokoro and had been posted to Kwibale, some six miles away to the west. There Obote lived happily for some time, although his life was still not without adventures. One day, while playing with other children on the bank of the Nile, he saw a little girl seized by a crocodile. Although two of the swiftest runners went for help and the rest shouted as loudly as they could in an attempt to distract the predator, the girl was dragged under the water and drowned. On another occasion, Obote was returning home in the darkness when he saw two leopards on the path ahead of him. He had been singing to let his parents know he was approaching, but the sight of the two animals froze his vocal cords. His father guessed there was something wrong and shouted to him not to move. Stanley then quickly drove his goats, with as much noise as possible, into a nearby compound and, armed with two spears and a club, took up a position in a tree. The leopards did not attack the goats, but in the disturbance Obote was able to retrace his steps cautiously to the house of the friend he had been visiting.

The friend in question, Ocao, was a renowned athlete and games player and trained Obote and his friends in a variety of sports. Obote was not very interested in games, at none of which he excelled, but he was very attracted to another of his mentor's accomplishments. Ocao was a great hunter and trapper and made his living by bartering game meat and birds for grain and other foodstuffs. In his company Obote added to the skills he had learned from his grandfather, Oceng. Even after the episode with the leopards he continued to go out hunting with Ocao, but made certain he was home before dark. He had no desire to kill animals; only to be able to track and observe them. Following the footprints of a duiker, a tiny antelope, he was just in time to see a python coil itself round the little animal before swallowing it. Withdrawing slowly, as he had learnt to do when he encountered the leopards, he made his way to the house of Ocao who later killed the python and sold its skin. Even at home there were dangers. One evening, when they had been sent to bring in lamps and some fruit their mother had gathered during the day, he and his sister discovered a black mamba in the roof of their house. They explained what they had found without mentioning the name of the snake because, according to Lango tradition, the name must not be mentioned until the creature was dead. If the name was spoken, it was believed that the snake would be forewarned and would make its escape, to strike on another occasion. Now, however, Stanley killed the mamba.

This interesting and at times exciting period of Obote's life came to an end when Stanley was transferred to Apac early in 1933, by which time the boy was still only seven years old. There was no accommodation in Apac for the whole of Stanley's family so the rest, including Obote, went to live with grandfather Akaki, a mile from Akokoro. Akaki being away from home when they arrived Obote went to stay with his great-uncle, whose name he bore, and then with his maternal grandfather. Still his gift for getting involved in danger persisted. Accompanying his uncle, Laban, to herd the family's goats, he broke away to scramble into a clay pit intending to mould a musical instrument. His uncle, meanwhile, climbed a tree, from which vantage point he could watch the goats. Other herds came by, and one of the older boys accompanying them threw a double-barbed fish spear into the clay pit. The spear entered the lower part of Obote's back, near the spine. Laban saw Obote lying face down-wards and immediately sounded a call of grave danger on his horn. This call was taken up across the countryside and a large group of people assembled, including Obote's grandparents and the local chief. Oceng wanted to try to remove the spear, but the chief resisted, pointing out that, because of the double barb, the removal of the spear would be more dangerous than its entry had been. With great reluctance Oceng agreed that the boy should be carried by relays of porters in a hammock made from one of Oceng's own fishing nets to the nearest dispensary at Aduku. The journey took a day and a half, but by good fortune Obote's arrival in Aduku coincided with the monthly visit of the medical officer from Lira.

Having had the spear removed and his wound treated, Obote divided his time between the homes of his grandfather, Akaki, whose stories he enjoyed so much, and of his father, Stanley, who, having been promoted to sub-county chief, now lived only a mile away in Akokoro. Stanley was extremely anxious that all his sons should learn the nature of chieftain-ship – above all, that it was not simply a matter of giving orders. A chief, he insisted, must learn to listen to his people so that he would know them and understand their complaints. At first, Obote preferred the more lurid tales of his grandfather, who held court among his admirers in the evenings when he would sing and accompany himself on a drum. His songs had moral themes or told stories of great deeds of earlier days. Gradually, however, Obote became fascinated by the procedure in the sub-county court, the presentation of evidence, the arguing of cases and the judgements that were given. In this way, although only nine years old, he came to learn a great deal about Lango customary law. One day he met an *askari* (soldier) who had come on leave, bringing with him a book containing the alphabet and a number of simple sentences in the Lwo language. The askari taught Obote the alphabet, which the boy learned in a single day, and the following day a junior chief saw Obote trying to read the book. The chief asked Stanley which school his son was attending, and Obote was summoned to read aloud from the book to the elders as they ate their midday meal. As a result it was decided that the boy should be sent on a baptismal course taught at a centre for Protestant children. This was deemed to be preferable to sending him to school, because the course there took only one year to complete, while the more varied curriculum in the school meant that children did not reach the standard of education in religious subjects required for baptism until the end of two years.

The centre was situated at a distance of eight miles from Obote's home, so it was arranged that he would live there in the home of the man in charge. Even now adventure was not far away. Obote travelled to the centre, with his luggage, on the back of a bicycle ridden by a friend of the family. Three miles from home, the rider drove the bicycle into the gutter at the roadside where both he and his passenger fell off. He whispered that it had been no accident. There were four lions on the road ahead. Cautiously the two travellers made a wide detour through the long grass and regained the road some distance further along.

The working day at the centre was a long one. The pupils awoke at six o'clock – at five o'clock during harvest time – and did some agricultural work or, if they were too young for such labour, they swept out the huts. Academic work began at eight o'clock, and for the first three months of the course there were no days off. During the second three months the boys had one weekend's holiday a month, and during the third, two weekends per month. In the final three months, however, there was no break. Obote passed his examination at the end of the course and told his father he would be baptized in December. Asked by a young man who was studying at Makerere College, a college of higher education located on the outskirts of Kampala, the largest town in Uganda, what name he had chosen for his baptism Obote was at a loss. His father quickly intervened and said that the boy would be named Apolo after a Mugandan missionary, Apolo Kivebulaya, who had worked among the pygmies just over the border in the Belgian Congo and about whom a book had recently been published in the Lwo language. Hearing that Obote had learned the alphabet in one day the student then said that he should also be named Milton, after a fine English scholar and writer. Thus the boy acquired two great names to act as an inspiration to him in the future.

In January 1936, at the age of ten, Obote was enrolled in the Ibuje Elementary Vernacular School for Boys. There were only two boys in the lowest form who were younger than he was, but in spite of that he was top of the class in the examinations at the end of the first term. In the second term there occurred another of those adventures which seemed to befall Obote throughout his childhood. After heavy rain, the roof of the dormitory collapsed, and Obote, along with a number of other boys, was housed at a farm some two miles away. The householder insisted that the boys should get up at five in the morning and work in his fields before going to school. All went well until the school ordered the boys to be innoculated against smallpox. Three days later, Obote and some of the other boys ran high temperatures, but the farmer still insisted they should work in the field before going to school. Two boys, who lived nearby, were taken home by their parents, but Obote's home was too far away for such an arrangement to be practicable. The farmer then told him that if he did not work he would not be fed. After two days without food Obote decided to run away. The journey home in his weak condition was only made possible by the help of a friend of his father who fed him and arranged for him to travel on the bicycle of the mail carrier who was going to Akokoro. Stanley accepted his son's story, and after a clan meeting had ascertained fully what had happened, quiet man though he was, he poured out his anger on the farmer.

A month later, when Obote had recovered, he returned to school and was housed with a senior clerk, but his absence had adversely affected his work and he came only third in his end-of-term examinations. His father was well satisfied with that result. Not so his mother, who said that her father, Oceng, had never stood behind anyone, and it ill behoved his first grandson to let him down, an opinion endorsed with interest by Obote's maternal grandmother. At that, Obote himself determined that Oceng's grandson would never again stand behind anyone, and with that decided he returned to school and was once more top of his form at the end of the third term.

The second year went well until, in the final term, there was a repetition of what happened when Obote was staying with his uncle, Isaka. He was the youngest of the boys staying at the home of the senior clerk, and the clerk's wife ordered him not to go to school. Instead, he was to help her cook her husband's lunch and look after her children. On the days that followed he was required to do other household tasks, but was still able to attend lessons. After three weeks, however, he was again told to stay at the house. It was the day on which half-term tests were to be held and Obote determined to disobey the woman's orders and go to school to take the tests.

On his return in the evening the woman was so angry that she refused to let him eat in the house. He made his way to the home of the county chief, where he was fed, and then he returned to bed. During the night he was awakened by the senior clerk who accused him of insulting his wife and told him to leave the house immediately. Obote gathered his belongings and set out, but having nowhere to go he spent the rest of the night in a patch of undergrowth before presenting himself at dawn to the cook of an Indian shopkeeper. The cook, who knew the boy, gave him food and then Obote waited for his schoolmates from the senior clerk's house to pass by so that he could accompany them to school. He asked them to corroborate his account of what had happened when he reported to the form teacher, but the boys told him that the senior clerk had warned them to support his own lurid account of Obote's behaviour on pain of being sent away from his house. At that, Obote dared not go to school but went into hiding in the ruins of the school dormitory. After several days, during which he lived first on raw and then on cooked cassava gathered in a nearby field, he learned from a boy, Uma, who worked for the head of the church in Ibuje, that his absence had come to the attention of the headmaster. The latter, concerned that Obote might have returned home because of troubles similar to those he had encountered the previous year, managed to discover from his classmates, who were interviewed one by one, the date of the boy's disappearance. He then sent urgently to Obote's home to ask if he were there. This caused profound consternation, but Obote, informed by Uma of what had happened, now decided to call on the headmaster and tell his story.

The following day Obote was able to join his father, who was attending a court hearing in Ibuje, and later accompanied him to Akokoro. At home he was met with great rejoicing, because it had been feared he might be dead. There was much feasting and celebration before he returned to Ibuje where, for the remainder of the year, he lived with the county chief. After this tumultuous week the rest of the term proceeded quietly, and once again Obote was top of his class in the examinations at the end of the school year.

The new year began with a new headmaster for the school and a new form master for Obote himself. Both new teachers were extremely popular because they were well-known footballers. Obote had two successful terms before being suddenly promoted to the fourth form. This presented him with some difficulties because he had a lot of ground to make up. By this time he was living at the headmaster's house and, by a stroke of luck, the two other boys who were also there were his friends. One of them was in the third form, which Obote had just left, and the other was in the fourth which he had now joined. By a judicious use of notes from both of them Obote was able to cover the course, but his task was made more difficult because he had been chosen to read two passages in an inter-school competition and also to sing in the school choir on the same occasion. The time spent in practice and rehearsal was demanding, and a further distraction occurred in October when the county chief and the headmaster introduced a series of talks on world affairs for senior boys in the school every Sunday evening. Obote was fascinated to learn about what was taking place in Europe. With a map of the world in front of the audience the speaker described the activities of Hitler and Mussolini and explained the crisis developing in Czechoslovakia. This was a new and engrossing experience for Obote, whose horizons had hitherto been limited to affairs in Lango District, with a leaven of local history learned from his grandfather, Akaki.

With Obote's time fully occupied with revision, learning new subjects, reading practice, choir rehearsals and the exciting news from Europe, the remaining weeks before the examinations and competition passed quickly. The examinations were written in the last week of November and the boys then went immediately to Boroboro to take part in the inter-school competition. Obote came first in the reading competition in both

the Gospel and Epistle classes, and his school, Ibuje, was third out of
seventeen participants in the overall competition. After this success the
period of waiting for the outcome of the examinations was tense. The
results were finally brought to the school by Canon T. H. Lawrence, an
Australian from Tasmania who had been the founder of Protestant
missionary work in Lango District. Eight boys from Ibuje had passed
sufficiently well to be allowed to proceed to class five, among them Obote
who, in spite of the obstacles he had had to overcome, was given a mark
of sixty-eight, the highest mark in his school being seventy-three. It was
an achievement to be proud of, but Obote was dissatisfied, because the
grandson of Oceng must never stand behind anyone. Canon Lawrence
took a less severe view of Obote's performance. When he learned from
the headmaster that the boy had been in the fourth form for only one
term, he was so impressed that he offered to drive Obote home in his
car, although Akokoro lay in the opposite direction from the one he had
intended to take.

Promotion to class five meant that Obote had to leave Ibuje and
transfer to another school at Boroboro. He detested the thought of
fagging for another boy, which was the practice in the new school, but
fortunately he had an older cousin in the school who, together with his
friends, made sure that Obote was not badly treated. Ever ambitious,
Obote set out at once to discover which of the thirty boys in his class
had attained a higher mark than he had in the recent examinations.
After he had performed particularly well in a general knowledge test, his
history teacher invited him to lunch and he was able to ask about the
examination marks. The list was with the headmaster, he was told.

In due course Obote was summoned to the headmaster's home. The
headmaster, Stanley G. Moore, had been at Boroboro little more than a
year and spoke no Lwo. Obote, on the other hand, spoke no English, so
their conversation was carried on through an interpreter, the headmistress
of the Boroboro girls' school, an Australian. The headmaster asked Obote
why he was interested in the examinations list and Obote replied that he
intended to do better than any of the boys who had got higher marks.
Obote's English teacher, Miss Phoebe Brown, who was present at the
meeting, told Obote to forget the list and to concentrate on improving
his own mark by 10, 20 or even 30 per cent. It was advice which Obote
took to heart and remembered throughout his life. At the end of his first
term at Boroboro he came third in the examination, beaten by the two
boys who had achieved the highest marks in the entrance examination,
but at the end of the second and third terms Obote was top of his class,
behind no-one.

In his first year at Boroboro Obote came into contact with the boy
scout movement. He liked what he saw of it and enquired if he could
join without taking the scout oath. Asked by the scoutmaster why he did

not wish to take the oath, Obote felt unable to answer. He did not want to admit that his grandfather, Akaki, had told him never to accept British rule, and the oath required him to promise to do his duty to the King of Great Britain. To his regret Obote never became a scout.

In Obote's second year at Boroboro, 1940, Mr Moore was transferred to Gulu to take the place of the headmaster there who had volunteered for war service. This left Miss Brown as the only teacher for whom English was her first language. Protests from the students led to arrangements being made by the new headmaster, Stanley Owiny, for Miss Brown to be assisted in her English teaching by Miss Wilkinson, the headmistress of the girls' school, and by Mr Hart, who was head of the nearby teacher training college. Obote himself made considerable progress while at Boroboro and in his second year was singled out to make a prepared speech during the ceremonies to mark the end of the course. Ten county chiefs were present on that occasion and Obote's performance was loudly acclaimed, but his triumph was quickly followed by disappointment. His ability and application had resulted in his passing first from his school in the entrance examination to a secondary school. It had been customary for the boy who topped the list to be awarded a three-year scholarship, tenable at his next school. On this occasion it was announced by the chiefs that the precedent would not be followed because Obote's father was a salaried local government official and could afford to pay the fees. Stanley's salary was 70 shillings a month, not unreasonable at that time, but he had ten children at school, so this was bad news and worse was to follow. At the selfsame meeting at which the chiefs made the decision regarding the scholarship they also decided to dismiss Stanley. The announcement created considerable ill feeling in Stanley's sub-county where he was extremely popular, and there were those who said it was envy of Obote's outstanding performance at school that had led to Stanley's dismissal. This later proved to be true, and the chief source of the envy was Obote's uncle, Yakobo, who, together with a number of his friends, had conspired to block any further educational opportunity for his nephew and for several other boys from Lango District.

The question of how the school fees were to be met appeared to have been resolved when Stanley told his son that the selfsame uncle, Yakobo, had agreed to pay. It was only gradually that Yakobo's perfidy became clear. One after another he contrived to place obstacles in Obote's way, beginning with his failure to provide adequate transport to get the boy to school in Gulu, 42 miles away in the neighbouring district of Acholi. One of Yakobo's aides tried to drop Obote off 15 miles short of his destination so as to discourage him from proceeding further, but Obote resisted strongly and the aide eventually continued the journey after telling the boy how his uncle had plotted to prevent him from going to school. As a result, during the years he attended school at Gulu, Obote walked the 42 miles to and from his uncle's residence seventeen times, at first taking nearly three days to complete the journey and later reducing the time to two days.

In Gulu all teaching was in English, and during official school hours all communication had to be in the same language. Obote regarded this as a challenge that he must accept as a means to success. He took an immediate liking to the headmaster, S. G. Moore, whom he had met briefly at Boroboro and who now questioned him about his knowledge of world affairs before putting him in charge of producing the maps for his weekly talks to the school about the war. Because Gulu served several districts, Obote now came into contact with boys from different ethnic groups. The ages of the boys also varied greatly. Some were already married and had children. In spite of having little spending money, Obote was able to eke out the rather meagre provisions offered by the school by making friends with several of the older students who had plots of land and produced some of their own food. He also made a point of getting to know as much as possible about all the boys in his year, especially those from other schools whom he had not previously met.

Although he greatly enjoyed his early months in his new school, Obote felt a deep sense of anger against those who had tried to prevent him from furthering his education. Hitherto he had worked hard to please his mother, as well as from a personal desire to excel. Henceforward he resolved to work to give his father cause for pride, and his aim was to do so well that he would be awarded a Lango District scholarship for the final stage of his secondary education after Gulu. He was encouraged by the opportunities for reading which Gulu offered. Although the school possessed no library, the boys were given a wide selection of books, including novels by Dickens and other classics of English literature. Obote never confined his reading to set texts. Anything readable he read, and in Gulu reading became his chief pastime. Although he tried hard to perform well on the football field he never excelled at the game.

At a lunch party to which he had been invited one Sunday by a local primary school headmaster Obote was urged by a chief, who was also present, to appeal, through Mr Moore, to the district commissioner against the decision not to award him a scholarship. This he did, but the district commissioner, T. R. F. Cox, said the case could not be reopened. Cox was a friend of Yakobo, and Obote wondered if he had consulted him. Some years later he was to suspect Cox of having been a party to another disappointment he was to have over the award of a further local government scholarship.

In the examinations at the end of the first term at Gulu, Obote came first. His cousin, Benjamin Odur, Yakobo's son, who was a close friend of Obote and was himself a student in Gulu, brought the news to his father ahead of Obote's arrival, the latter having had to walk to his uncle's home. Obote was disappointed by the cold reception he received from Yakobo, but he enjoyed his holiday because of the kindness shown him by Ben and his other cousins. He regaled them all with the stories his grandfather, Akaki, had told him, and they listened, enthralled by all he had to say.

During the holiday Obote met a man named Mudunguti who impressed him greatly. Mudunguti – that was probably not his real name – had been a senior chief in Rwanda but had been deported to Uganda, ultimately settling in Lango District. He had no source of income and lived in abject poverty. Yet he never complained and never sought sympathy. Obote was deeply moved by his stoicism and regarded him as an example to be followed. Later he came to think of Mudunguti's case as a powerful argument against colonialism. But when he discussed the matter with his father some years afterwards, Stanley, wiser than he, pointed out that Mudunguti may have suffered at the hands of a colonial government, but there were many who suffered at the hands of their own Ugandan chiefs. Thinking about that, Obote concluded that Mudunguti was an argument against bad government by anyone.

Soon after his return to school for his second term in Gulu, Obote went for a walk with some of his friends on a Sunday afternoon. Their objective was a Roman Catholic mission school nearby. As they approached the place it seemed empty, but suddenly they were pounced upon by white soldiers and roughly thrust into a store room where they were locked up. The next day they were paraded before the Gulu police commander who then summoned Mr Moore. After some discussion the boys were released and they learned that, during the holidays, the school had been closed. The missionaries there, Italians of the Verona Fathers Mission, had been interned, and the school had been turned into a transit camp for South African soldiers en route for Juba in the Sudan. When, that afternoon, Moore gave his weekly talk about the war, he was asked why Britain and South Africa were allies when the South Africans appeared as racist as the Germans. That experience, and Moore's sincere but halting attempt to explain the position, only served to confirm for Obote the wisdom of Akaki's advice to resist foreign rule.

During a holiday in his second year which, like all previous holidays, he spent at the home of his uncle, Obote learned from Ben Odur that Yakobo had decided he should not return to school, but that he would be employed as a servant around the house. Ben proposed that Obote should pretend to be ill and that he would do the work for him. Yakobo was fond of his son and would not let him work, but Ben was obdurate, so Obote returned to school. But the same sort of problem arose at Christmas 1942, and again it was Ben's intervention that induced Yakobo to pay Obote's fees and provide the additional equipment he needed for his final year. It was a time of hardship at the school. Food was scarce, and the fields in which the school grew its cassava were raided from time to time by thieves. The boys had to take turns to be on duty to guard the fields and several were injured while trying to drive away robbers.

The next crisis for Obote arose at the end of the second term of his final year, when the headmaster gave each boy a letter to take to his guardian asking what the boy hoped to do when his time in Gulu came to an end, and setting out the fees and other expenses which would be incurred at a variety of other educational establishments. Obote was keen to go to a senior secondary school and thence to Makerere College, the highest form of education then provided in Uganda, and his cousin, Ben, planned to do the same. Yakobo, however, said Obote should apply for a teacher training college or for the Mulago Paramedic School near Kampala. On the advice of a friend Obote wrote to his father explaining his dilemma. Stanley held a meeting with a number of senior members of his clan at which it emerged that Yakobo had only nominally been paying Obote's school fees. In fact, Stanley, along with several other members of his clan, had been sending money regularly to his brother to be invested in a bank account in Jinja. The sums paid by Stanley were considerably in excess of any school fees paid by Yakobo, and it was Stanley's money that had paid for Obote's education and would be made available for his further studies. This was pointed out firmly but tactfully to Yakobo, who then asked Obote to make his choice of senior secondary school but to avoid the ones selected by Ben Odur so as to avoid competition.

The next task was to pass the senior secondary entrance examination, a competition open to the whole country. Obote was determined not only to pass but to pass well enough to win a local government scholarship. His performance in his sessional examinations throughout his time in Gulu augured well for his performance in the entrance examination, and, true to his expectations, his result was the best of any student from Gulu. Yet he heard nothing from any of the schools to which he had applied for admission until, after some delay, he was rejected by his first choice, the Roman Catholic school at Kisubi, between Kampala and Entebbe. He later discovered that this was probably due to a reference written by his headmaster, Moore, who, fearing pressure might be brought to bear on Obote to convert to Roman Catholicism, had suggested in his letter that the boy was a strong candidate for the Anglican priesthood. Obote's second choice had been Nyakasura, near Fort Portal in Toro District in Western Uganda. Unfortunately, because of a lack of teachers, the school had had to cut out its senior forms, and the new pupils who were to have been admitted were offered to other schools. For that reason the school term was already in its third week when Obote received an offer from Busoga College, Mwiri, near Jinja, in the Eastern Province. He was thrilled by the news, as were all his family, and another week of celebration delayed Obote's journey to Mwiri still further. These diversions, together with other preparations for his departure and the slow journey to his destination, meant that five weeks had elapsed before Obote took up his place in Mwiri. He was just eighteen. Meanwhile an attempt was being made by his friends to get him a local government scholarship. Because the offer of a place had come so late, an award had already been made to another boy, and this was given as the reason why another scholarship could not be given. It was a specious argument, but was said to be final.

Three things immediately impressed Obote on his arrival in Mwiri. The first was the headmaster, Francis Coates, the second was the school library and the third was the school's motto, 'For God and my country'. Coates was extremely kind to Obote throughout his three years at the school. On the first day he reassured him that there would be no problem arising from his late arrival. His performance in the entrance examination had given a clear indication of his ability, and there would be ample opportunity during the first term to make up for the time he had lost. Through the help of other boys Obote found regular periods when he could do extra work. He also discovered that mathematics had been so well taught in Gulu that he had little to make up in that subject. Only in geography and in laboratory work was he really behind.

Mwiri, Obote soon learned, had been founded for the sons of chiefs, but most of the boys there came from poor homes and had little money to spend. Obote felt comfortable, being neither poor nor the son of a wealthy chief. He regretted that the school had no chapel, but he read his Bible daily, taking illegal advantage of the fifteen minutes of 'silent time' during which each boy was supposed to sit on his bed and reflect. Obote was caught reading the Bible by another student, Tucker Nabeta, who was hoping to be ordained in the Anglican Church. When the two met later in the day they discussed their mutual interest in Bible reading and at once became firm friends. Nabeta was a Musoga, as were the majority of boys in the school, and Obote was pleased to be able to widen his circle of acquaintances by getting to know students from that district. After ordination, Nabeta was to become chaplain at Makerere College and became eventually assistant bishop of Busoga. He died in 1984. The Western Province was represented by only one youth, a solitary person whom Obote never got to know very well, but the following year a student arrived from Kigezi District, in the extreme south-west. His name was E. N. Bisamunyu and, following his grandfather Akaki's advice to try to understand foreigners, Obote came to know the new arrival well.

The school library opened a new world for Obote. He slipped away there whenever the opportunity presented itself. He had read everything upon which he could lay his hands while he was in Gulu, but here was untold wealth, books on every possible subject, as well as bound copies of old newspapers. When he left Mwiri the headmaster wrote on his report, 'he reads widely'. This, Obote regarded as almost the supreme accolade. He still found time to try out new sports, including cricket, tennis, hockey and rugby football, but showed no great aptitude for any of them.

The examinations at the end of Obote's first term in Mwiri brought a considerable shock. Although confident that he had made up for his late arrival, he was placed only fourth. Characteristically, he determined to work much harder. On the train that carried him home to Lango he met a number of boys from another school, King's College, Budo, which was in Buganda, and subsequent encounters led to other friendships which were to ripen still further when the youths all went to Makerere. These contacts opened Obote's eyes to issues which, in Lango and even in Gulu, had scarcely impinged upon him, and the friendships were to stand him in good stead throughout his later life.

Back home he found himself in the midst of a dispute of which he had been the unwitting cause. It was widely believed by a number of younger men, who had formed the Young Lango Association to promote their ideas in a society where traditional authority was still very strong, that the senior chiefs were deliberately preventing children of those who were not chiefs, or at least were not their friends, from getting higher education. Obote's failure to get a local government scholarship had proved to be the spark which ignited their anger. They took action by encouraging Samwiri Okello, the headmaster of Obote's former school, Boroboro, to expel a number of the children of chiefs. He gave no reason for his action, and the chiefs were at a loss what to do. Yakobo, some of whose children had been expelled, sought Obote's advice, saying he was inclined to send the children to Catholic schools. These schools had attracted few pupils because Lango was essentially a Protestant district. Yakobo's proposal was likely to cause heated argument, but after consulting several of his friends and giving the matter deep thought, Obote agreed with his uncle's plan. He recognised that Yakobo's generation would find it difficult to effect any sort of reconciliation with Roman Catholics, but the children needed education and here were the means to get it. His own generation, he said, would have to reach an accommodation with the Catholics if the country was to make any progress. Thus, at an early stage, Obote demonstrated both pragmatism and tolerance, qualities to which he attached the greatest importance throughout his later career. His advice, too, proved to have been sound. As a result of the campaign launched by friends of Yakobo, education in Catholic schools became wholly acceptable in Lango within ten years. The fears that this would lead to divisions in the district proved unfounded. Twenty years later, when elections were held for membership of the new national assembly, both Catholics and Protestants voted solidly for one party rather than dividing along religious lines as happened in several other districts.

Obote's second and third terms in Mwiri were uneventful, but he came first in each of his progress examinations and continued to hold that position for the rest of his time in school, apart from one occasion in his final year when unusual circumstances prevented him from revising as he had intended. Shortly after the second term had begun, a new student arrived at the school. He was James Oluk, son of the most senior chief in Lango. Along with two other boys from Lango, Oluk was invited to tea with a family living near the school. A man from Lango was present on the occasion and proposed that opium, *waragi* (a crude form of local spirits), and cigarettes should be smuggled into Obote's box so as to get him expelled. The other two boys told Obote what they had heard, but Oluk never mentioned it, although he tried hard to establish close contact with Obote. Obote never made the plot known to the headmaster because he did not want to implicate the two who had warned him, and he never confronted Oluk, hoping that one day the latter would tell him what had happened. Forewarned, however, Obote was able to ensure that the plot never came to fruition. It seemed to have sprung from rivalry between Oluk's father and Yakobo, both of whom were candidates for a new post which would be superior to all the county chiefs in Lango. Oluk's father was the senior office-holder, but could neither read nor write, while Yakobo could read and write in Lwo, Runyoro, Luganda and KiSwahili. The plot had been intended to discredit Yakobo by bringing disgrace upon his nephew.

It was in the third term of his second year that Obote gained prominence outside the academic field. He had been unaware that caning was practised at Mwiri. One night he was awakened by a prefect who summoned him to a meeting attended by only some of the other prefects. There he was told he was to be caned for encouraging junior boys to be disobedient. The matter had arisen over the question of fagging, about which the school rules were silent. Few of the prefects had fags, so Obote, who disliked the idea intensely because of the implied inferiority of some of the boys, had urged the younger boys to resist. Thinking quickly, Obote grabbed a ruler and backed into a corner, from which he threatened his assailants and said that he was ill and was due to go to hospital the following day. If anyone touched him he would die and they with him. It was true that he had been to the school dispensary that very day, after having been severely bitten by an insect, and had been told that he would have to go to hospital for treatment. This was known to some of the prefects present who, nonplussed, said they would postpone the caning until he returned from hospital. Obote took no chances and jumped out of a window before they could change their minds. The next morning he complained to the headmaster that he had been given no opportunity to state his case before being threatened with punishment. Coates, very wisely, did not criticize the prefects but himself took Obote to hospital in Jinja. The punishment was never carried out, and a week later Obote was himself made a prefect. He was at once given the special task of persuading the younger boys who were not involved in games to work in a citrus garden which the headmaster had created to serve the needs of the school and in which Coates himself worked alongside the young volunteers. Because of the reputation he had built up by his stand over the fagging incident, Obote had no trouble in raising recruits, as Coates doubtless anticipated. The following year caning was abolished.

The academic year ended happily. His friend, Nabeta, had won a place at Makerere, he himself had been made a prefect, and once again he was top of his form in the sessional examinations. During the journey home he again met his friends from Budo and was invited by them to spend a few days at each of their homes in neighbouring Teso District. It was a useful experience. The boys were sons of chiefs and he was introduced, in conversation with their families, to problems peculiar to Teso, particularly to one concerning boundary issues which gave him a foretaste of a similar problem, of much greater magnitude, with which he himself had to deal later in his life.

When the school reopened for Obote's final year there was an acute shortage of food. He was determined to draw the attention of the school's authorities to the seriousness of the matter, and when he was duty prefect he arranged to have the food meant for breakfast for the whole school to be served only to the boys in the junior section. The older boys protested vigorously, but it was too late, the food had already been eaten before they arrived at the dining hall. The supervising teacher and the head prefect were extremely angry, and along with them Obote was summoned to the headmaster's office. There, he argued that the entire school had constantly complained about the food shortage and the prefects had, on several occasions, urged the head prefect to make the complaints known to the supervising teacher. On that particular morning he had been deeply moved by the obvious signs of hunger among the junior boys. He went on to say that he would accept any punishment for what he had done, even including expulsion. But he was not expelled, nor was he punished in any other way. Instead, a second breakfast was served, this time for the older boys, and henceforward the school bus was sent foraging for food daily in order to increase the boys' rations.

Later in the year, the sixth form was taken to climb Mount Elgon, on the border between Uganda and Kenya. It was a very demanding expedition, the climb itself being extremely tough and the cold near the summit was intense. To get to the top took four days, and only seven boys reached it. One of the seven was Obote. Towards the end of the second term, a friend of Obote, Wilson Aguma, developed trouble with one of his eyes while playing football. At the dispensary the nurse inadvertently put something in both eyes which caused Aguma acute and prolonged pain. He was taken to hospital in Jinja immediately, Obote accompanying him. Obote stayed in Jinja for ten days, visiting his friend daily. He returned to school just in time to sit the progress examinations, but because of his absence he had not revised and came only third. This rankled greatly, not that he had any regrets about helping his friend, but the boy who came first in this examination became head of the school for his final term and had his name inscribed on an honours board. Years later, when Obote was prime minister of Uganda, he talked about his disappointment to Coates, who said he hoped Obote no longer blamed the school nurse for what she had done to his friend or for the effect he believed her action had had upon the examination results. Contrite, Obote felt that some restitution was needed and recommended that both Coates, to whom he and all his fellow students owed so much, and the nurse, now long since retired, be appointed OBE.

In the last term most of the time was devoted to revision, and this provided the headmaster with an opportunity to introduce a new subject. The course began with the study of some of the writings of Plato. Obote was deeply impressed by what he learned about Socrates, and he and his fellow students argued in lively fashion about the *Republic*. In general, the class preferred Aristotle to Plato, but they enjoyed most of all reading Plutarch's *Lives*. To introduce young people to books of that sort in Uganda in the 1940s was proof of considerable enlightenment on the part of Coates, and it brought Obote into contact with political and ethical concepts which were to play an important role in forming his character.

Before sitting the Makerere entrance examination, Obote and his friends went home and took part in a number of celebrations to wish them well in their forthcoming ordeal. Yakobo seized the opportunity to solicit Obote's help in translating into English a letter he was sending to the district commissioner. The district commissioner was impressed by the quality of the translation and offered Obote a job as interpreter at the district headquarters. Obote was warned, however, that the offer could be a barbed one. There was some political agitation at the time in Lango, and papers critical of the administration, written in English, had been widely circulated. It was suggested to Obote that the district commissioner might suspect him of having been in some way responsible for the papers and was hoping that by offering him an appointment at district headquarters he could keep a watchful eye on him. Obote, in any case, had no intention of being diverted from his plan to go to Makerere and turned down the proposal.

The examinations were to be written in the eastern town of Tororo, and thither Obote went with the other members of his class. The papers proved to be far less fearsome than had been anticipated, but there followed a painful wait until the results were known. Rehearsals for a

Christmas carol service took place at the school, but the timing of the service was dependent upon when the Makerere results were published, the theory being that the service would be a celebration of the outcome. Eventually the telegram arrived. A bell rang to summon the whole school to assemble and the headmaster announced that only two candidates from Mwiri had been successful. One was the solitary youth from the Western Province who had made no friends while at Mwiri. The other was Obote. Now he was to be a fully-fledged student, after a boyhood which had brought many problems and which had subjected him to many tests. But he had overcome them with patience and courage. His experience was already wide, partly because of the help he had been given by members of his family and his friends, and partly because of his own determination to meet people, to learn about them and to try to understand them. He had shown a considerable capacity for friendship, but he had always been prepared to stand upon his own feet. He was on the verge of being twenty-one and his boyhood was at an end.

Chapter 3

The young politician

Makerere College only achieved the status of a university college attached to the University of London in 1950, three years after Obote arrived there. Located on the outskirts of Kampala, the main town although not then the capital of Uganda, the college had been in existence for nearly thirty years and was the highest centre of education in East Africa. Students came to the college from Kenya, Tanganyika and Zanzibar, as well as from Uganda, and there were even a few from Nyasaland and Northern Rhodesia. The course was of two years' duration and successful students were awarded a college diploma which was about equivalent to a good A level standard in three subjects. After that there were professional courses in education, in medicine at the already famous Makerere medical school, in agriculture and in veterinary science.

Obote had set his heart on reading law, and when he learned that no courses in law were available at Makerere his first inclination was to surrender his place there. He was persuaded by a fellow student to seize the one opportunity for further education which had so far presented itself, and he began what was to be an enjoyable period of study at Makerere in March 1947. He had firmly decided that he did not wish to become a teacher, and although his performance in scientific subjects in the entrance examination had been about the same as in the humanities, he believed his weak performance in biology would preclude him from going on to a professional course in one of the applied sciences. The humanities seemed to offer a wider choice of occupation after completing his studies. Unfortunately, no course in history, one of his favourite subjects, was on offer, so he eventually opted for English, geography and what were described as general studies, which mainly consisted of political science and sociology. He particularly enjoyed English, which was taught by an imaginative lecturer, John Sibly, and he was especially pleased when he was chosen by the other first-year students to play the title role of Julius Caesar in the department's annual Shakespeare production. Geography, which in retrospect he recognized as having been very well taught, he found less enthralling. From time to time he absented himself from classes in that subject in order to attend the meetings of the Uganda Legislative Council which were held in nearby Kampala. The legislative council was at that time a rudimentary body. Although in 1945 three senior African chiefs had, for the first time, become nominated members, they were unlikely, and were certainly not expected, to challenge the Protectorate administration's policies. The only criticism of authority came from the handful of European and Asian unofficial members whose interests were almost exclusively commercial. Nevertheless, the legislative council, albeit primarily a forum in which the administration could explain its proposals to a captive audience, was the nearest thing Uganda possessed to a parliament, and as such it attracted Obote's profound interest.

During this period, too, he read whatever law books the college library possessed and his determination had its reward when he learned that he had been awarded a local government scholarship by the Lango District Council to read law in England. Although only in his second year at Makerere he at once gave up his college place in order to prepare himself for the adventure that lay ahead. His elation was followed by bitter disappointment when he was told that the Protectorate administration had ordered the withdrawal of the scholarship because law studies were thought to be an inappropriate subject upon which to spend public funds. His disappointment turned to distrust when he learned that T. R. F. Cox, who had been involved in an earlier scholarship dispute, now occupied an influential post in the secretariat.

He was briefly at a loss as to what he should do next. He did not think he could return to repeat his second year at Makerere, but his only qualifications for employment were the Cambridge School Certificate he had gained at Busoga College and the resilience he had acquired as a result of the hardships and setbacks he had undergone in his years as a student. He had, however, made many friends at Makerere, including a number of students from Kenya from whom he had learned of the very different conditions prevailing in their country. He determined, therefore, to spend some time in Kenya, trying to understand a society in which a small, white, settler population could virtually dominate government policy.

In the event, he saw little of the settlers. In Nairobi, where he found accommodation and work, the chief manifestation of white domination he encountered was when he was refused admission to the city library. This was offset by the opportunity to read in the libraries of the US Information Service and the Indian High Commission. He also met Jomo Kenyatta, at that time a vigorously outspoken critic of British rule in Kenya. Interesting though this experience was, he knew that if he were to seek permanent employment he must return to Uganda. He still had little idea of what he wanted to do, but an opening occurred in the costing department of the large construction company, Mowlem, in Jinja. Although he became involved in the rudimentary trade union activities taking place in the town, the next two years were relatively uneventful. In 1952, however, a number of Baganda formed the Uganda National Congress, the first political party to be set up in the Protectorate. The intention was to found a country-wide political movement which would campaign for immediate self-government and would be open to members of all races. This objective, however, meant that in practice the membership of the party was almost exclusively African and, because of a lack of financial backing, its main efforts were concentrated in and around Kampala. Remembering his grandfather's views on British domination, Obote was deeply interested in this new development. He at once became a member of the UNC, but the demands of his work meant that he could not take part in the central activities of the party, which took place fifty miles from Jinja. The Jinja branch played a relatively minor role and was dependent upon the far from vigorous liaison efforts of a Musoga lawyer, David Lubogo, whose practice was in Kampala and who brought sporadic news from the centre to the branch members.

Towards the end of the year a new prospect opened before Obote when his company transferred him to Nairobi. Before leaving Uganda he was given a letter, signed by Lubogo and other members of the UNC leadership, declaring him to be the accredited representative of the Congress in Kenya. This was not, at the time, a particularly significant honour, but it did lead to an introduction to Walter Odede, a former lecturer at Makerere who had recently become president of the Kenya African Union. He had succeeded Jomo Kenyatta, who had been arrested on a charge of managing the movement among the Kikuyu people known as Mau Mau which had declared war on the Kenyan government. It was through Odede that Obote first met Tom Mboya, who was to become Odede's son-in-law and who was already playing an important role in the trade union movement among Africans in Kenya. At this stage Obote was too anxious to hold onto his job to renew his acquaintance with trade unionism, but his path was soon to cross that of Mboya once again.

His stay in Nairobi was short. In 1953 he was transferred to the Kinangop region where his employers were building an important dam. In this area the Mau Mau movement was becoming increasingly active and it was not long before Obote came into contact with it. Late one night he was awakened and taken, along with a number of other young men, to take part in a Mau Mau oathing ceremony. He refused to eat the ritual meat and drink the ritual beer, pointing out that he was not a Kikuyu and that the oath would not therefore be binding on him. He then produced the letter accrediting him as the representative of the UNC in Kenya, and to his relief that evidence was accepted as proof of his good faith. Some time later he was approached by a member of Mau Mau who asked him to assist by allowing supplies for the movement to be transported on Mowlem's lorries travelling from Nairobi. He protested that it was the drivers of the vehicles who should be asked for help, and because they were Kikuyu there should be no problem. It was explained to him that his role would be to turn a blind eye to any contraband he might encounter when checking the contents of the trucks. This he willingly agreed to do. His sympathies had been fully enlisted by the struggle being put up by Mau Mau against what he regarded as an unduly repressive and unresponsive government.

He was equally receptive when he was approached by the Mau Mau leader, Dedan Kimathi himself, with a further request. As a result of the bombing of their camps by RAF aircraft, Kimathi said, they were desperately short of cooking facilities. If Obote would arrange for some Mowlem employees to bring stoves and parafin from Nairobi he would gladly pay for them. Obote again agreed to help, but in face of the increasingly indiscriminate violence used by Mau Mau against both African and European civilians he became disillusioned. To wage a campaign against troops and police might be justifiable; the methods of terrorism employed by Mau Mau in his opinion were not. He was not sorry, therefore, to be transferred to Nairobi in 1955 and thence, briefly, to Mombasa.

On his return to Nairobi in 1956 Obote left Mowlem and began working for an oil company. By this time the Mau Mau guerrilla campaign was virtually at an end, although the enormous task of rehabilitating the thousands of people whose lives had been disrupted by the struggle still lay ahead. It had also been announced that, for the first time, Africans would be allowed to elect eight representatives to the legislative council on a qualitative franchise. The number was raised to fourteen the following year. Members of the Kikuyu, Meru and Embu groups would not be allowed to take part because of their involvement in the Mau Mau rising. African political organizations had been proscribed during the state of emergency, but in order to promote the elections approval was now given to the formation of political associations on a district basis, although not at a national level. Excited by the prospect of sharing in these new political opportunities, Obote joined the Nairobi District African Congress (NDAC) which had been founded by C. M. G. Arwings-Kodhek, the first qualified African barrister in Kenya. The NDAC soon rejected its founder, and although he was not himself present at the meeting at which the decision was taken, Obote learned that he had been elected chairman. The group then threw its support behind the candidature of Tom Mboya, whose main backing came from the trade union movement and who was standing against Arwings-Kodhek in the Nairobi constituency. Mboya was victorious, and by his participation in the election campaign Obote gained political experience and established a lasting friendship with the rising star of Kenya's politics.

It would be a surprise to many of his later critics to learn that it was during his stay in Nairobi that Obote first took heed of the warning to abjure communism. It would be even more surprising to discover that his mentor was Apa Pant, the aggressively nationalist Indian consul-general in Kenya. By offering scholarships to enable Africans to study in India Pant had convinced the British rulers of both Kenya and Uganda that he was bent on disseminating communism in East Africa. At that time anyone who openly criticized British administration was deemed to be inspired by communist ideals. Pant it was, nevertheless, who warned Obote to avoid communism when Uganda became independent, because democracy could never survive in a communist state.

Soon after the 1957 legislative council elections Obote was arrested on suspicion of having connections with Mau Mau. After being kept in prison for three days he was released because of the lack of evidence against him. Nevertheless, he deemed it wise to leave Kenya and to see what Uganda had to offer. He had no plans and certainly gave little thought to the possibility of involving himself with the political life of his own country.

In Obote's absence Uganda had undergone a political revolution as fundamental, if far less bloody, than that he had witnessed in Kenya. Under the inspiring governorship of Sir Andrew Cohen, who had arrived in Uganda in 1952, the year in which the Uganda National Congress had been founded, a new spirit was abroad in the country. Cohen had not been immediately impressed by the leaders of the UNC and looked for better-educated Africans whose political utterances were not restricted to over-simplified demands for immediate self-government. Although such men existed, Cohen soon recognized that they were men of words rather than of action and were unlikely to win popular support. His next plan was to increase the African membership of the legislative council so as to provide a controlled forum for would-be politicians who could command public confidence. The council, which, in spite of its name, was essentially a consultative body, was to be the training ground for the future leaders of the country.

There was one obstacle to the plan – the kingdom of Buganda. In so many ways Buganda, upon many of whose leaders the British had relied heavily in the early years of the century when the Protectorate administration was being extended to regions where local chiefs, like Obote's grandfather, Akaki, were slow to adapt to the new regime, had advanced far ahead of the rest of the country. To have held it back until other parts caught up would have been unjust. After setting up an inquiry into the situation in Buganda, therefore, Cohen concluded that the only fair way to ensure the kingdom's co-operation in his constitutional plan was to offer additional powers to Buganda's leaders in the conduct of their local government on condition that they agreed to work with the rest of the country towards a unified state. Even at that time it had seemed a risky undertaking, but Uganda could not advance without Buganda and alternative plans were not forthcoming.

The immediate result was not to arouse resentment in the rest of the country, as some civil servants had feared it might do, but to stir up powerful opposition in Buganda itself against what was seen as an attempt to undermine the special position its leaders believed the kingdom already enjoyed. They were proud of their country, of its traditions, its culture and its system of government. The Baganda, by and large, were prosperous – the leaders themselves especially so. All this could, in their view, be jeopardized by too close an association with peoples whom they regarded as distinctly less sophisticated than themselves. Moreover, in a united Uganda their voice could so easily be lost amid the clamour of the more numerous inhabitants of the rest of the country. Even after the large accession of territory made with British help in the 1890s at the expense of neighbouring Bunyoro, Buganda still comprised, in area, only a quarter of the Protectorate, and its population amounted to only a third of that of Uganda as a whole. Pressure was accordingly brought to bear on the *kabaka*, the ruler of Buganda, to resist Cohen's overtures. When he did so, the governor, in a moment of frustration, deposed him and sent him into exile. This act, far from ensuring the acquiescence of the Baganda, only served to unite any waverers behind the move to resist any further British interference in the kingdom.

A powerful, pro-Bugandan lobby was immediately mustered in England – a response which Obote was himself later to experience in similar circumstances. It was backed by united action on the part of the Baganda in Uganda itself and the British authorities had to back down. Ostensibly the Baganda, too, made concessions which would limit the powers of the *kabaka* by means of constitutional restraints and would result in Buganda's agreement to taking part in the activities of the legislative council. But the *kabaka*'s exile had strengthened his hold over his people in a manner which could not be restricted by constitutional means. It would, too, have been a poor Muganda who could not find a way to circumvent the provisions regarding membership of the legislative council. An attempt by Cohen to woo the Baganda by suggesting they should take the lead by being the first region to hold direct elections to the council foundered just when it seemed an agreement had been reached.

Meanwhile, under Cohen's skilled tutelage, the council had become a seminary for aspiring politicians from the rest of the country, but its success only encouraged the division between Buganda and the rest of Uganda. But Cohen pressed ahead and, just before Obote returned to Lango District, he had introduced a ministerial system with five of the ministers drawn from the general public while the rest were civil servants. Three of the five were Africans. In addition, the membership of the legislative council had been increased to sixty, and it was intended that representative members of the new legislative council, to be elected in 1958, should be chosen by means of direct elections on a wide franchise in those districts which decided to avail themselves of the opportunity. Moreover, although an official majority had been retained, already thirty of the sixty members were Africans.

These reforms had not been carried out without considerable upheaval, not least because of the fears they had aroused among the leaders of Buganda who were concerned that the preferential treatment hitherto accorded to the kingdom in return for its co-operation was being eroded. Moreover, the leaders had been able to enlist the support of the vast majority of the Baganda by playing upon their pride in their identity and by emphasizing their unique traditions, although some of those had been radically modified to benefit the leaders themselves since the imposition of the Protectorate.

The suspicions about British motives would have been relatively insignificant had it not been for the geographically central position which the kingdom occupied within Uganda. Kampala, the commercial and later the political capital, was located in Buganda. All communications, by road, by rail, by lake steamer, and even by air, radiated from Buganda. The Protectorate administration had its headquarters at Entebbe, in Buganda. The high court was located in Kampala, and the university college which served the whole of East Africa was on the outskirts of the town. The kingdom of Buganda was more central to Uganda than the home counties are to England. Through the chance development of British administration in the region, Buganda had become the very core of a country to which its leaders, and possibly many of its people, did not particularly wish to belong. Whatever the future held for Uganda, however, Buganda must be an integral part of it. Unfortunately, the British authorities did not know how to achieve that essential objective and the Buganda question was to grow until it became the dominant factor bedevilling further constitutional advance.

Obote, meanwhile, had more immediate problems. His return to his home district of Lango followed hard upon disturbances occasioned by hostility to legislation recently introduced by the Protectorate administration in the hope of encouraging the spread of individual ownership of land. The Uganda National Congress was rightly suspected of having helped to foment the unrest and some of its local members were arrested, Obote among them. In spite of the recent constitutional reforms, possibly even because they had readily instituted those reforms, the Protectorate authorities were not well disposed towards politicians who demanded still more, and who were prepared to promote their claims by stirring up opposition to any or all of the government's measures. Obote protested that he had only just returned to Uganda and had no knowledge of the

Land Apportionment Act – and could certainly have played no part in
the disturbances. He was told, therefore, that he must accompany officials
around the district explaining to the public the importance of the legislation. The fact that he performed the task with extreme reluctance and
with little understanding of what he was required to say was to stand him
in good stead, for it introduced him to the whole population of Lango
as a man who was not in favour with the British authorities. Shortly after
these events, the Lango representative in the legislative council, Jacobo
Omonya, who had been elected by the district council acting as an
electoral college, resigned. Obote, angered by his encounter with the
British authorities but pleased to find an opening for his talents, decided
that this was his opportunity to seek election in Omonya's place.

There were three other candidates, two of whom were teachers. Obote
presented himself to the electors as a critic of the British administration
who had already suffered at its hand – witness his recent clash with
authority over the Land Apportionment Act and, even more painfully, by
having had his scholarship to study law withdrawn. By contrast, the two
teachers had benefited greatly from their willing subservience to foreign
rule. They had both received overseas scholarships and now enjoyed
secure employment by the state. In the uneasy conditions prevailing in the
district his appeal fell on receptive ears and he was elected convincingly.

Obote travelled to Kampala and took the oath as a representative
member of the legislative council on the afternoon of 10 March 1958.
His first feelings were not of triumph but of profound loneliness. The
council was in its final meeting of the session and virtually all the other
members had held their seats for more than four years. They were familiar
with the proceedings of the council and, under the skilled handling of
Sir Andrew Cohen, who had until recently presided at the meetings, they
had begun to feel at home there. Obote knew some of the leaders of the
UNC who sat in the council, but in this milieu they seemed unfamilar.
Dr B. N. Kununka had practised in Lango District. Now, in Kampala, he
debated with a smooth eloquence which reflected his professional training. He was, too, surrounded by a circle of Bugandan friends who were
totally unknown to Obote. At the same time he was at ease in the company
of European and Asian members of the medical profession who, as far
as Obote was concerned, inhabited another world. The elderly Muganda
chief, Y. K. Bamuta, another member of the UNC, shared neither Kununka's sophistication nor his fluency in English, but he was part of the
traditional hierarchy of the Bugandan kingdom, and it was to Buganda
and not to the political shibboleths of the UNC that he gave his ultimate
allegiance. Even the president of the UNC, Ignatius Musazi, had spiritual
roots which reached still further back into Buganda's past than did those
of Bamuta, back to the time when the clans were predominant, before
the *kabakas* claimed authenticity by adopting the title *Sabasajja* (head

of the heads of clans), by which the present holder of the office was still addressed. The other African representatives who were not members of the UNC seemed to Obote to be of little significance. Although they criticized the administration, they did so as individuals, debating enthusiastically but with little apparent expectation of achieving any notable response.

The European and Asian members of the council were, in Obote's eyes, out of place there. They represented an era in Uganda's history that was already drawing to a close. The official members, confident, as colonial civil servants often were, in their unassailable authority, listened with a fair measure of politeness to the arguments put forward by representatives on the opposite side of the council, but showed little inclination to change their views. Even Jimmy Simpson, the leader of the representative members and a vigorous critic of bureaucratic caution, was no radical opponent of the system. Nor, indeed, was the professionally irascible Handley Bird, who, in any case, had surrendered his right to criticize openly by accepting a ministerial portfolio, from which vantage point he attacked his former colleagues with all the assumed venom he had formerly used to chastise the administration. The artificiality of such behaviour was new to Obote and accorded ill with his own feelings about the way in which the country's affairs should be conducted.

The brilliant Indian, Sir Amar Maini, had also joined the front bench of the administration. His prodigious memory for facts was matched only by his ability to marshal them and project them in debate with the speed and deadly accuracy of a machine-gun fed by an endless belt of cartridges. Stenographers gave up the unequal struggle to keep pace with him. Instead of giving him proofs of his speeches for correction, they resignedly handed him blank sheets of paper in the hope that he, at least, might be able to recall what he had said. Other council members, for the most part, sat in dazed incomprehension, too mesmerized by his eloquence even to seek refuge in the bar. Obote was impressed, but for him Maini's was not the voice to speak for the people to whose aspirations he himself wished to give utterance – the small farmers, the wage-labourers and the petty traders. Only one non-African member aroused his sympathy: Mrs Barbara Saben, the wife of a Kampala businessman, seemed to him to speak with a sincerity and fervour he himself set out to emulate.

His maiden speech, delivered on 11 March in the course of a debate on the administration's three-year capital development programme, was, like most maiden speeches, competent but undistinguished. It was, essentially, the speech of a sound constituency man. He drew attention to the absence of any rail communication with Lango District and to the poor quality of its roads. He spoke, too, of the prolonged drought that had made it impossible for his constituents to produce the cotton quota demanded by the administration as a pre-condition for the establishment of a cotton ginnery in the district. Finally, he addressed a theme to which he was to return several times during the rest of the session – the lack of any senior secondary school in Lango. He contrasted this with the abundant provision of secondary education in Buganda, another issue he was to raise in subsequent speeches. The entire contents of the development programme demonstrated, he said, a lack of appreciation of the needs of the Northern Province. Congratulating Obote on his maiden speech, as was customary, Maini murmured that brevity was the soul of wit – and then proceeded to speak for three times as long himself, albeit with his usual fluency and linguistic felicity.

Obote was given the opportunity to comment on a more directly political topic the following day, when Bamuta introduced a motion calling upon the British government to initiate negotiations that would lead to self-government for Uganda. Bamuta's opening address seemed confused because of his poor command of English, but he maintained that when Uganda did achieve self-government there would be no all-powerful President Nkrumah, who exercised unchallenged authority over traditional rulers and commoners alike. Hereditary rulers would retain their authority. Thus was Obote introduced to the problem which would bedevil not only the remaining years of the Protectorate but would carry over into independence and lead to his own downfall. At this time, however, he did not comment on the statement. Instead, he supported Bamuta's main proposal. Britain, he said, had originally offered its protection to Uganda, but had subsequently overstepped its role by acting as if Uganda were a colony. Here was the authentic voice of grandfather Akaki speaking. But the training given by Obote's father, Stanley, could not be summarily set aside. Obote conceded that it would be unjust to underestimate Britain's contribution to the country's development, but he believed the time had come to plan a timetable for the hand-over of power to the people of Uganda. His statement was couched in moderate terms and he was later to admit that he had no clear idea of what self-government would involve. But that was the era of national claims to self-determination, and India had provided an example which had, at that time, an impact upon the attitudes of East Africa's budding politicians more potent even than had events in Ghana. Needless to say, the motion was noted by the government's representatives and rejected.

Obote asked his first question in the council on 5 May on a matter concerning his own constituency, but he returned to wider political issues the following day when he asked if the ministerial system the administration proposed to introduce in Buganda would be extended to the other provinces. When the minister of local government, L. M. Boyd, said that it would not, and gave what appeared to be an equivocal explanation for the government's decision, Obote raised the issue again in an adjournment debate on the same day. He made it clear that he was not criticizing the Baganda for going along with the proposals. The fault lay with the central administration which, in spite of maintaining that its long-term aim was to create an independent and unitary Uganda, was bent upon setting up a state within a state. When independence was eventually achieved, would Buganda wish to surrender the privileges it was now acquiring, he asked. It seemed very doubtful. He was ably supported by Dr Kununka, who proposed that a constitutional adviser should be invited to hear the views of the rest of the people of Uganda and to make recommendations for the country's future development as Professor Keith Hancock had recently done for Buganda. The member for Teso District, C. J. Obwangor, also spoke in favour of the motion.

The acting chief secretary, G. B. (later Sir George) Cartland, although a practised negotiator of uncertain ground, found it difficult to argue convincingly against these criticisms. He stressed the fact that, since the establishment of the Protectorate, the various parts of the country had had to be developed along different lines for a variety of irreproachable reasons. The current situation was simply a continuation of a natural historical process. Earlier in the day, however, J. K. Babiiha, the member for Toro District, had challenged this assumption in the course of a debate on another topic when he had argued that, from the outset, the British authorities had encouraged Buganda to enjoy internal autonomy and had continued to do so irrespective of malfunctions and more obvious misdeeds. Obote's contribution to the argument, was, therefore, only one among many expressions of dissatisfaction with the role of Buganda within the Protectorate. At this early stage of his career in the legislative council he was far from establishing himself as a leading speaker from the representative benches.

In one respect Obote had, nevertheless, begun to develop an individual line of thought which was to become more significant as time passed. Unlike the other representatives, he felt no resentment towards the Baganda. He could recognize their powerful sense of national identity, their pride in their traditions – even if some of them had been considerably modified under British influence – and their self-sufficiency. He was prepared to respect those feelings while realizing that they must somehow be curbed in order to create a unitary, independent Uganda. It was for this reason that he was prepared to accept the administration's decision to allow districts to decide for themselves whether they would adopt direct or indirect methods of election in the forthcoming contest for seats in the new legislative council. Although his strong preference was for direct elections which would allow as many people as possible to cast their vote, he recognized that the only prospect of winning the co-operation of Buganda lay in permitting the kingdom's leaders to direct operations by using their local council, the *lukiiko*, as an electoral college. Buganda's participation in the central legislature, was, in Obote's view, more important at that moment than a rigid insistence upon democratic principles. In the event, even the offer of indirect elections was not enough to win Buganda's support. The leaders of the kingdom argued, speciously, that the protectorate administration had broken the agreement recently made between Britain and Buganda by introducing a speaker to preside over the legislative council instead of the governor, thereby making a fundamental change in the nature of the council. Until the question was settled by the high court, Buganda claimed the right to stand aloof from the council's proceedings.

For the remainder of the session Obote remained in the shadow of more practised speakers in the council. Later in May, for example, at the request of the other representative members Kununka became the first African to open the debate on the budget on their behalf. Obote himself took no part in the debate except to raise a number of constituency issues at the committee stage. Babiiha, meantime, renewed his attack upon the administration for creating a state within a state by its attitude towards Buganda. Bamuta and a former senior official in the Buganda government, S. W. Kulubya, spoke up in defence of the kingdom, while Obote, observing the simmering conflict of opinion, held his peace. In September, when the session reopened after a long recess, Babiiha persisted in his campaign, asking for a uniform judicial system for the whole country instead of allowing Buganda to have its own hierarchy of judges. Uncharacteristically, Obote himself asked if it was the administration's intention to make agreements with the other districts similar to those which had been made half a century earlier with Buganda and the three other, smaller kingdoms of the south-west. His object in asking the question is unclear, but for the rest of the session he left Kununka to take the lead in expressing regret that the administration had not seen fit to adopt the representative members' proposal for a reasonable increase in the number of Africans to be elected to the next council and in asking for the appointment of a constitutional committee early in 1959, to prepare the way for major constitutional changes. Obote spoke late in the debate on the first motion but added nothing original to what had already been said by earlier speakers. If he had intended to contribute to the discussion about a constitutional committee he was prevented from doing so by the ending of the session, and, in any case, the government conceded this important point.

If he had made no profound impression during the six months he had been in the council, the experience had whetted Obote's appetite for political life. He had every intention of standing for re-election on a much wider franchise and he had been reorganizing the Lango branch of the UNC with that end in mind. He had, too, begun to understand the workings of the legislative council better. Most of all, he had begun to feel that British overrule would not last for ever and that he himself could play a significant role in restoring independence to his people. He had had little opportunity to assess the character of Sir Andrew Cohen. By the time he became a member of the legislative council the governor had ceased to preside over the council's meetings, his place having been taken by a speaker. But Cohen had left his mark. A convinced liberal, he had spent some years in the colonial office before taking up his appointment in Uganda, and he had become deeply conscious of the stirrings of political life in different parts of Africa. He had, too, the encouraging example of the Gold Coast, where a liberal governor was working closely and successfully with African political leaders and thereby setting a pattern that might have some exciting implications for other colonial dependencies. So the years of Cohen's governorship had been full of innovation, and Africans who had been only tentatively contemplating political change in some remote future had begun to feel themselves part of a tangible scheme which would lead to self-government. There had been other Africans who resented what Cohen was trying to do, but their opposition had only stoked the fervour of those who had begun to see Cohen not so much as a colonial governor but as an African leader.

It was, however, upon reports of Cohen's actions, rather than upon personal acquaintance, that Obote had to base his opinion. He was particularly impressed by the easy manner in which Cohen had cut the ground from under the feet of the UNC leaders by conceding much of what they had been preparing to demand, even before they could fully articulate their requests. Obote's admiration for Cohen was to develop into a close friendship later in his career. But Cohen was to be replaced as governor before the end of the year. His successor, Sir Frederick Crawford, had a more conservative view of Uganda's future. A colonial administrator first and foremost, Sir Frederick concentrated upon sound administration rather than upon visions of imminent independence for Africa. So Obote was to find himself in an uneasy atmosphere, when the momentum built up by Cohen was still carrying the country forward, but now intermittently, with occasional setbacks interspersed by sudden forward surges.

Chapter 4

Gaining experience

Preparations for the new elections by the Protectorate authorities had been both intensive and thorough. A supervisor of elections, C. P. S. Allen, had been appointed soon after the decision to hold elections had been taken and a training course was held for election officers. As early as January 1958 a publicity campaign had been launched, and on 1 February registration of voters began in the Northern and Western Provinces and in the eastern province on 1 March. To the disappointment of Obote – and of the Protectorate administration – the Bugandan government decided after lengthy negotiations that the kingdom would play no part in the proceedings. In the early stages, the menfolk of Lango District, too, were slow to register, fearing that the whole process was a European ruse to deprive them of their land. In the first six weeks only 15,271 potential voters had registered their names. Intensive touring by the district commissioner and his staff overcame these suspicions and by the closing date there were 58,951 names on the register, nearly 74 per cent of the estimated number of people entitled to vote.

Obote himself campaigned vigorously for re-election. Having to appeal to a much wider electorate he travelled the district on a bicycle, talking to anyone who would listen. His rivals were the same three men who had stood against him at the previous election, and the substance of his campaign remained the same as before. He introduced himself as the protest candidate and dismissed his opponents as government men. As the sitting member he had already demonstrated his willingness to present the case for improvements in his constituency and was clearly not afraid to challenge the protectorate authorities when opposition was needed. Although Allen recorded that there was considerable tension in Lango, the elections themselves went off quietly. In the event, Obote's appeal to the electorate proved as effective as it had been to the district council the previous year. His victory at the polls was overwhelming. Of the 52,416 votes cast in his constituency he polled 40,081, a striking tribute to the effective manner in which he had organized the constituency party as well as to his own campaigning skill. When the result was announced Obote and his supporters organized a large-scale victory parade which, in spite of the forebodings of the administration, proved to be a thoroughly good-humoured occasion.

The die was cast. Obote decided there and then to become a professional politician. Deeply committed to the principles of democracy even at this early stage in his career, he was greatly encouraged by the strength of the support he had received. His attendance allowance as a member of the legislative council, which still sat relatively infrequently, was not princely, but during the council sessions he could stay with friends in Kampala. He had little taste for the company in the Uganda Club, founded on the initiative of Sir Andrew Cohen as a meeting place for members of all races with an interest in politics. In other respects, too, his needs were small, and money was never, either then or subsequently, of great importance to him. He could survive, and he would be doing what he now realized he had always wanted to do.

The new council met on 17 November 1958 and was addressed by the governor, Sir Frederick Crawford. The heady days of Cohen, when Africans had felt inspired to hasten to keep up with his ideas for reform, were a thing of the past. Crawford, although invariably courteous in his dealings with people in all walks of life, was far from sharing Cohen's vision of an early move towards self-government. The content of his speech was not such as to encourage any hope of great political change. He spoke at length about the need to maintain law and order. The economy, too, must be strengthened, he said, and there must be further developments in the field of education. He mentioned native courts, new proposals regarding land tenure and the need to increase African participation in the civil service in preparation for the time when self-government might eventually be granted. Only at the very end and, it seemed to some of his listeners, with some reluctance, did he refer to the possibility of constitutional change. Even then he spoke in guarded terms, and nothing appeared to be in prospect beyond what had already been agreed in the previous session. Self-government, it seemed, was more remote than before.

This was in line with Britain's consistent refusal to propose a timetable for constitutional advance, a refusal which had aroused grave doubts about the British government's honesty even during Cohen's governorship. A timetable, even a long term one, with all the necessary caveats about the need for training and time to gain experience, would have given some indication that Britain was serious about handing over power.

The majority of the elected members were clearly unimpressed by Crawford's address, but they had yet to establish themselves as an effective opposition. In some respects they were in a weaker position than they had been previously. Dr Kununka, probably the ablest African speaker in the former council, was no longer a member because of Buganda's refusal to send representatives. John Lwamafa, re-elected to represent Kigezi District, had accepted the post of parliamentary secretary for education and now sat on the government side. K. B. Katiiti, from Ankole, had been chosen by the *eishengyero*, the council of that kingdom which had rejected direct elections, so he allied himself with the nominated European and Asian members on the unofficial side of the council who now constituted the rump of the representative members's association. The rest of the unofficial African members formed themselves into the elected members's association, but even within that group there were divisions. W. W. Rwetsiba, also from Ankole, George Magezi from Bunyoro and M. M. Ngobi from Busoga District joined together to found the Uganda People's Union which, however, made no attempt to enlist widespread popular support. Their aims were to shrug off the naturally-assumed leadership of Bugandan politicians, to distance themselves from the self-centred ambitions of the Bugandan kingdom, to promote the interests of the other districts and to work for a unitary government in an independent Uganda. Obote, however, remained loyal to the UNC; his belief in democracy prevented him from doing otherwise. Although the Congress had failed to fulfil its early aspirations, it still set out to be a people's party.

Some of those divisions became apparent in the African members' response to the governor's address. Katiiti and Rwetsiba appeared to welcome what he had said because he had spoken in defence of the dignity and status of the hereditary rulers, of whom the *Mugabe* of Ankole was one. Babiiha, however, moved an amendment regretting the brevity of the reference to constitutional change and seized the opportunity to range widely over the whole field of government policy. Obwangor followed suit, while Magezi concentrated his remarks mainly on constitutional matters, concluding that there seemed to have been some retreat on this front. Obote, as had become his custom, spoke late in the debate. Often this meant that he had little opportunity to add any original comment, but on this occasion he concentrated his attention upon the composition of the legislative council to demonstrate the shortcomings of government policy. Drawing attention to the absence of members from Buganda, he deplored the government's failure to pursue the question of the kingdom's participation more effectively. He was saddened, too, by the fact that dissatisfaction with government policy had meant that Bugisu District was represented by a nominated rather than by an elected member. Overall, the proportion of nominated members of council was still far too high, he claimed, and Africans should have been invited to hold office as ministers in some of the fields of particular importance to them, such as education and trade. He was critical, too, of the special representation of minorities, although on democratic rather than on racial grounds. All in all, it was an effective speech, because it dealt with specific issues within a general context.

Earlier in the meeting he had asked a number of pertinent questions about the recent elections, drawing attention to the role played by religious affiliation in certain constituencies and also asking if it was normal government practice to tape the speeches of politicians campaigning for election. The significance of the first enquiry related to the Roman Catholic origins of the main rival to the UNC, the Democratic Party, founded in 1954. Obote was not a protagonist of the view that religion and politics are mutually exclusive, but he was concerned about the impact of sectarian religion upon the concept of a united Uganda. The taping of speeches, the government maintained, was done only when, as in some cases in Lango District, it was thought they might be prejudicial to peace and good order. Obote, it seemed, was already attracting the critical attention of the Protectorate authorities.

Events outside the legislative council now took precedence over political debate. In December 1958 Ignatius Musazi, president-general of the UNC, suspended six of the party's leading members, including the chairman, J. W. Kiwanuka, and the secretary-general Dr Kununka. In justification he claimed that the six had supported the setting up of a Cairo office of the party which, in his view, would open the way for communist and Egyptian imperialist intervention in Uganda's affairs. Obote joined with Kiwanuka and Kununka in issuing a counter-statement in support of the Cairo office, because they wanted to bring Uganda into the mainstream of international politics, and in announcing the suspension of Musazi.

Musazi immediately summoned a general assembly of the UNC and won the support of a majority of the hundred or so members who attended. When the annual party congress met in Mbale in January 1959, however, his supporters walked out alleging that the meeting was irregular because it had been called by men who had been suspended. Tactically this was a bad move. The rump which remained in the meeting expelled Musazi from the party and elected Obote as president-general in his place. Kiwanuka and Kununka were re-elected to their former posts. Although pleased by his elevation to high office, Obote had no feeling of triumph at the downfall of Musazi. He recognized clearly enough the former president-general's shortcomings as a negotiator with the government and his lack of constructive ideas in policy-making sessions, but he respected the work Musazi had done in founding the UNC. Musazi may have been ineffective as a debater in the more sophisticated setting of the legislative council, but as an open-air orator under the tree of liberty in Kampala he had made a great impact on his audiences.

Obote's relations with Kiwanunka and Kununka did not run smoothly for long. He had always admired Kununka's skill in negotiation and his ability to present a case clearly and cogently, but he found Kiwanuka erratic and unpredictable. They, for their part, with their longer experience of politics, were inclined to look upon Obote's role as that of a figure-head, leaving them to get on with party business. It was a position Obote was most reluctant to accept and within a few months he clashed with his associates. The two main causes of friction were, first, his realization that the external aid which financed the Cairo office was being administered by Kiwanuka as if it were his own money. China was the main source of the aid because, at that time, relations between China and Russia were strained and the former hoped that by strengthening its links with the Afro-Asian Solidarity Movement, which was based in Cairo, it would gain allies in the Third World. Second, he discovered that both Kiwanuka and Kununka were opposed to the idea of a common roll for people of all races in the elections for a future national assembly and that they had adopted that stance in response to pressure from the Bugandan hierarchy. Obote was disturbed both by his colleagues' attitude and by their reason for adopting it. If democracy was to mean anything in Uganda it must mean equal rights for members of minority communities just as much as it must mean the abolition of minority privileges. The UNC had always aimed at being a national and a non-racial party and it would have been a denial of both those principles to permit one group within the country to dictate terms which were contrary to the party's constitution. Within the party itself it would be suicidal to permit ethnic loyalties to supersede allegiance to a united Uganda.

In August 1959 Obote summoned a meeting of his supporters within the party in Kampala at which it was agreed to suspend Kiwanuka, Kununka and the party treasurer, P. Ssengendo. B. K. Kirya, a legislative council member, became party chairman and A. K. Mayanja, who had been one of the founders of the party while he was still an undergraduate at Makerere, was elected secretary-general. The meeting accused Kiwanuka of acting in an overbearing fashion, issuing statements without consulting the executive committee and travelling abroad without seeking the committee's approval. The others were said to have aided and abetted him. The suspended members refused to accept the decision and called their own meeting later in the month, at which Obote and Mayanja, now the only Muganda among Obote's supporters, were expelled from the party. As a result, two groups, each calling itself the UNC, existed in rivalry with each other for several months, but Kiwanuka's group steadily declined in importance. Its Bugandan orientation discouraged support from other areas, and inside Buganda the vast majority of the people, other than those who had joined the Democratic Party, were committed supporters of the *kabaka*'s government.

While the UNC indulged in internecine conflict, the members of the Uganda Peoples' Union (UPU) had taken the lead in attempting to seize the political initiative from Buganda, but conducted their campaign almost entirely within the confines of the legislative council. This was of particular significance because, in February 1959, a committee had been set up to look into the constitutional future of Uganda. The committee was to be chaired by a civil servant, J. V. Wild, and the majority of its members were to be African representative members of the legislative council. Horrified by the prospect of the future constitution of the country being determined by a predominantly non-Bugandan group, the Bugandan leaders responded by refusing to meet the committee. At the same time, they urged the people of Buganda to register their disapproval of what was happening by boycotting non-African goods and by refraining from buying from shops owned by non-Africans. The UPU spokesmen were outraged when the British secretary of state appeared to give in to Buganda's threats by proposing on 9 April 1959 that separate constitutional negotiations should take place with the kingdom. In a question in the legislative council on 4 May, Ngobi expressed the view shared by other UPU members that any such discussions were bound to enhance the position of the *kabaka*'s government at the expense of any hope of creating a unified Uganda. The chief secretary replied that, in his view, such apprehensions were groundless, an opinion which was certainly not shared by the UPU. Magezi therefore moved the adjournment of the council in order to discuss the matter further, arguing that the government's attitude would only encourage other districts to demand some sort of federal system for an independent Uganda. This would be financially ruinous and would destroy the harmony needed for future development.

Obote stood aloof from these recriminations and took no part in the demand for retribution against those who had inspired the boycott. He could see no solution to the problem of Buganda's refusal to be swallowed up in an independent Uganda, but the more he travelled the country with the Wild Committee, which began its hearings in April, the more he was convinced that there could be no valid settlement which excluded the kingdom. He was not even convinced that the apparent unanimity of the other elected African members reflected any real unity of purpose in the country as a whole. How could there be real unity, he asked, when there was such a diversity of languages, of religions, of cultures and of political traditions. He himself could not campaign effectively outside his own district because he would only be understood by those who spoke English, and they were few in number. The centralized authority of Buganda had no parallel in Lango or Teso or Acholi Districts. Even within Buganda itself there was an incipient political split between Protestants and Roman Catholics. It was all very well for the Protectorate authorities to talk of the need for nation-wide political parties, commanding the allegiance of people from all districts. The UNC had failed to achieve that objective, and not only because of the early preponderance of Baganda among its leaders. The Uganda People's Union (UPU), too, although its spokesmen came from all over the country, was united only at legislative council level. The electorate had chosen men to represent constituency interests and knew little of national issues.

It was a gloomy forecast, and one which Obote did not make too public. He fully realized that, without confidence in the future, there was no hope of progress towards an independent, democratic Uganda. He could claim some reassurance from the extent to which political parties had aroused an awareness of political issues, as was evident in the representations made to the Wild Committee all over the country outside Buganda. Even in Karamoja District, which was often regarded by Europeans and Africans alike as a kind of anthropological museum, the district council had presented the committee with fourteen points for consideration, of which the first two consisted of requests for additional representation in the legislature and universal adult suffrage. The other points were not, in fact, of a constitutional character, being concerned with the government's handling of the endemic problem of cattle theft and protests against the harsh measures adopted by the district administration to prevent overgrazing. The councillors were, however, disconcerted when Wild gently reminded them that universal adult suffrage implied votes for women. Ancient prejudices and local difficulties were probably of greater concern to the majority of Uganda's population than any consideration of the nature of the future government of the country. But if the leaders of opinion were beginning to show an interest, as all the evidence presented to the committee suggested that they were, the rest of the people would probably follow suit in time.

In the meantime there were some who already had strong views about the constitution to be reckoned with. In a brief speech in the legislative council in June, Obote opposed those who, in response to Buganda's obduracy, were demanding that other district councils should also deal directly with the central government. The districts, he said, were essentially tribal units, and nothing should be done to strengthen tribalism. At the same time, he did not favour the suggestion that Buganda's separatism should be challenged by calling upon the Protectorate authorities to abolish the *lukiiko* (the kingdom's parliament) and the government of the *kabaka*, the kingdom's traditional ruler, to both of which the Baganda were deeply attached. The first step should be to strengthen the role of provincial councils, with the dual objective of providing a more powerful but less provocative counterbalance to the position of Buganda and of overcoming tribalism in the rest of the country. It should, he hoped, also act as a preliminary move in the direction of national unity. This latter suggestion may not have had much substance, but the whole speech underlined Obote's desire to create a unified Uganda and to ensure that Buganda was not excluded. Unlike the other African representative members of the council, he was at pains to ensure that Buganda's claims should be investigated with sympathy, not simply dismissed out of hand.

Shortly afterwards he again spoke out against criticisms that Buganda received an unfair share of financial assistance for local government. This, he said, was because the kingdom had more than its share of law and order problems, and that these were caused, in part at least, by the behaviour of the Protectorate administration. He was once more prominent in the debate in November on a proposal to amend the penal code in several respects, all of which were aimed at dealing with the troubled situation in Buganda, where the boycott was being enforced by acts of terrorism including arson and murder. Buganda had already been declared a disturbed area on 23 May 1959. Now the government proposed to make it illegal for a society which had been proscribed to resurface under a different name but with the same officers. It would also be unlawful to attend meetings or to claim membership of such a society. In speaking against the proposal, Obote again appeared to be defending Buganda, but in this instance, bearing in mind the chief secretary's reply to his earlier enquiry about the taping of political speeches, he was more concerned lest the measures, if adopted, should be levelled against any party to which the government took exception. He was conscious of the fact that, although the bill ostensibly gave powers to the governor, they would in practice be exercised by district officers, of whose disapproval he had already had personal experience.

More directly orientated towards dealing with the situation in Buganda was the proposal to make incitement to boycott an offence if the boycott was deemed to be aimed at bringing into disrepute either the central government or the *kabaka*'s government, at damaging the economy of the country or at arousing feelings of ill-will or hostility towards particular races or classes in the country. Representative members of all races spoke against the amendment, but only Obote argued that there was no reason why the Baganda should not boycott European-owned shops if they wished to do so. To prevent them would be an arbitrary act by an unelected government. In any case, he continued, those whom the government deemed to have been the leaders of the boycott were already in detention, so that the question of incitement was no longer relevant. It was against those who broke the law and indulged in acts of terrorism that the government should proceed, and it already had adequate powers at its disposal to deal with criminals of that sort. The attorney-general agreed that a boycott was not in itself illegal and that the measure was intended to deal only with cases were incitement to boycott constituted a threat to law and order, but Obote was unconvinced. He was very much afraid that the legislation might be directed against any opposition to unpopular measures if resort were had to a boycott. It would, he knew, be difficult if not impossible to say at the outset that a boycott was unlikely to lead to violence.

Obote's speeches were to have repercussions in an unexpected quarter. Towards the end of the year he had a telephone message from a nominated member of the legislative council, Mrs Pumla Kissosonkole, the step-mother of the wife of the *kabaka*, inviting him to call on her in her office. When he did so she told him that a number of people had been impressed by the tenor of his arguments, among them the *kabaka* himself. She thought that much might be gained if Obote were to have a private meeting with her son-in-law. Obote was excited by the prospect, but while recognizing the need for a measure of secrecy at this tentative stage in the discussions, he was wary of becoming involved in any activity which might not have the approval of his party. He therefore asked if he might take with him a member of the party's executive, proposing the name of Abu Mayanja.

His choice of partner may, had it been made public, have appeared surprising in view of Mayanja's record *vis-à-vis* Buganda. Mayanja had been sent down from Makerere for organizing a student strike in protest against the standard of cooking in one of the halls of residence. Thanks to the intervention of Sir Andrew Cohen, who liked the young man's lively intelligence and regarded his Makerere escapade as less than venal, he had then been awarded a scholarship to enable him to study in Britain. From the safe haven of Cambridge he had written letters to the Ugandan press, berating the *kabaka*'s government for its failure to co-operate with the rest of Uganda. After qualifying as a barrister he had returned to Uganda in 1958 and had opened a legal practice in Kampala, but soon became involved once more in the activities of the UNC, a move which did not endear him to the Bugandan leaders.

Seeing Uganda's political life with fresh eyes after his return from Britain, Mayanja was greatly impressed by the new member of the legislative council from Lango, recognizing more swiftly than many other observers the power which resided in Obote's spare frame. When the first split within the UNC took place Mayanja had already concluded that his old colleague, Musazi, was no longer the man to lead the party through the constitutional complexities which faced Uganda. Later, when Obote broke with his allies, Kiwanuka and Kununka, Mayanja threw his weight behind Obote, whom he already saw, perhaps uniquely at that early stage, as the future leader of an independent Uganda. The two were in many ways complementary. Obote, in spite of his clear mind and strength of purpose, lacked the sophistication of manner and of speech to impress more superficial observers of his suitability to become the country's leader. Mayanja, on the other hand, had no desire to be the leader, and his irrepressible sense of fun deprived him of the *gravitas* needed for such a responsible position. But he was wholly at ease when dealing with the press and he actively enjoyed taking part in complicated negotiations. Obote's decision to take him as his companion in the discussions with the *kabaka* was not, therefore, wholly illogical. Moreover, Mayanja was, after all, secretary-general of Obote's wing of the UNC, and the party chairman, Balaki Kirya, whom Obote might perhaps have chosen to accompany him, was not a Muganda and he was renowned neither for his intelligence nor his skill in negotiation.

Although for these various reasons Mayanja was an appropriate choice for Obote to make, his acceptance by the *kabaka* was surprising, but the latter made no demur. There was then some discussion between Obote and Mayanja about their conduct in the *kabaka*'s presence. Both because he was not a Muganda and because he did not wish to suggest that he was in any way subservient to the *kabaka*, Obote said that he would behave with utmost civility but he did not intend to prostrate himself before Mutesa or give any other indication that he acknowledged any sort of subordination to the *kabaka*. Mayanja, however, fulfilled all the obligations expected of a loyal Muganda subject, even insisting on sitting on the floor in the *kabaka*'s presence. The *kabaka* himself showed every courtesy to Obote, shaking hands with him and indicating that he should sit on a chair beside him.

From that time the three conducted intermittent talks in private, from which it transpired that the *kabaka*'s main aim was to prevent the Democratic Party from taking the lead in Uganda's affairs. The leaders of that party were Baganda who patently wished to see an end to the powers of the *kabaka*'s government in their existing form. Obote's apparent sympathy for Buganda's predicament had encouraged Mutesa to seek his co-operation in the face of this internal challenge. Although he was fully aware of the delicacy of his position, Obote nevertheless consistently urged the *kabaka* to permit his people to vote in elections for the central legislature. Above all, he stressed that, if the Democratic Party was to be defeated, Buganda must play its part in whatever national assembly might emerge as a result of constitutional discussions. Without such participation, he said, the kingdom would be in no position to influence events. The *kabaka* replied that he could offer all Buganda's seats in such an assembly in support of Obote, but the latter said he would be happier to see direct elections in the kingdom so that the people could give their support freely.

Obote was not dissatisfied with what had taken place. He found the *kabaka* a likeable man who seemed to be under heavy pressure from his advisers to take a cautious line in dealing with the constitutional issues which had Uganda in their grip, and who was fully aware of the difficulties he faced. Obote was not unsympathetic, and he believed their conversations had helped the *kabaka* to adopt a more co-operative attitude towards the British government's efforts to reach a constitutional settlement. At no point, however, did Obote say, as the *kabaka* was later to claim,[1] that if he became prime minister after independence, he would stand down and allow Mutesa to name his successor. The *kabaka*'s statement is all the more open to question since Obote had always insisted that a party leader could only be chosen by the party, or at least by its national executive. In any case, the *kabaka* would have been in no position to choose a prime minister for the whole country because he was only ruler of Buganda. At no time was any other member of the UNC allowed to become privy to the discussions. Obote was far too anxious to protect whatever progress might be made towards the integration of Buganda from the hostile scrutiny of those who still eyed the kingdom with deep suspicion.

The Wild Committee completed its deliberations in October and its report was published on 24 December. In spite of the limitations of the committee's brief, the impact of the report was enormous, foreshadowing as it did early responsible government, with a chief minister and universal adult suffrage. There had been a minority report signed by the non-African members of the committee recommending special representation for non-Africans in the national assembly, but the remarkable thing was the unanimity of the members on every issue of importance. This owed a lot to the judicious chairmanship of Wild. Obote's own overriding impression of the committee's proceedings was of the scrupulous fairness of the chairman and of the clarity with which he had expounded the various issues under consideration. On the question of special representation, it was significant that the Asian communities had at first been anxious to ensure that they should be represented in the legislature by people of their own choosing. A number of younger Asians, however, had argued strongly that their future in Uganda depended upon their being integrated with the population as a whole without asking for any special concessions to be made to them. It was this latter view that triumphed. In the event, the creation of small urban constituencies in Kampala and Jinja ensured that Asians were able to elect their own representatives, and because the arrangement had neither a racial nor a communal basis it was acceptable to the African political leaders.

It was after the committee had completed its travels that Obote became involved in a bizarre adventure. A Muganda visiting Sweden pretended that he was Obote and a reception was organized by the Swedish government in his honour. Before it took place, a Swedish student who had attended a course at the labour college in Uganda denounced the imposter and an invitation was sent to Obote to visit Sweden himself. Obote sought the approval of the UNC executive, which agreed to finance the trip, and, being anxious to see as much of the world as he could on this first opportunity to travel abroad, he followed a circuitous route, through Nairobi, Khartoum, Lagos and Monrovia, regretfully spending only a few hours in each place as he changed from one aircraft to another. From Monrovia he travelled to Madrid in the company of a Spanish journalist with whom he had struck up an acquaintance, and thence flew on through Paris to Stockholm. As an opportunity to see the world it had been disappointing, but then his fortunes changed.

In Stockholm he met a number of people, including Olaf Palmer, who was private secretary to the then prime minister of Sweden. One of the main attractions of the Swedish visit was the opportunity Obote hoped it would provide to learn about Scandinavian socialism because the UNC had already begun to consider the possibility of introducing a socialist form of government into Uganda. This was no naive pursuit of an ill-digested ideology. Obote was not alone among Africans in recognizing that, whatever benefits British administration had brought to Uganda, equality of opportunity was not one of them. All senior posts, whether in the government or in business, were still held by Europeans or Asians, while historical fortune had left a number of Baganda as the only Africans owning large areas of land and able to accumulate notable wealth from rents and the sale of produce. Socialists, unlike the British authorities or the wealthy Baganda, at least appeared concerned with discovering means to iron out some of these inequalities. In the course of two meetings with the Swedish prime minister, at a reception and in the prime minister's office, Obote was given documents to study and he also acquired a number of books that might assist him and the members of his party to understand what the Swedish government was trying to do. The prime minister stressed very firmly, however, that in Sweden socialism was not to be equated with communism. It was a distinction of which Obote was already well aware. For him, even socialism would never become an ideology to be sanctified, only a tool to be used, pragmatically, when it seemed to suit the needs of the people of Uganda.

Nevertheless, Obote was soon to make contact with communists. While he was staying in his hotel in Stockholm he was contacted by two Germans who said they had been following events in East Africa and that they had friends in Berlin and Moscow whom they felt sure he would be interested to meet. Obote realized immediately that they were communists, but considered that if he accompanied them with his eyes open he had little to lose and might even derive some benefit. Following the plan proposed by his new friends he travelled to Paris and spent a night there. The following day he was to catch an aircraft to Berlin, so he left his hotel after breakfast, only to discover that Paris had two airports. His ticket was with the two Germans, and he did not know on which flight he was to travel or from which airport he was scheduled to fly. Disappointed, he returned to his hotel where, at about midday, French police arrived and demanded to see his visa. Never having been in Europe before he was unaware that a visa was required to visit France, but fortunately the two

Germans, having waited in vain for him at the airport, came to his rescue and an onward flight was arranged for the same afternoon.

In Berlin he was introduced to a large number of people, most of them communists, but some were members of Christian groups and one was a prominent member of the Social Democratic Party. The communists told him they would like to open an embassy in Uganda when it became independent. Obote hastened to point out that independence was still a thing of the future, and that even when it was achieved Uganda would inevitably have strong links with Britain for some considerable time. If East Germany were to open an embassy, he said, West German disapproval might lead to British reprisals against Uganda. He was, in fact, playing for time. At that stage he had given little thought to the future foreign policy of Uganda and was wary of entering into any premature commitment with overseas powers.

While he was in Germany he visited Leipzig, where he met a handful of students from Uganda and other East African territories. Then, back in Berlin, he was told he had had an invitation to visit China. He soon gathered that China had been his ultimate destination all along and his stay in Moscow was consequently brief, although he was given the opportunity to meet a number of East African students there. In Peking he met the foreign minister, Marshal Cheneyi, who was to be his host. He found the marshal a friendly, talkative man, always happy to recount how the communists struggled to seize power in the 1940s. Cheneyi's main concern, however, was with the future of the Afro-Asian Solidarity Movement, but Obote remained carefully non-committal on that subject. Nor, following the line to which he had adhered in Berlin, did he ask for any assistance from the Chinese government. He was particularly anxious not to jeopardize the prospect of constitutional progress by appearing to have become an associate of the Communists. In the overcharged atmosphere of the cold war he had little hope of escaping the latter charge, as he was to discover on his return to his own country.

Obote began his journey back to Uganda by travelling to Berlin. From there he went to Ostend, and took ship for England. He was extremely seasick, and it took him some days to recover when he went ashore. He was anxious to get back to Uganda after a month's absence into which he had packed a remarkable amount of travelling, some of it to little purpose. He had, however, learnt something of the ways of diplomacy and he had sharpened his awareness of the extent to which Uganda might become prey to foreign interests if care were not taken.

His reception by the Protectorate authorities was less than welcoming, as he might have anticipated had he been a more seasoned politician. He was summoned to Entebbe where he was censured by Sir Frederick Crawford for having failed to attend a meeting with the governor, for which Obote himself had asked, and for getting involved in injudicious contacts with countries hostile to Britain. The governor said he was angry that Obote should have been so easily beguiled into accepting the invitation of the communists, but he probably recognized that the young man was still only a novice in the realm of international intrigue. As for Obote himself, the encounter left him in some doubt as to whether the ever-courteous Sir Frederick was more distressed by the bad manners he had displayed in absenting himself from a prearranged meeting or by his apparent flirtation with the Eastern Bloc. The governor did suggest, however, that any further escapade of a similar nature might lead to the withdrawal of Obote's passport.

It was a lesson Obote took to heart, and when he himself took office he changed the regulations restricting travel to communist countries and placed an embargo only upon visits to South Africa. In one respect Obote's travels had served him badly. Many senior civil servants who had already convinced themselves that he was a crypto-communist concluded that their opinion had been confirmed by his unexpected trip to the East and so became more confident than ever that he could not be trusted as Uganda's future leader. The DP, too, when it suited it to do so, was inclined to describe Obote's party as being dominated by communists.

Before the report of the Wild Committee was formally discussed Obote was to make another journey, having been invited by Air India to join its inaugural flight from Nairobi to Bombay in January 1960. Magezi and a brother of the *kabaka* were also among the guests, together with a number of African politicians from Kenya. From Bombay the visitors travelled to Bangalore, where they attended the annual rally of the Indian National Congress. Mrs Indira Gandhi was president of the congress and Obote was considerably impressed by her skilful conduct of business and the diplomatic manner in which she handled the participants. He was impressed, too, to discover that she also acted as hostess for her father, the Indian prime minister, and was present and took a full part in the conversation when Obote and his companions had lunch and dinner with Jawaharlal Nehru.

To Obote Nehru seemed a dominating figure. Although unassuming in manner, he was unquestionably in charge of his country. His knowledge of the complex problems of India seemed encyclopaedic, and in private conversation he talked as freely and incisively as he did in the meetings of congress. He appeared to have well-digested views on every topic that was raised, from the disturbing behaviour of China to India's own struggle to establish itself on a firm base. He talked with his guests about India's policy towards Africa, mentioning the scholarships his country had awarded and urging his guests not to send students to pursue liberal studies. Obote was unfamiliar with the term and when he sought clarification Nehru replied that while he himself was a lawyer he had also read physics. He believed African students should concentrate mainly on scientific subjects, because that was the area in which there was the greatest lack of expertise. From Bangalore Obote travelled to New Delhi, where he met other congress leaders as well as some Ugandan students. He also found time to do some sightseeing before returning home after his second experience of the world outside East Africa.

In his absence disturbances had broken out in Bukedi District. Taxation was the ostensible reason for the rioting, but more fundamental was the feeling that chiefs should not act simultaneously as tax collectors, as controllers of the police force called upon to arrest defaulters and as judges at their subsequent trial. Obote had no doubt that his party had helped to instigate the protest, but while he had considerable sympathy with the people's complaint, he was critical of the violence they had employed to make their point. He was glad to have been out of the country when blame was apportioned. Kirya was not so fortunate. He was arrested but was later released, although the subsequent inquiry into the origins of the disruption laid some at least of the responsibility at his door. It was a relief to Obote that no blame was attached to the UNC or to any other political party, although the secretary-general of the UPU had taken it upon himself, in Magezi's absence, to accuse the police of 'impetuous and highly irresponsible conduct' in opening fire upon the rioters. He did, however, go on to urge the people of Bukedi to refrain from further acts of violence, and his criticism of the police was later reinforced by the report of the commission of inquiry which stated that constables had opened fire without orders from the officer in charge.

There had been another development while Obote had been in India which worried him far more than the events in Bukedi. In the middle of January a pamphlet had been published to which Michael Kintu, the *katikkiro* (chief minister) of the Bugandan government, had written an introduction. In it he had asked unequivocally for the restoration of Buganda's sovereignty and ordered the people of Buganda not to recognize anyone whose authority did not derive from the *kabaka*. In spite of his anxiety not to alienate Buganda, Obote could not allow such an overt challenge to his hopes of an independent, united Uganda to go unanswered. On 3 February he called a press conference at which, speaking on behalf of all the elected members of the legislative council, he said that an independent Buganda would never be tolerated by the rest of emergent Africa. African nationalism could not countenance excessively small states. It was a risky statement to make, putting in possible jeopardy any gains he may have made as a result of his private conversations with the *kabaka*. But Obote was convinced that unless pushed into a corner by the excessive demands of the other districts, the *kabaka* himself had no desire to sever links with the rest of Uganda.

While these problems were troubling the Ugandan scene early in 1960, the British government had been considering the Wild Committee's report and had decided to make a guarded response. When the governor opened the new session of the legislative council on 22 February 1960, constitutional matters were not relegated to the end of his speech but he did not give outright approval to the Wild Committee's recommendations. The secretary of state, he said, had agreed that the next legislative council should be elected on a common roll with no special safeguards for minority communities. There would, too, be a majority of non-officials in the executive council and, as far as possible, they would be chosen from the elected members of the legislature. But, and here the caution of the government became apparent, for the time being the governor would preside over the executive council and it would continue to have only an advisory role.

To pacify the kingdoms, the governor concluded his remarks on constitutional issues by saying that the dignity and status of the hereditary rulers would be upheld. Quite what this would mean in practice no-one knew and Sir Frederick himself did not vouchsafe any explanation. But, bearing in mind the problems arising from the differing political arrangements already in existence in various parts of the country and the difficulty of satisfying the conflicting claims of each kingdom and district, a relationships committee was to be set up to inquire into ways and means of reconciling those claims. This, as the governor was later to reveal in a speech to the chief executives of all the country's local governments, was the reason for the British government's hesitation about accepting the Wild Report in full. To have done so in ignorance of the likely consequences would, Sir Frederick said, have been dangerous in the extreme. It is to be regretted that this explanation was not given at the time the matter was discussed in the legislative council. By his failure to do so the governor had reinforced the disappointment felt by most of the non-official council members, who had expected a more appreciative response to the Wild Committee's recommendations. They had become even more gloomy when he rounded off his address with a reprise of the theme of law and order which, he said, had been seriously threatened during the previous year, not only by the boycott in Buganda but also, more recently, by the outbreaks of violence in Bukedi and parts of Bugisu District and in the Eastern Province. Constitutional reform was not, it seemed, high on the British government's agenda.

The widespread optimism engendered by the publication of the Wild Report having been markedly diluted as a result of the governor's statement, Obote's immediate reaction was to say that African members were faced with no alternative but to seek immediate independence. More mature consideration led him to modify that view, but Africans in the legislative council derived little consolation from the speech of the chief secretary, Sir Charles Hartwell, when he opened the debate on the governor's address. The resolution he proposed was that the council should merely take note of the Wild Committee's recommendations. The African elected members unanimously supported an amendment, moved by M. M. Ngobi, urging the council to endorse the majority recommendations of the committee. Speaking last for the elected members, Obote argued vehemently that, after sixty years of British administration, Ugandans must surely be ready to run their own affairs. If they were not it was a disgrace to British rule.

In spite of the unanimity of the views expressed by the elected members their amendment was defeated on 8 March. Obote, who was steadily emerging as the leading spokesman for the critics of the government, thereupon announced that the elected members would take no further part in the debate on the chief secretary's motion and they left the chamber. Hartwell, rounding off the debate, concluded that although Ngobi had moved the amendment Obote was the ringleader of the opposition, and he attacked him accordingly. But it was not only in this debate that Obote demonstrated his new status. The following day an announcement was made that showed the extent to which he had become the dominant figure in African politics in Uganda.

For some time Obote had been concerned by the differing attitudes of the various political groups in the country towards both the form which Uganda's constitutional development should take and the means by which such developments might best be achieved. A greater degree of consensus was called for on both counts, particularly in view of the problem presented by the wary and consequently obstructive attitude of the *kabaka*'s government. Obote had been approached some time earlier by Ssenteza Kajubi with the suggestion that his UNC might unite with the Democratic Party to promote direct elections throughout the country. The Democratic Party was the other leading nationalist party in Uganda. Founded shortly after the UNC and largely through the instrumentality of the Roman Catholic Church in Uganda, its strongest support came from those parts of the country – Acholi, Buganda, Ankole and Kigezi – where Roman Catholic missionaries had been most active. Like the original UNC, most of its leaders, Kajubi among them, were Baganda, many of them well-educated and either concerned that, as Roman Catholics, their hopes of advancement within what was officially a Protestant heirarchy were slight or else genuinely believing in the virtues of a united Uganda. Again like the UNC, the DP had failed to make much headway among the general public in the kingdom because of the power of the chiefs and the loyalty of the Baganda to their *kabaka*. Nevertheless, joint action by the UNC and the DP could not fail to have a powerful impact on Ugandan politics.

In spite of his prominent role in the DP, Kajubi emphasized that he was making the suggestion at the instance of a number of like-minded people rather than as an official representative of his party, but added that he felt sure the DP would insist upon there being a distinguished, independent person as chairman of the amalgamated party. He suggested as a suitable candidate Serwano Kulubya, a leading Muganda who had been treasurer in the *kabaka*'s government and was now a nominated member of the legislative council. Obote replied that the UNC constitution required both the president and chairman of the party to be elected. For that reason he could not agree that Kulubya, or indeed anyone else, should be simply nominated to the office of chairman.

The matter ended there, but Obote approached Magezi shortly afterwards with a view to discussing the possibility of co-operation between the UNC and the UPU. Magezi warily suggested that negotiations to this end should be conducted under a neutral chairman and proposed Yusufu Lule, another Muganda, who had formerly been a lecturer at Makerere College and had since become a non-official minister in the Protectorate government. Obote agreed to the suggestion and the three, Obote, Magezi and Lule, had a number of private, nocturnal meetings at Lule's house along the Bombo road just north of Kampala. In the course of the talks it was suggested that the DP should be approached with a view to enlisting its co-operation if the members were willing. The DP leader, Benedicto Kiwanuka, himself a Muganda, was invited to take part in the discussions but he attended only one meeting. While he agreed that a united front would be of value in dealing with the problems presented by the behaviour of Buganda, he insisted that co-operation must take the form of the other parties joining the DP. This proposal was firmly rejected. Kiwanuka then left the meeting and took no further part in the discussions.

Obote and Magezi next considered inviting Apolo Kironde, yet another Muganda, to join them. Kironde had recently founded a political party, but although its membership was still very small he disliked Lule so much that he felt unable to take advantage of any benefits that might accrue from becoming involved in discussions with him, even if they might lead to the formation of a larger, and consequently more influential, organization. Obote was not unduly worried by this decision because Kironde's party carried little weight. There was yet another small party, led by another Muganda, Jehoash Mayanja-Nkangi, to which an approach was briefly contemplated. It was finally decided that Mayanja-Nkangi was too closely wedded to the ideas of the Bugandan establishment to fit into the proposed new political pattern.

Having failed to spread their net more widely, the two leaders agreed to recommend to their supporters that their parties should amalgamate. They recognized that the prospect of gaining support from their party members would now be easier because of the absence of any significant Bugandan politicians in their proposed organization, although Obote himself deeply regretted this. He was particularly saddened by the loss of

Abu Mayanja, who had been in the US during much of the period of negotiation with Magezi. While there he had been approached by representatives of the *kabaka*'s government with an invitation to join them as minister of education in the kingdom. It was clear that the *kabaka* felt he could control the lively spirit of Mayanja more effectively within his own establishment than if it were left to flourish with the UNC. To Obote's dismay Mayanja accepted the offer, explaining that he believed he could influence the *kabaka*'s government from within better than by staying outside it as an ostensible opponent. Obote was sceptical about this but could not dissuade Mayanja from taking up his new post.

Magezi and Obote now decided they must send messengers into the districts, asking for delegates to be appointed to a meeting at which the proposed amalgamation could be discussed and, they hoped, accepted. But news of their deliberations had leaked out and it was feared that misunderstandings would arise if a public announcement of their proposal were not made immediately. To give the plan substance in advance of the announcement a meeting of supporters of both groups who were available in Kampala elected Obote as president of the new party, which it was decided should be called the Uganda People's Congress (UPC). W. W. Nadiope, an influential, ambitious and politically unprincipled man, who had been the senior chief of Busoga, was elected vice-president. Obote had no liking for Nadiope but he had to accept him as a colleague in view of the electors' decision. In the same way Magezi became secretary-general of the new party, but to preserve democratic principles the three elections were later confirmed by delegates of the UPC from all parts of the country when general agreement to the amalgamation had been reached.

Obote's first speech in his new role as leader of the UPC took him back to his favourite theme of Buganda. He was supporting a motion proposed by Obwangor which called upon the government to rescind the deportation orders against people accused of having illegally advocated a boycott of non-African shops and goods who must, the government said, share responsibility for the lawlessness and intimidation that had subsequently occurred. There were ten deportees at that time, all of them Baganda. Obote had never been convinced by the reasons vouchsafed by the government for its restrictive action and he argued that if, as it was now claimed, the boycott was declining, the reasons were still less valid. In any case, innumerable other, more effective measures had been adopted to control the boycott. This was the moment for a gesture of goodwill which would be far more effective in reconciling the Baganda than would the perpetuation of punitive measures.

Obote's approach did not endear him to the leaders on the government benches. When, two days later, he supported Magezi's adjournment motion, drawing critical attention to the government's attitude towards labour issues, and particularly to its handling of a recent strike of workers on the tea estates of Kijura and Kiamara, the chief secretary responded in disparaging terms. He dismissed as irresponsible rubbish the arguments of the opposition members and added that he had hoped for better from Obote, but would know what to expect in future. It was a gratuitous attack, reflecting the pique of a senior civil servant whose actions a mere member of the legislative council had had the temerity to criticize, rather than suggesting a measured judgement upon what had been said. In fact, Obote's motive in speaking as he had done was not solely or even primarily intended as an attack upon the government. As the pressure for constitutional change grew stronger he was anxious to involve as many people as possible in the movement so as to strengthen the democratic base of a self-governing Uganda. Bearing in mind the achievements of Mboya in building up the trade union movement in Kenya as a powerful political force, Obote believed it was time to arouse the interest of wage-earners in Uganda in the politics of their own country. What better way to do this than to champion their cause when he believed it to be a just one.

Obote's next speech in the council demonstrated how unjustified the chief secretary's attack had been. After Obwangor had spoken for nearly two hours in response to the governor's address at the opening of the session, Obote took only ten minutes to deliver one of the most measured and cogent speeches the council had heard for some time. He was totally opposed, he said, to the crime and violence so prevalent at the time. Criminals were not nationalists. Nevertheless, it would help considerably if the government would take elected members into its confidence when it was determining policy to deal with crime. Nor would it do any harm if administrative officers were no longer empowered to act in a judicial capacity. The same should apply to chiefs, so that the dispensing of justice could be seen to be separate from policing and prosecution. On a different but equally conciliatory note he sought to reassure those who feared that when Africans came to power there would be no place for non-Africans in the country. When Uganda achieved self-government, he maintained, there would be a continuing need for expatriate civil servants. Indeed, even more of them might be required.

In a similar vein, Obote supported the extension of the state of emergency in Bukedi for a further six weeks. He had visited the district several times, he said, and could find no justification for the violence that had taken place there. There was no doubt that grievances existed, but if the government would trust the elected members of the legislative council and consult them, the nature of the grievances might be more clearly understood and they could be dealt with appropriately. It was important, if the trouble was not to spread, to ensure that restrictions were not imposed indiscriminately upon innocent and guilty alike.

The plea for greater trust in the elected members was not without justification. Since the departure of Sir Andrew Cohen the role of elected members in determining policy had notably diminished. Civil servants once more made their decisions and acted upon them as if their authority was above question. Criticism was regarded as presumptuous, particularly if couched in the naive terms frequently employed by members of the legislative council whose command of English was sometimes limited and who, on their own admission, had had little opportunity to shoulder responsibility for taking important decisions.

When the question of prolonging still further the state of emergency in Bukedi was raised towards the end of April, Obote once again did not demur. He was not equally acquiescent when a similar proposal was made with regard to Buganda. The state of emergency had, he argued, proved wholly ineffective in checking violence in the kingdom, and the government would be better employed in seeking out the ringleaders who were really responsible for the disturbances. Now, beyond any doubt, he was making his mark as the most effective critic of the government, not by the violence of his language, nor yet by the variety of topics upon which he was prepared to speak. It was by his concentration upon the main issue of Uganda's political future, and by the importance he consistently attached to the part Buganda must play in it, that he was gradually able to assert his pre-eminence among the emergent African politicians in Uganda.

Yet it was at this point, and certainly without his recognizing it, that the first threat to his future leadership appeared. One of the most intelligent, if unassuming, of the representative members of the legislative council, W. W. Rwetsiba, accepted an appointment as parliamentary secretary in the ministry of natural resources. Obote expressed surprise that such a valuable member of the opposition should have been poached by the government at a critical time in the country's progress. But it was not the loss of Rwetsiba that was to trouble him in the longer term. The difficulties were to arise from the character of the man who was to be Rwetsiba's replacement. The Ankole district council elected in his stead G. S. K. Ibingira, a lawyer and distant relative of the ruler of Ankole, who had studied at the university college in Aberystwyth and who was to prove an uneasy colleague and ultimately a powerful opponent of Obote.

Chapter 5

Independence

In June 1960, Obote took part in the first of a series of visits to England by political representatives from Uganda which were to culminate in independence. The venture did not suggest that success was near at hand. The group consisted of representative members of the legislative council, and it was in the course of their discussions with British parliamentarians and members of the foreign office that Obote's admiration for the determination and persuasive powers of Barbara Saben was powerfully reinforced. Mrs Saben had not been a member of the Wild Committee, but her devotion to the committee's recommendations was total.

Disappointed by the Ugandan government's lukewarm response to the recommendations, Obote issued a statement on his arrival in London setting out his position. The UPC, he said, supported by the majority of the people in Uganda, wanted immediate independence under a strong government, and was prepared to uphold the dignity and prestige of the hereditary rulers. His party, he went on, was disturbed that the government had consistently ignored the country-wide appeal of the people of Uganda, and its representatives had come to England to impress upon the colonial secretary that it would be in the best interests of the people of Uganda and of Britain to grant responsible African government to Uganda at once. Among their specific requests the delegates as a whole asked for universal adult suffrage and the appointment of a chief minister.

At that time neither Obote nor any of the other members of his party distinguished at all clearly the difference between responsible government and complete independence, nor had they any idea what independence would entail. But if Buganda could have ministers and take responsibility for much of its own business, they could see no reason why the rest of the country should not do the same. In any case, Obote had already made it clear that Uganda did not wish to dispense with British civil servants in the immediate future. He showed even greater naivety in his attitude towards the hereditary rulers of Buganda and the western kingdoms, about whose future role the British government had justifiable doubts. It was Obote's idea that they should play the same sort of constitutional role within their own kingdoms as did the queen in Britain. What he had failed to grasp, in spite of his conversations with the *kabaka*, was that Mutesa could not begin to comprehend such an idea and, equally important, that the Baganda could never envisage their ruler occupying such a position. Instinctively they believed that 'kabakaship' and constitutional monarchy were contradictory terms.

The British government was far more aware of the predicament than was the Ugandan delegation. Lord Perth, the minister of state for the colonies, listened courteously to what the delegates had to say but insisted that the cabinet had not yet reached any decision. It would, however, take into account Ugandan opinion when it did so. He offered no immediate prospect of self-government, arguing that, as yet, no coherent pattern of political parties had emerged in Uganda and the problem of a suitable form of government remained unsolved. If the next legislative council elections were to produce a clear and coherent result it would be possible to consider the situation more positively. It was not an encouraging response, and the only real benefits the delegates derived from their visit were the opportunity it provided for them to state their case and the number of people with whom they were able to discuss their aims. Obote himself was introduced to the Liberal leader, Jo Grimond, by the delegates' legal adviser, the Liberal peer, Lord Ogmore. He also met Fenner Brockway and John Stonehouse. Both were campaigners for an early end to British imperialism and both had been to Uganda and were not unfamiliar with its problems.

On their return to Uganda the politicians met another setback when the Protectorate administration agreed to postpone the registration of voters in Buganda although it would go ahead in the rest of the country. The Bugandan government, it appeared, was not confident that the election ordinance was applicable to the kingdom, and the Protectorate authorities did not argue the matter. The appointment of the promised relationships commission was also delayed because Buganda was dissatisfied with its terms of reference and had threatened not to take part in the elections if they were not altered. To the utter dismay of the elected members of the legislative council, the secretary of state invited the *kabaka*, with eight advisors and two personal staff, to visit him in England. The *kabaka* was known to be opposed to a unitary state, and the latest developments seemed to suggest that the British government no longer thought it essential.

There was a more hopeful sign in September when Ian Macleod, the British secretary of state for the colonies, having made no impression upon the *kabaka* and those accompanying him, wrote to Sir Frederick Crawford expressing his dissatisfaction with Buganda's unwillingness to co-operate and insisting that the registration of voters should go ahead for the whole country after all. Buganda did not give in so easily. The word went out from the *kabaka*'s government that loyal Baganda should disobey the Protectorate administration's edict. So, when the rolls closed on 31 October, only 33,133 Baganda had registered, about 5 per cent of those entitled to do so, compared with 75 per cent in the rest of Uganda.

Meanwhile, on 19 September, one significant symbol of constitutional change was revealed to the country when the magnificent new legislative council building, intended as the home of a future national assembly, was opened by Macleod. Sir Frederick Grawford, whose wife had recently died after a protracted illness, presided over the ceremony with his customary dignity and courtesy in spite of his sad experience. In his address he referred to the picturesque ruins dotted about the African continent and went on, 'It may be that one day men may count the stones of Kampala among their heritage, but let us all strive to see that when they do so its name is firmly linked to a vision of parliamentary democracy, of just and wise rule by the freely elected representatives of the people.' All too soon those words would mock those who heard them with such high hopes. The speech of the secretary of state, too, would arouse sad echoes in the years ahead. 'Sometimes,' he said, 'when I look at the Ugandan scene I have had moments of depression, because there is such great potential in the country, and yet, so it has seemed from time to time, instead of being in the vanguard of advance in this part of the continent of Africa, little progress had been made because divisions remain, the arguments continue and the problems seem quite intractable.' He concluded on a more optimistic note, but his earlier remarks cast their shadow over the future.

When the council reopened on 22 September its first business was to debate a bill aimed at preventing intimidation in the elections for a new legislature which, it had been decided, should take place in 1961. One after another, Gaspar Oda, the only member of the Democratic Party in the council, Babiiha, Katiiti, Ibingira, Ngobi and Magezi gloomily spoke in support of the motion. Obote was ill, so took no part in the debate. Had he done so, he would doubtless have agreed with his colleagues, although taking care to emphasize that the ordinance should apply to the whole country and not only to Buganda. He was not so ready to play a conciliatory role the following day when he joined in the condemnation of the Protectorate administration for paying the expenses of the recent Bugandan delegation to London. To his surprise and gratification, when he called for a vote on the motion he was joined in the lobby, not only by the other elected African members, but also by all the European and Asian representative members.

He was, nevertheless, very careful in what he said about Buganda. When the chief secretary moved that the county of Buyaga should be declared a disturbed area because coffee trees owned by Baganda, as well as official buildings in Mubende District, had been attacked, he made no comment, although several other elected members criticized the motion. The government, they said, was not tackling the root of the problem, which was that the majority of the inhabitants of Buyaga did not regard themselves as Baganda. They were descendants of people who had, for generations, owed allegiance to the rival kingdom of Bunyoro, and it was with Bunyoro that their loyalty still lay. The fact that, with British assistance, the Baganda had conquered their forebears and annexed their land at the end of the nineteenth century did not alter their point of view. In former days, Buyaga had been part of the very heartland of Bunyoro, and the burial places of many of its rulers were still located there.

The issue of the future treatment of expatriate civil servants stirred him from his silence. With the best of intentions the British government had offered money to all colonial governments to assist in the payment of expatriate civil servants after self-government, but had stipulated that requests for a share in these funds should be made before 1 April 1961. In order to take advantage of the offer the Protectorate authorities proposed to enter into negotiations with Britain, but Obote demurred in the strongest terms. He had always maintained, he said, that expatriate civil servants might well be needed after independence, but a decision on that point, and on the terms upon which they would be invited to stay, was one which must be reached by the electorate through their representatives in parliament. He showed his irritation at this attempt to predetermine the actions of an independent Uganda by remarking that expatriate civil servants would be expected to think of themselves as servants and not as rulers.

In speaking as he did Obote struck an uncharacteristically sour note, which could only be justified on the grounds that it was an expression of a genuinely deep-seated commitment to upholding the dignity of black people. He was concerned, too, at the apparent indifference shown by the British government to the sense of urgency felt in Uganda over the issue of constitutional advance. On 4 October the Buganda *lukiiko* had shown its disregard for British authority, for its own word as set out in the Agreements of 1900 and 1955, and for public opinion in the rest of Uganda, by adopting a resolution stating that Buganda would become an independent state on 31 December. Still, Obote protested, the promised relationships commission had not been appointed, in spite of the great store the British government professed to set upon its attempts to provide a solution to the problem of the kingdoms.

His remarks were not appreciated by senior civil servants, who increasingly regarded him as a troublemaker. In fact, Lord Munster was named as chairman of the commission before the end of the month, and he arrived in Uganda a little over a week later on 8 December. He came at an exceptionally difficult moment in the affairs of the Protectorate, and on 31 December the *lukiiko* confirmed its resolution concerning Buganda's independence. The Protectorate authorities refused to be stampeded into any retaliatory measures and their restraint paid off. Few people acknowledged the new status claimed by the *lukiiko* and the conduct of affairs in the Protectorate continued as before.

The non-Baganda members of the legislative council were not satisfied with the passive response of the government. They considered that the Bugandan leadership should be shown who was in control. In the closing days of the council, in early February 1961, M. M. Ngobi introduced a motion criticizing the ineffectiveness of government policy *vis à vis* Buganda. By failing to react to the provocation repeatedly offered by the *kabaka's* government, the Protectorate authorities had left the Baganda uncertain as to where their loyalty should ultimately reside, he claimed. Rehearsing the events of the past months, he recalled that, in direct contravention of the 1955 Agreement, the *katiikiro* of Buganda had failed to submit the names of those who would represent the kingdom in the legislative council. On several occasions the *lukiiko* had passed resolutions denouncing political parties. On 24 September 1960 the *lukiiko* had passed another resolution rejecting direct elections to the central legislature and threats had subsequently been made against any persons who had sought to register as voters. On all these occasions the Protectorate authorities had done nothing. Finally, there had been a totally negative response to the declaration of Buganda's independence in spite of Britain's professed commitment to the creation of a unitary Uganda. It was not enough, Ngobi went on, to say there would be no secession as long as the Protectorate remained in being. The government must act to ensure that there would be no secession when the Protectorate came to an end. Or perhaps Britain was deliberately pursuing a policy of divide and rule with a view to perpetuating colonial government in Uganda?

The dilemma facing thoughtful Baganda was reflected in the speeches of two nominated government back-benchers, both of whom had been senior officials in the *kabaka's* government. M. E. Kawalya Kagwa, former chief minister, and S. W. Kulubya, former treasurer, urged the government to act with caution and not to require the Baganda to jettison their ancient traditions and loyalties precipitately. By contrast, a former chief justice in the *kabaka's* government, M. Mugwanya, who, like the others, was now a Protectorate government back-bench member, took the opposite line, stressing the extent to which the Bugandan leadership had acted illegally, even by their own rules, by denying him and other elected members of the *lukiiko* the right to take their seats, or by dismissing them for no valid reson. Mugwanya, it should be said, had been a founder member of the Democratic Party, which made him an obviuous target for the Bugandan leaders' displeasure. Magezi, Babiiha and Obwangor all spoke openly in support of Ngobi's motion, but it was noticeable that

Obote's influence had begun to be felt. No longer did they denounce the Baganda indiscriminately. Their attacks were now levelled solely against the leadership, and they admitted that the chief sufferers from the misdeeds of the *kabaka*'s government and the *lukiiko* were the Baganda themselves.

Obote was as sensitive as ever to the dilemma in which the Baganda found themselves, but he was in no doubt that their leaders had gone too far in declaring independence. With elections to the central legislature only weeks away, it would be disastrous if Buganda were allowed to opt out. He was convinced that, if only the *kabaka*'s government would trust its own people and give them the right to vote for their representatives in a national assembly, some sort of compromise could be reached. This would enable the Baganda to make their rightful contribution to the future of the whole country while benefiting from the greater resources that unity would make available. In his profound anxiety for the future, he spoke out against the *kabaka*'s government for the first time, because at this critical stage he recognized that only the Protectorate authorities had the power to act to save the country from breaking apart. If the chiefs of any other district had behaved as the Baganda chiefs had done, he said, the chief secretary would immediately have urged the governor to have them forcibly replaced. Were the Protectorate authorities powerless to act in the case of Buganda?

The chief secretary, G. B. Cartland, though better able than his predecessor had been to sympathize with the strength of feeling among council members, remained convinced that there would be little to gain from open confrontation with the Bugandan leadership. He preferred to await the views of the relationships commission on the pattern for Uganda's future development and also to test the strength of the political parties in the forthcoming elections.

The nomination of candidates for the elections took place late in February. Obote was unopposed in his Lango constituency because the would-be Democratic Party candidate arrived to pay his deposit by cheque when the rules stated that payment must be in cash. For that reason, when polling took place Obote was in Kampala instead of making a last-minute effort to stir up support in his own constituency. It quickly became clear that in Buganda, where only a handful of people had dared to register and still fewer had had the courage to vote in face of the overt hostility of the chiefs, Democratic Party candidates were heading for a sweeping victory. Obote then received a telephone message from the *kabaka*'s office asking him to go there immediately. When he met Mutesa, the latter said urgently, 'We have got to defeat them [the Democratic Party].' Obote replied that it was too late, that by urging his subjects not to take part in the elections, the *kabaka* had paved the way for a DP victory. Even though only a tiny minority of the people had cast their vote there was nothing that could be done to change the outcome.

The two slept in the *kabaka*'s office that night, but the new day brought no relief. Although, in the country as a whole, the UPC had polled a total of 488,334 votes to the 407,416 polled for the DP, the DP had won 20 out of 21 seats in Buganda, making their overall total 43, to the 35 gained by the UPC. The UNC gained only one seat, and two were won by independents. For the Bugandan leaders this was the worst possible result, but they alone were responsible for the outcome. Salt was rubbed into their wounds when the leader of the DP, Benedicto Kiwanuka, a Muganda and, still worse, a commoner, was appointed leader of the house. Obote became leader of the opposition. It was little consolation that, when the council met, Sir Frederick Crawford announced that the secretary of state was not ready to accede to Kiwanuka's request to be appointed chief minister.

The governor's subsequent statement that it was hoped there would be a further constitutional conference in September was received with mixed feelings. Obote seized the opportunity to ask Sir Frederick to consult with the secretary of state with a view to reopening talks with Buganda. His aim was to ensure that future constitutional discussions should not be bedevilled by the old problems. Writing much later, Ibingira claimed that it was about this time that he personally urged the UPC leadership to adopt a strategy of co-operation with the *kabaka*'s government. The leaders, he wrote, were not enthusiastic, and Obote himself was persuaded only after some resistance. Such was Obote's reluctance, he went on, that he, Ibingira, even went so far as to discuss with Nadiope the possibility of the latter's becoming president of the party in Obote's place.[2]

Obote may well have been less than anxious to talk with the Bugandan chiefs, whom he regarded as a malign influence upon the *kabaka*, but Ibingira's claim can have little substance in so far as discussions with the *kabaka* himself were concerned. Obote had, after all, already had talks with Mutesa, and he had consistently spoken up for the Baganda in so far as it had been possible to do so. Mutesa himself made no reference in his own account of these events to the role Ibingira claimed to have played.[3] What is of interest is that Ibingira should have contemplated the replacement of Obote at this early stage, if indeed he did so.

On 1 June the last of those parts of Buganda which had been declared disturbed areas were freed from restrictions. This was a prelude to discussions of the report of the Munster Commission which the governor held, individually, with Benedicto Kiwanuka, Obote and the *kabaka*. The report recommended that Uganda should be a single, democratic state with a strong central government, but with Buganda in a federal and Bunyoro, Ankole and Toro in a semi-federal relationship with the rest of the country. The prerogative of the *kabaka*, his civil service, the *lukiiko* and traditional customary matters should be protected from central government interference, but foreign affairs, defence, the national police and nationality should all be the preserve of the central authority. As far as elections to the national assembly were concerned, there should be universal adult suffrage on a common roll for the whole of the country, except that Buganda alone should be permitted to choose between direct and indirect elections.

This was a formidably complicated set of proposals and to implement them would call for a hitherto unprecedented degree of goodwill between the various groups involved, as well as a level of political sophistication unlikely to be found in Uganda or, indeed, in many other countries. The one overwhelmingly important recommendation, in Obote's opinion, was that Buganda should take part in elections to the national assembly. It was a minimum concession to the idea of unity, but it was better than independence for Buganda. The question remained as to whether the *kabaka*'s government would accept the proposal.

There was some doubt on this score when Benedicto Kiwanuka, so hated by the Bugandan hierarchy, was named chief minister on 2 July. Cartland ceased to be chief secretary and became, instead, deputy-governor. Although the governor himself retained a number of reserved powers, Uganda was now virtually self-governing as far as internal affairs were concerned. But if the status of Kiwanuka displeased the Baganda, Obote was also less than happy to learn that Sir Frederick Crawford was to retire in October and was to be succeeded by the chief secretary of Kenya, Sir Walter Coutts. Crawford's governorship had always seemed to Obote unimaginative and excessively paternalist, but the appointment of his successor offered no improvement. On behalf of the UPC Obote protested that Coutts was already unpopular in Kenya because of his opposition to Kenyatta's release and his generally negative attitude towards African political leaders. He, surely, was not the man to stand as figurehead in a Uganda now set on the road to independence.

It was a vain gesture on Obote's part and he left for England with mixed feelings in September, together with the other African leaders, to take part in what was hoped would be the final constitutional conference before full internal self-government was achieved. Buganda was still the main stumbling block, but Obote had paved the way for a *modus vivendi* by talking with the *kabaka* a week before the conference and agreeing that, so far as the UPC was concerned, many of Buganda's claims could be met. Nevertheless, the British colonial secretary, Iain Macleod, who chaired the conference, had a difficult task in trying to balance the conflicting demands of the various parties to the discussions.

Meeting each group separately, Macleod sought to discover the issues upon which they were reluctant to make concessions. The Bugandan leaders were particularly anxious to maintain control over the method of

electing Bugandan members to the national assembly. They were concerned lest direct elections should provide a link between the voters and
the central government which would bypass the traditional hierarchy, thus
providing the Baganda with a new focus of loyalty. They were anxious, too,
to protect the privileges they had acquired under British rule, particularly
with respect to landholding and to controlling the administration of
justice and the maintenance of order through their own police force. Like
Obote, Macleod considered it was essential Buganda should recognize the
central government after independence. If the only way of getting it to
do so was to make the concessions the Baganda demanded, then there
was no point in arguing further.

Kiwanuka could not accept that point of view. He knew full well that
indirect elections in Buganda would mean the total defeat of his party
in the kingdom. Any electoral college would be controlled by the chiefs
and they would ensure that DP candidates were not elected. He took his
stand, however, on the ground that direct elections had already been
held in Buganda. To allow the *kabaka*'s government to decide how elections should be held in future would not only be a retrograde step, but it
would also set at nought the courage of those who had been brave
enough to court their chiefs' displeasure by voting in the recent elections.
It was a powerful argument, which Obote could only partially counter by
pointing out that the recent elections had not been truly direct because
the majority of the electorate had been persuaded not to vote.

Sensing that the colonial secretary was inclined to give in to Buganda's
demands, Kiwanuka led his followers out of the conference, but was
persuaded to return by the offer of the title of prime minister when self-
government was achieved. In an aside, Sir Walter Coutts asked Obote
what he wanted, in view of the fact that everyone else seemed to be
getting what they wanted. Obote replied that he wanted new elections
before independence, and this too was conceded. The conference having
apparently reached agreement and the framework of an independence
constitution having been prepared, it was announced that Uganda would
have full self-government on 1 March 1962, and that elections would be
held in April. Macleod was on the point of bringing the conference to a
close when Obote insisted that its work would not be complete until
a firm date for independence had been agreed. Macleod said that was a
matter to be decided by the British cabinet, but Obote persisted. After
the conference had been adjourned three times to enable Macleod to
take soundings with other cabinet ministers it was agreed that, if legal
arrangements could be made in time, Uganda would become independent on 9 October 1962.

There were still a number of obstacles to surmount. The dispute
between Buganda and Bunyoro over the Lost Counties – those areas
conquered by Buganda with British help in the 1890s – was unresolved,

but the British government said that three privy councillors would be sent to Uganda to make recommendations for the settlement of the problem. It was a considerable relief to outside observers when, on 26 October, the Bugandan *lukiiko* endorsed the agreement reached in London by 70 votes to 0 with two abstentions, and Buganda's secession, which most people had forgotten, came officially to an end.

It was a shock to Obote when, early in November, a movement known as *Kabaka Yekka* ('the *kabaka* alone') was inaugurated. Although denying that it was a political party, it appeared to incorporate all the groups within Buganda that supported the kingdom's claim to a distinct identity. Obote's objective, therefore, had to be to ensure that the new movement played a full part in the affairs of Uganda, an objective which became doubly important when direct elections to the *lukiiko* were held in February 1962 and *Kabaka Yekka* candidates were overwhelmingly victorious. The UPC leaders had decided not to contest the *lukiiko* elections for a number of reasons. In the first place, they did not think they could win enough seats to influence any decisions the *lukiiko* might ultimately take on the nature of elections to the national assembly and they did not wish to be party to an inevitable vote in favour of indirect elections. Secondly, Obote was anxious not to antagonize the Bugandan leaders and thereby jeopardize the prospect of their participation in the central government. Kiwanuka was not so circumspect, and won for himself and his party still greater hostility from the Baganda by his insistence upon the DP's taking part in the elections, although without significant success.

Obote consoled himself with the fact that direct elections had at last been held in Buganda, and although the chiefs had clearly determined the outcome, it would be difficult, he hoped, to reverse the process at a later stage. Bearing in mind Buganda's past record, it was not a very logical hope, and he was unduly sanguine in claiming that 800,000 people had been introduced to the electoral process. Nevertheless, he urged the *kabaka* to allow direct elections for the national assembly, pointing out that a similar victory for *Kabaka Yekka* would be assured, but his arguments were in vain. Direct elections to the *lukiiko* were an internal affair. It would be an entirely different matter to allow the Baganda to vote for representatives to sit in a body beyond the control of the Bugandan authorities. It was a measure of the strong sense of Bugandan loyalty to the idea of a distinct identity that, when the *lukiiko* voted on whether or not to hold direct elections, even such strong Ugandan nationalists as I. K. Musazi and E. M. K. Mulira voted in favour of an electoral college.

On 1 March 1962 Uganda became self-governing with Benedicto Kiwanuka as its first prime minister, and a cabinet was sworn in to replace the council of ministers. The same morning Obote had issued a statement urging the people of Uganda to uphold the virtue of tolerance. The Bugandan government was not represented at the ceremony marking

Uganda's new achievement, the *kabaka* being engaged at the opening of the kingdom's own high court. In the evening, when the Ugandan government held a celebratory dinner party, the Bugandan government held its own reception. Yet Kiwanuka did his best to bridge the gap that yawned between his DP and *Kabaka Yekka*. In his inaugural address he announced that he was in favour of federal status, not only for Buganda but also for the kingdoms of Ankole, Bunyoro and Toro and for the district of Busoga. It was clearly the first salvo in Kiwanuka's election campaign and Obote and the UPC tried to call his bluff by introducing a motion into the assembly to guarantee such federal status after independence. Kiwanuka revealed his inexperience of parliamentary sword-play by proposing an amendment demanding federal status at once, even before the elections took place. It looked like a brilliant riposte until Obote countered by pointing out that there was no time to change the constitution before the elections, fixed for 25 April – or perhaps Kiwanuka was deliberately trying to delay the elections?

Kiwanuka's ineptitude had already been demonstrated when he had sought to curry favour by raising the price paid to coffee growers by 20 per cent. It was an inopportune moment to make such a gesture and the objective could only be achieved by providing a heavy government subsidy at a time when prudence suggested a tight rein on public spending. He was forced to abandon a similar measure in favour of tea growers because of the opposition put up by Sir Walter Coutts. He did, however, raise the wages of the lower ranks of government servants to a minimum of 4 shillings a day, which in some cases amounted to a 100 per cent increase. Obote made no attempt to win popularity by such clumsy methods. As leader of the opposition he had, in any case, no opportunity to distribute such largesse. Instead he maintained a low profile, touring the country to make his presence felt, but saying little that was likely to stir up strong political feelings. Above all, he sought to reassure expatriate civil servants who had been worried by Kiwanuka's precipitate actions. By contrast, the Bugandan government had no doubts about its hostility to Kiwanuka. On 14 March the whole Bugandan cabinet called upon Coutts to protest about the prime minister's tactics. The ministers were particularly incensed by Kiwanuka's recent visit to the sensitive Mubende District, the former heartland of the old Bunyoro kingdom and the centre of the Lost Counties dispute. He had, they maintained, been stirring up hostility to Buganda's authority in the region.

Kiwanuka was undeterred. He had got the bit between his teeth. His suggestion that Uganda might consider leaving the commonwealth if full federal status were not given to the kingdoms of Bunyoro, Ankole and Toro and the district of Busoga inflamed an already heated situation. The rulers of the three kingdoms, accompanied by the senior chief of Busoga, went to London early in April to promote their case. They were pursuing an impossible dream. None of them could sustain the sort of government they sought without substantial assistance from the central government. The new secretary of state for the colonies, Reginald Maudling, was fully aware of this, and was conscious, too, of the more pressing issues in need of his attention. Inevitably he stalled, suggesting that some guarantee of the status of the rulers and of the distinctive, traditional institutions of the kingdoms might be incorporated in the independence constitution, and with that vague assurance they had to be satisfied.

In the event, outside Toro the status of the kingdoms and Busoga played no significant role in the elections to the national assembly, with more specifically local issues taking precedence. Voters in two Toro constituencies refused to vote until federal status had been granted, but later the two seats were won by the DP. The UPC campaigned hard in Bunyoro but lost one seat, not on account of the federal issue but because the leaders of Bunyoro feared the UPC might be more favourable to Buganda over the Lost Counties. In Busoga the result was completely different, the UPC winning all seven seats in spite of the DP's commitment to federal status for the district. Local and personal loyalties had triumphed. In the south-western district of Kigezi religious affiliations determined the outcome of the voting, a clear indication that the people of Uganda as a whole were still unable to think primarily in terms of national issues. The politicians might strive for a united Uganda but their efforts did not bind together the hearts of the people.

As in the previous year, the UPC won almost twice as many seats as the DP outside Buganda, but on this occasion voting within the kingdom followed a very different pattern. Acting as an electoral college, the *lukiiko* ensured that the KY won 21 seats. Kiwanuka himself had not been proposed as a candidate and he had no alternative constituency upon which to fall back. Obote could not, however, feel wholly confident about the future. Although half the KY members elected to the assembly belonged to what might be termed the progressive persuasion, Abu Mayanja, who was a prominent member of that camp and had played an active role in the independence movement, had not been elected, while among those chosen was the arch traditionalist, A. K. Sempa. This left Buganda's future role in doubt. Nevertheless, if any progress were to be made Obote must work on the assumption that there must be co-operation between the UPC and KY, even if no actual alliance existed between the two groups. He therefore invited a number of leading KY members to join his cabinet, among them A. K. Sempa himself, who was given the finance portfolio, and Jimmy Simpson, former leader of the representative members in the legislative council who had sworn allegiance to the *kabaka*.

Mutesa soon stirred up unease by sending a message to Reginald Maudling, the new British secretary of state for the colonies, on 4 May rejecting the recent recommendation of the privy councillors dealing with the Lost Counties issue which proposed that two of the counties should be returned to Bunyoro. The commissioners had been anxious to settle the matter before independence to avoid what they saw all too clearly as a potential cause of strife and bloodshed. The *kabaka*, rightly in view of the terms of the agreement between Britain and Buganda, claimed that they had exceeded their terms of reference in suggesting a change in Buganda's boundaries. The senior minister of Buganda, Michael Kintu, told the *lukiiko* that he would resign rather than agree to any transfer of Buganda's territory.

These difficulties surfaced more fully at the constitutional conference held in Lancaster House, in London, in June. The representatives of the DP argued consistently that the Lost Counties issue must be resolved before independence. At the same time the other kingdoms, led by the ruler of Toro and emboldened by the apparent success of Buganda's brusque tactics, demanded immediate federal status. Obote, prime minister since 30 April after the UPC victory at the polls, recognized that a lot of compromises were called for. To ensure Buganda's participation in an independent Uganda it was clearly necessary to concede federal status to the kingdom. It was not an ideal solution and Obote had no clear idea of how the arrangement would work. At the lowest level it meant that a complicated constitution must be drafted, because it would be difficult for a country with an elected government to accommodate within its borders a kingdom with an autocratic, hereditary ruler. It was essential, too, that Buganda's relationship with the rest of the country should be spelled out in minute detail if conflict were to be avoided. As far as the other kingdoms were concerned no similar arrangement could be tolerated and Obote was determined to make that clear.

The ruler of Ankole presented no problem. He was not a strong character and had only added his support to the movement for federal status under pressure from the forceful ruler of Toro. The senior minister of Busoga, Henry Muloki, was open to argument. Obote pointed out to him that he was not, like the others, a hereditary ruler, but the elected leader of his people. It might well be that, in the not too distant future, the people of Busoga might resent the imposition of the trappings of hereditary rule. Muloki accepted the argument and ceased to press the matter further. The ruler of Bunyoro was less concerned with federal status than with the future of the Lost Counties. Recognizing the combustible nature of this issue, Obote would have been glad to see it settled immediately. He was equally aware that to try to dispose of it at once would cause endless delay to the independence process. In the last resort it was an internal issue and Obote was prepared to postpone a decision provided a temporary compromise could be found. In the event, the British government was forced to impose a solution with which neither

Buganda nor Bunyoro was content. This took the form of a promise by the Ugandan government to hold a referendum in two years's time in the two counties to which Bunyoro attached most importance. The remaining five counties would be recognized as forming part of Buganda. The two disputed counties would be administered directly by the central government until the referendum. It was an arrangement fraught with danger, but for the sake of independence Obote was prepared to take the risk.

There remained the question of federal status for Toro, and here Obote tackled the ruler of Toro head-on. In the course of private discussions the issues were divided into two parts. First, there were the questions of the prestige and dignity of the ruler, and Obote conceded at once that these should be upheld. Turning to more substantive matters, he stressed that there was no question of Toro having a high court and ministers, as had been agreed for Buganda. In the first place they would cost too much. The people of Toro would obviously not shoulder the burden of additional taxation that such institutions would require without some resistance. The result could well be the overthrow of the ruler by his own people. The *mukama* retorted that the money could be obtained from the Kilembe copper mines in the west of the kingdom. Obote pointed out that a form of civil war already existed between the government of Toro and the Bakonjo people who inhabited the western part of the kingdom. The Bakonjo would not be happy to see the wealth of Kilembe used to reinforce the selfsame authority to which they took such great exception. Reluctantly the *mukama* gave way.

By these various machinations Obote got his promise of independence on 9 October, but at a price. Although Buganda had been kept within the fold, its position there was precarious. The distribution of power between the central government and the authorities within the kingdom had involved give and take on both sides. Much now would depend upon the continuing goodwill between the various parties to the constitutional agreement. However, the central government was given full authority for the maintenance of public order throughout the country. Although Buganda was to have its own police force, the central government would retain ultimate control over all police forces in the country and the Ugandan police could be employed in any part of Buganda at any time. It was less than reassuring, nevertheless, that, on his return from the conference, the *kabaka* told his people that he was sorry the dispute over the Lost Counties had grown worse, while the acting *katiikiro*, Francis Walugembe, said that Buganda would never agree to any part of the kingdom being administered by anyone else.

These tense and intricate negotiations had been preceded by what could later be seen as a fortunate escape by Obote from a potentially embarrassing set of circumstances. For some months before the conference he had been constantly importuned by a representative of the Israeli government seeking closer relations with Uganda. Eventually Obote had agreed to pay a short visit to Israel on his way to London. The main delegation, led by Felix Onama, minister of works, went straight to England while Obote had meetings with General Moshe Dayan and General Allaun in Israel. Onama, meanwhile, met his opposite number in the British government, and when Obote arrived in London Onama told him that they had been invited to a party in the evening. Obote said he was tired after his journey and would decide what to do when he had rested. About 4 p.m., Onama called on him again and Obote repeated that he was still very tired and did not intend to accept the invitation. He strongly advised Onama not to do so either, but instead to prepare himself for the conference. With some reluctance Onama agreed. The party, Obote later learned, was at Cliveden, and it was the occasion of a meeting between John Profumo and Christine Keeler.

Obote began the run-up to independence with greater political problems than were faced by most of the leaders of other African states, but with, on the whole, better economic prospects. On the political side the position of Buganda underlined one of Obote's greatest disadvantages. Few, if any, African states had any profound sense of identity at the moment of independence. They all consisted of peoples with differing languages and cultural traditions, brought together arbitrarily by colonial rulers and left, when independence came, with little alternative but to accept the boundaries drawn by the retiring colonial masters and the administrative framework they had left in place. In lieu of a sense of nationhood, however, most of the newly independent countries had an undisputed leader who had brought them through the travails of the independence struggle and now provided a focus for their loyalties. Nkrumah in Ghana, was the archetypal figure in this respect, but there were many more. In Senegal, Leopold Senghor filled the bill. No-one challenged the pre-eminence of Julius Nyerere in Tanganyika or of Félix Houphouet Boigny in Ivory Coast. In spite of the initial fears of some of the smaller ethnic groups in Kenya, Jomo Kenyatta soon established himself as the undisputed father figure of all the people in his country.

Obote, by contrast, had never occupied such an unassailable position. Accepted as overall leader of Uganda only after tenuous negotiations with the real leaders of the largest and most influential ethnic group, he did not even command the undivided loyalty of the rest of the country, having to compete for the people's support with a vigorous opposition party. His every action had to be preceded by a careful contemplation of the conflicting reactions it might arouse. Not for him the unquestioning adulation of a grateful people; only a precarious balancing act that could be upset in a moment if the pride of the Baganda should appear to be threatened. He would need all the patience and negotiating skills learned from his father to see him through.

At the very outset of Obote's term of office, one of the potentially most important developments for the future of Uganda had to be abandoned because of the political and constitutional problems with which the country was faced. For some years under colonial rule a number of valuable services in the three mainland territories – currency, postal services, railways and harbours, customs, and several other operations – had been jointly administered by an East African high commission. With the approach of independence Julius Nyerere believed the time had come to take this arrangement a step further by the creation of an East African federation which might, at some stage, lead on to the achievement of pan-Africanism. He had even offered to postpone Tanganyika's independence until the other two countries had reached a similar stage of development if this would help to promote his plan.

Kenya was willing to co-operate but Uganda held back. Obote himself was not as concerned as Nyerere about the dream of a united Africa because he considered Uganda, albeit a colonial creation, to be a reasonable unit of government in which Africans might fulfil their potential. Nevertheless he favoured the scheme for closer union within Eastern Africa, recognizing the wider market the plan would guarantee for Uganda's produce at a time when world markets were becoming more competitive. But he could not carry his cabinet with him. The KY members staunchly resisted any suggestion that Buganda should be drawn into an even wider political union and thus find its power still further diminished. Several other cabinet members were worried by the confusion they feared would arise if a country that already had a mixed federal constitution were to be incorporated in a larger federal arrangement. Obote knew that he could not press too hard and the proposal was dropped, to be revived at a later date in a diluted but probably more practical form with economic co-operation as its main objective.

Obote was not unduly pessimistic in his assessment of Uganda's economic future. For years, relying mainly on sales of cotton and more recently of coffee buttressed by a range of other products such as tea, sugar, tobacco and copper, Uganda had maintained a favourable balance of trade, to the envy of most of its neighbours. In its election manifesto the UPC had announced its intention of carrying on a similar programme, with an economy based upon the three Cs, coffee, cotton and copper, backed by the three Ts, tea, tobacco and tourism. But, as Obote had noted, the price offered for coffee was falling sharply and it had become increasingly difficult to sell cotton on the world market. Kiwanuka's injudicious intervention in the economy during his brief period of office had not helped matters and, as Sempa's budget presented on 5 June made clear, there was a considerable deficit to be met on the previous year's activities. This would mean that both the general revenue balance and the capital development fund would have to be run down. There would be a further deficit in the recurrent budget in the forthcoming year which could only be met by an increase in customs and excise duties on a wide range of goods, notably petrol and diesel fuel, and this would have repercussions in many areas of the economy.

On the other hand there were a number of hopeful signs. The government still had the advice of several experienced expatriate civil servants and Obote was by no means reluctant to seek their aid. When most of them left the country in 1964 the prime minister was able to appeal to the head of the new Labour government in Britain, Harold Wilson, who willingly sent other advisers, thereby laying the foundations for a warm and lasting personal relationship between the two men. In addition, and as a result of earlier discussions between the British and Ugandan governments, a World Bank mission had visited Uganda and on 30 April 1962 submitted a report recommending a £53 million public investment and development programme covering the period up to June 1966. £34 million, of which half should be financed locally, was to be spent by the central government, and the remaining £19 million by public authorities. This meant an increase of £2 million annually in central government spending compared with the situation in recent years. The mission also recommended that expenditure on agriculture, livestock farming, manufacturing, mining and tourism should be more than doubled, with special emphasis upon broadening the country's agricultural base in order to reduce dependence upon sales of coffee and cotton. It was a demanding programme, but not beyond the scope of a country the soil of which was remarkably fertile and one which had never suffered seriously from drought or any of the crop diseases to which its neighbours were prone. Above all, there was at that time no shortage of land for those who wished to farm, either as landowners or as tenants.

It was now time for Obote to consolidate his own foundations in anticipation of independence, and the annual convention of the UPC, which took place in August, did this for him in full measure. He was re-elected as president of the party with overwhelming support and John Kakonge was re-elected as secretary-general. By contrast, the annual conference of the DP was a depressing affair for the party leaders, only three hundred members appearing at the opening session. But, as far as Obote was concerned, the DP constituted only a minor problem. His main task lay in holding together the shaky framework of UPC relations with Buganda once the restraining hand of Britain was withdrawn on 9 October. His goal was a free, united Uganda in which the dignity of every inhabitant was recognized, but there were a significant number of influential people who had other plans.

Chapter 6

Prime minister

Looking back upon the events following independence, there is a natural tendency to concentrate attention upon the political struggles which shattered the high hopes entertained by most of the people of Uganda on 9 October 1962. In fact the immediate post-independence years held no such traumas for the majority of the population. Political independence provided a deep feeling of emotional fulfilment, but what people were really looking for was an improvement in their standard of living. The new regime duly announced that it was intent upon achieving economic as well as political independence, but in spite of all Uganda's advantages that was easier said than done. To make an immediate break with the colonial economic pattern was impossible. Obote was determined to keep external borrowing at a minimum, but if Uganda was to earn the money needed for development, it could do so only by exporting the produce the world market needed. Fortunately, this did not mean that food production for internal consumption must suffer. The fertility of the soil meant that food and export crops could be produced in sufficient quantities to meet both the needs of Uganda's own population and the demands of the external market. The balance of trade with a number of countries remained consistently favourable and, in addition, by an arrangement with the USSR made in 1963, Uganda was able to avoid the quota restrictions imposed upon coffee sales to Western markets by exporting coffee to Eastern Bloc countries.

Nevertheless, development was held up, not through lack of external aid, which was made available from a rich variety of sources, but because of the educational legacy left by Britain. Since the early 1950s Makerere had been producing a steadily increasing number of well-educated university graduates for all the East African territories, although not on the scale to meet the requirements of independent countries, particularly in the field of applied sciences or in the business and commercial sector. Consequently, Uganda still had to rely heavily upon the expertise of expatriates and, in the fields of commerce and business, upon the large Asian community, which had been mainly responsible for building and sustaining the country's commercial life from the earliest days of the Protectorate.

The shortage of trained and educated Ugandans was even more marked in the vital intermediate stage between the primary schools and the university. From the introduction of secondary schools, of which the number at independence was still chronically small, the aim of secondary pupils had been to obtain the academic education which would get them to Makerere or, failing that, into a teacher-training college or a clerical appointment in the Protectorate administration. No-one wanted the sort of training which might lead to employment as an artisan or mechanic or, worst of all, as a small farmer. Obote had always been aware of the acute shortage of secondary education and technical training, but to remedy the deficiency was not easy. Although his government set to work to increase the provision of secondary education, the availability of teachers and teaching equipment, coupled with the natural inclinations of the pupils and their parents, meant that the emphasis continued to rest upon the production of boys and girls suited primarily to clerical or minor executive work.

The more able among those young people, not unnaturally, aspired to higher posts in the administration, attracted by the salaries and apparent security enjoyed by those who had been fortunate enough to step into the shoes of the expatriate civil servants immediately before or after independence. As Africans had begun to take the jobs formerly held by Europeans, it was desirable that they should not be offered salaries far in advance of the general income level of the population. But to have discriminated on what would have appeared to be racial grounds would have been invidious, and neither the British authorities nor Obote's government when it took their place felt able to grasp the nettle. It proved to be a source of grievance to those who acquired high educational qualifications at a later stage, but it is open to question whether the majority of Ugandans were pleased or displeased by the sight of some of their compatriots enjoying the rewards formerly restricted to expatriates.

Another problem faced by the government in enlisting the whole-hearted support of the population, even outside Buganda, was the continuing lack of any strong sense of political unity. The UPC candidates in the elections earlier in the year had mustered an impressive number of votes. But, in spite of Obote's own attempts to forge a strong party organization, the electors had cast their votes less for the UPC and its policies than for individuals, well-known locally, who, they believed, could be relied upon to promote local interests.

As prime minister, Obote had duties outside Uganda as well as at home. In August 1962 he was invited to attend the meeting of prime ministers and heads of commonwealth countries which was held in London.

Because Uganda was not yet independent he went, not in his own right but as an observer, the guest of the British delegation. It was at this meeting that the British prime minister, Harold Macmillan, argued persuasively in favour of Britain's seeking admission to the common market. He was strongly opposed by John G. Diefenbaker, the prime minister of Canada, and by Eric Williams from Trinidad and Tobago, who feared the effect Macmillan's proposal might have upon the West Indian sugar trade, Britain being the West Indies' principal market. Obote was greatly impressed by the case Macmillan made and even more by the skill with which it was presented. Before he had heard the arguments he had simply assumed that if Britain joined the common market the members of the commonwealth would also be drawn in. This, so far as he could see, must bring considerable benefit to all parties. The doubts expressed on this score by Diefenbaker and Williams and, perhaps most of all by the New Zealand prime minister, K. J. Holyoake, unsettled him. But he still judged Macmillan to have presented a convincing argument and was far from disturbed by the prospect of Britain's making an approach to the EEC.

Obote met Macmillan again, briefly, in October when on his way to the United Nations to seek membership of that body for Uganda. His conversation with the British prime minister was only of a formal character, although the meeting reinforced Obote's high opinion of the man. In New York Obote addressed the general assembly of the UN, but was not profoundly impressed by the potential of that body. Far more exciting were his subsequent conversations in Washington with the American president, John F. Kennedy, and his brother, Robert, the attorney-general. He found the president extremely well informed about Uganda and willing to help if help were needed. After more than an hour of discussion, interrupted unsuccessfully on several occasions by Robert Kennedy, who seemed anxious to remind his brother of another, more pressing engagement, the president reluctantly brought the conversation to a close. He said he would be unable to dine with Obote as had been planned because he had an important speech to make, but Robert Kennedy would take his place as host. The speech, as Obote learned that evening, was, indeed, important. It was the occasion upon which Kennedy denounced the USSR for establishing missile bases in Cuba and announced the imposition of a naval blockade to prevent the shipment of arms to the island.

Over dinner Obote asked Robert Kennedy if he thought the speech would lead to war, but the attorney-general did not think it would. He believed Kruschev would back down, but added that if he did not do so the US was ready for him. Obote also expressed some surprise that the president had seen fit to appoint his brother to such an important post and asked if this would not provoke accusations of nepotism. The attorney-general was amused and cheerfully dismissed the suggestion, as he did Obote's further query about the two brothers's campaign for the election of the inexperienced Edward Kennedy as senator for Massachusetts. Both the president and the attorney-general exuded confidence and competence, but Obote found the president the more genial conversationalist and he was very conscious of Robert Kennedy's ruthless determination and drive.

Although the return journey took him via London, Obote did not pause there because he was anxious to get back to Uganda. But he was again in England in January 1963, on this occasion in the company of Rashidi Kawawa, the prime minister of Tanganyika. Their aim was to discuss independence for Kenya, because the East African common services could not function properly while Kenya remained a colony after its two neighbours had achieved independence. In the meantime Obote had met Kenyatta again after many years and had found him a changed man. He was no longer the dynamic politician he had been at their last encounter ten years earlier. To Obote he now seemed an old man, reluctant to talk seriously about any political matter and determined not to speak about the past. Although Obote came to know him very well as the years went by, and had many conversations with him, Kenyatta remained silent about his years of detention.

The visit to London was apparently abortive. Obote did not warm to the secretary of state for commonwealth affairs, Duncan Sandys, who, he thought, took little interest in the dilemma of the East African countries and was offended when the two visitors refused his invitation to accompany him to the opera. The following day Macmillan called a meeting at Admiralty House and with his customary suavity and good humour smoothed over the differences between the two sides, but nothing further was achieved and Obote never discovered whether the visit made any impact upon Kenya's advance to independence. Macmillan's own account of those events, written nearly a decade later, shows him in the sort of affable role portrayed by Obote himself. He did, however, explain that the British government was meeting with genuine difficulties in arriving at an acceptable constitution for an independent Kenya. There were so many conflicting interests and the problem of defining regional boundaries was proving acute. This was especially true of the coastal region which, historically, had been a separate protectorate, and of the area in the north-east inhabited by the Somalis, whose loyalty to Kenya was in some doubt. Macmillan also paid tribute to Duncan Sandys for his efforts to produce a satisfactory settlement, but quotes from a note by Sandys about his encounter with the two East African leaders, written on 28 January 1963, which suggests that the antipathy felt by Obote was mutual. 'I have had to spend several hours being reproached (and almost insulted)', he wrote, 'by . . . Mr Kawawa and Mr

Obote, of Tanganyika and Uganda. However, it all ended amicably and they accepted a very harmless communiqué. They were complaining about the slow march of events in Kenya – which is only their affair to the extent that they are all there in the East African Organization.' The words omitted by Macmillan from the quotation might throw even more light upon Sandys feelings.[4]

After Kenya became independent, a determined attempt was made to put the economic community that had developed out of the high commission onto a firm basis in order to improve the economic prospects of the three territories. Early in 1964 a meeting was held in Uganda, which led to the signing of the Kampala Agreement. The underlying plan was that each country should specialize in certain areas of production to avoid duplication of effort and to improve the market for each of the products. In practice the scheme did not work because each country pursued its own interests. Uganda, for example, wanted a tyre factory, but before the enterprise could be set in hand Kenya had built a tyre factory of its own, financed by the Firestone company. So the agreement was never implemented.

A further meeting took place in 1966, at which the agreement was entirely recast and this became the basis upon which the community operated until its breakdown in 1977. The groundwork for the new agreement was laid by the appropriate ministers, but it was the leaders of the three countries who initiated and eventually adopted the plan. The aim was to organize the common services more effectively, but the colonial legacy had left the headquarters of all those services in Kenya. The result was that any earnings from them were used by Kenya to balance its budget at home and to speculate on the London market. Some sorting out of this anachronism was urgently needed. It was therefore agreed that the headquarters of the community itself should move to Arusha, in Tanganyika, and that the headquarters of East African harbours should be based in Dar es Salaam. The railway headquarters would remain in Nairobi, as too would the headquarters of East African Airways. The headquarters of the postal system were to have been moved to Kampala, but the building had not been completed when Obote's government was overthrown and so the staff remained in Nairobi. However, the air training school was transferred to Uganda as, too, were a number of community research stations. Until 1971 Uganda effectively sustained the community financially and got little material return, but the three countries did at least maintain very friendly relations during that period.

The collapse of the community in 1977 was a tragedy for East Africa. It was the outstanding example of regional co-operation in the whole of the African continent and provided a number of excellent services for the inhabitants of the countries involved. The breakup began in 1971 when, after the overthrow of Obote, Nyerere refused to recognise his successor. As a result there were no further meetings of the three heads of state. Although ministers from the three countries worked together for some time to fulfil the tasks already allocated to them, the absence of any new policy directives meant that the operation was gradually run down. The community was eventually dissolved after Kenya came to the reluctant conclusion that it was financing the services single-handedly.

Obote next represented Uganda on the international scene when he accepted the invitation of the emperor of Ethiopia to attend a conference of heads of states and governments in Addis Ababa towards the end of May 1963. A newcomer to the ideological struggles in Africa, Obote's impression of the meeting was that it suffered from a lack of preparation. In fact a great deal was achieved, and Obote's own contribution was of some significance. He had been anxious to meet President Nkrumah of Ghana who had played such an important role in arousing the political awareness of Africans and accordingly he requested a half hour's interview. In the event the meeting lasted for four hours, and Nkrumah was greatly impressed by the understanding shown by Obote. Nevertheless, the latter was not convinced by Nkrumah's enthusiasm for a political union of the African states, although he was strongly in favour of their working together. When he spoke at the conference the following day that was the line he advocated and his remarks made a deep impression upon his hearers. Even Nkrumah considered he had presented a convincing speech.

From the deliberations there emerged the Organisation of African Unity (OAU) which, while firmly rejecting President Nkrumah's powerful plea for a political union, adopted a charter under the terms of which signatories recognised the sovereign equality of member states, promised to respect their territorial integrity and inalienable right to independent existence and resolved to settle all disputes by peaceful means. The recent murder of President Olympio of Togo also led to the unreserved condemnation of political assassination, as well as of subversive activities against member states.

Many of these decisions were to have a profound influence upon events in Uganda in the 1970s, but at the time Obote was chiefly impressed and delighted by the unanimous agreement to pursue a policy aimed at putting an end to colonialism in every part of Africa. As Uganda's contribution to the undertaking he offered to provide a training ground for forces seeking to combat white supremacy in South Africa, but his offer was not taken up. Uganda did, however, become one of the nine members of a co-ordinating group, later known as the African Liberation Committee, with responsibility for controlling a fund to which all members of the OAU contributed with the aim of assisting people involved in the liberation struggle. Obote noted, without much sympathy, the intensity of Nkrumah's disappointment at the failure of the conference to support his aims. Concerned essentially with practical issues, Obote was too involved in trying to make a success of an independent Uganda and in helping others struggling to achieve independence to think in the grander terms of a pan-African political union. Nkrumah recognized the strength of Obote's powers of advocacy. Wishing to enlist his sympathy, if not his active co-operation, he returned with him to Entebbe when the conference ended and took the opportunity to praise the prime minister's role in Addis Ababa in an interview with the Ugandan press.

Membership of the OAU was to have an important influence upon Uganda's foreign policy. The OAU became a substitute for the alliances and alignments which had characterized inter-state relationships in other parts of the world. Diplomacy within Africa itself was not so much a job for professional diplomats based in foreign countries as a forum in which heads of state, or sometimes foreign ministers who reported to heads of state, determined the shape of policy. The same did not apply to Uganda's relations with countries outside Africa, although here again, with the possible exception of relations with Britain, far more decisions were reached as a result of negotiations carried out by ministers, or by the prime minister himself, than as a result of the efforts or advice of civil servants. This was due in part to the lack of trained diplomats in Uganda, as in other former colonial dependencies. In colonial times the dependencies did not have any foreign policies, but simply followed the lead of the metropolitan power. With the coming of independence there was little time to train career diplomats. More important, however, was the nature of the business conducted with foreign powers. For the most part this consisted of trade agreements or the negotiation of loans and aid. Such dealings were the function of those responsible for governing the country. Nevertheless, Obote did seek advice before reaching decisions on foreign policy, although not so much from professional diplomats as from members of the party. A foreign affairs group always had access to the foreign minister so that the cabinet was constantly informed about the views of party members. In this respect, as in others, Obote believed that public opinion should not be ignored. Consultative government was something for which he constantly strove; for that and for the election of office-holders.

There was one area of what might almost be described as foreign relations, although it was very much an internal affair, in which the prime minister ploughed a lonely furrow. In spite of the understanding between the UPC and KY, relations between Buganda and the central government remained precarious. Even at the time Uganda became independent Obote had had it in mind to try to solve the problem by engineering the appointment of the *kabaka* as ceremonial president of Uganda as soon as Sir Walter Coutts, who became governor-general in October 1962, could be reasonably invited to stand down. The situation did not arise until a year later, and even then Obote had some difficulty in winning the support of his cabinet for his plan, which was not surprising in view of the widespread doubts about Buganda's intentions. Some members went so far as to propose William Nadiope as an alternative candidate for president, and it was only Obote's threat of resignation that enabled him to carry the day. The UPC had no desire to publicize its disunity at this early stage.

The whole idea of making Mutesa president was a gamble. It was Obote's firm intention that the *kabaka* should be simply the titular head of state, but he hoped the dignity that office bestowed would gratify the Baganda and make them more amenable to the idea of co-operating with the rest of the country. It was a vain hope. Mutesa could not understand the concept of a limited presidency. He took up residence in the former government house in Entebbe, which was located in Buganda, and proceeded to act as if he had the same arbitrary authority in Uganda as he enjoyed within his own kingdom. He quickly demonstrated his extravagance in petty matters as in larger affairs. He would summon his Bugandan ministers to pay court upon him in Entebbe and while they were there they filled their cars with petrol at the expense of the Ugandan government. The treasury officials protested that they had made no provision for the *kabaka*'s idiosyncratic ideas on finance, but their dismay was only a prelude to far more fundamental disputes between the titular head of state and his government.

On 11 November 1963 Obote took time from his political problems to take part in a more joyful ceremony. On his return from a visit to London in 1961 he and a friend had taken presents from a Ugandan studying in England to the man's sister who worked in Kampala. This was the first occasion of Obote's encounter with Miria Kalule. From that meeting a strong bond of friendship developed and the two were married in November 1963. Learning of the forthcoming wedding, President Nkrumah invited the couple to spend their honeymoon in Ghana. They flew from Entebbe to Addis Ababa, where the emperor gave a formal lunch in their honour at which he politely avoided all political discussion. From there they took an Ethiopian Airways flight to Lagos where they had been invited to call on the prime minister of Nigeria, Sir Abubakar Tafawa Balewa, who gave a dinner party for them. After the meal the honeymoon couple had informal conversations with ministers of the Nigerian government during which several of those present criticized strongly the idea of an 'African personality' which was being popularized by the more fervent pan-Africanists of the time, particularly in Francophone countries.

From Lagos they travelled to Sokoto, in Northern Nigeria, where they were briefly the guests of Sir Ahmadu Bello, the prime minister of the Northern Region, and then they flew in a private plane, sent by Nkrumah, to Accra where they were met at the airport by the president himself. They were driven to Flagstaff House where Nkrumah both lived and worked. There, Nkrumah had a private conversation with Obote, lasting thirty minutes, before the visitors were taken to a house nearby where they were to stay. A programme had been prepared for them from which it was clear that there would be little time for private pleasure. It appeared that the president expected to spend every morning in conversation with Obote while Mrs Obote was taken on sightseeing expeditions. The guests would also take tea daily with Nkrumah. His invitation had not, it seemed, been an act of pure altruism, for it was of politics, and particularly of the role of the OAU, that he spoke constantly. Even in the afternoons and evenings the young bride found her husband engrossed in books he had acquired in Lagos and Sokoto dealing with federal government and the history of Nigeria, and he collected more books in Accra on agriculture and the co-operative movement.

On the afternoon of 22 November they heard the news of the assassination of President Kennedy. Both Nkrumah and Obote were deeply grieved, Obote, in particular, recalling that it was exactly thirteen months since he had enjoyed that lively conversation with the young American leader. He decided that it would be appropriate to bring his honeymoon to a close and after a farewell dinner at which the visitors were introduced to a cross-section of Ghanaian leaders – ministers, judges and other dignitaries – they set out for Uganda. They broke their journey in Monrovia where they had lunch with President William Tubman who, like Balewa, was quiet in manner but was clearly a man of authority. Mrs Obote was interested to note that the two men, as well as the dynamic Nkrumah and the regal emperor of Ethiopia, seemed to get on uniformly well with her husband, who constantly displayed an easy tolerance without ever giving ground on any matter of principle. She was also to learn that, unlike some of those others, Obote listened attentively to the views of his ministers and was sensitive to public opinion. In this respect Balewa, whose benign wisdom and patent honesty had impressed them both, seemed at that time to resemble him most, although at a later stage Mrs Obote thought that President Julius Nyerere of Tanzania was closest in style and manner to her husband. One thing she had already begun to appreciate: although her husband's affection for her was beyond doubt, and was to remain so, he was, first and foremost, wedded to his political career. Family ties, indeed all human relationships, meant a great deal to him, but at the moment of crisis they must take second place to his commitment to his country. It was not a question of ambition or self-seeking. He was passionately devoted to what he conceived as his duty to the people of Uganda.

At home once more Obote revealed another side to his character. During their honeymoon he had discussed with his wife how she should spend her time and they had agreed she should not rush into doing things until she had had an opportunity to decide what would most appeal to her. He was anxious she should see as much as possible of Uganda, but he stressed that this should not incur any unnecessary expense for the public purse. At the same time, she must not accept any invitations that might place them under an obligation to others. This meticulous concern for keeping both of them above suspicion of peculation went further when he produced files containing receipts for everything he had bought, in some cases as far back as 1960. All the objects in his official residence in Entebbe were itemized, together with proof of purchase, and the same applied to the two-roomed house he was renting at Naguru and the Kampala city council house he sometimes occupied. Bed linen, kitchen utensils and cutlery were all listed, and a second file contained a note of every expense he had incurred since June 1958. This almost obsessive attention to detail was essentially an attempt to be as honest with himself as he tried to be with others, but, by chance, it was to prove extremely important seven years later. He told his wife that he was not very interested in personal wealth. His main source of income was his salary as prime minister and he also had a share in the canoe business operated by his father on Lake Kyoga, which brought him an additional sum equal to about half his salary. He proposed that his wife should open a bank account of which she would take charge and into it he would pay his salary, endorsing each payment personally. He was prone, however, to forget to pay in cheques, using them instead as bookmarks until his wife tracked them down.

Their first Christmas together brought the customary gifts from businessmen who sought to encourage customers to buy at their shops. All these were politely returned. Later, when they toured the country, they received further gifts, which embarrassed Obote greatly. He knew it was the tradition in Uganda to do that sort of thing, but he was deeply worried lest the practice should encourage office-holders to live beyond their means or to accept bribes. He toyed with the idea of passing legislation requiring all gifts to be handed over to the state, but after consulting a number of people whose advice he respected, among them Sir Tito Winyi, the ruler of Bunyoro, he decided against it. Instead, he adopted the practice of passing such gifts to charitable foundations once a discreet time had elapsed so that the donor would not learn about it.

The new year brought a new problem for Obote's government. Before independence few potential African leaders had given much thought to the future role of the armed forces. Contrary to their practice in other parts of Africa, the British authorities had made no provision for training professional Ugandan officers for the army. With the sudden approach of independence hasty improvizations were called for. A number of senior warrant officers and NCOs were given a cursory training course and promoted to the rank of *effendi*. This did not put them on a par with British officers, nor were they ideal material for officer rank. Not surprisingly this intermediate status did not satisfy the ambitions of the men involved, and Obote considered it a thoroughly unsatisfactory expedient. After independence he made urgent arrangements for younger, better educated recruits to be sent, belatedly, to the Royal Military Academy Sandhurst for full officer training. As an interim measure some of the *effendi* were given commissioned rank. The two most senior of them were to play an important role in the near future. The more senior of the two, Shaban Opolot, hailed from Teso District, in the Eastern Province, but was married to the daughter of a former chief minister of Buganda. The other, Idi Amin, a Kakwa from the extreme north-west of Uganda, had been a popular figure in the army as a champion heavyweight boxer. Neither, least of all Amin, had any serious educational qualifications, and their promotion was an act of expediency rather than of sound judgement.

It was not, however, the delay in replacing the British officers and NCOs with Ugandans that was the immediate cause of dissatisfaction in the army, although there was undoubtedly a serious undercurrent of unease on that score. Chief among the army's grievances was the low level of pay for all African ranks. On 17 December 1963 the minister of the interior, Felix Onama, told the troops that no increases would be possible in the immediate future because of the more pressing demands of education and the medical services. News of a mutiny in the Tanganyikan army on 21 January 1964 was at first dismissed as unimportant because it was thought Nyerere's rule was so popular that no opposition could be sustained. When the mutiny entered its third day, however, the government became deeply concerned, fearing a similar rising might follow in Uganda. The borders with Tanganyika were closed and police took up strategic positions in Kampala, Entebbe and Jinja. In a misjudged attempt to stabilize the situation, and contrary to the advice given him by Obote, Onama had announced considerable pay increases for senior NCOs on 22 January. In the light of his recent statement that no money was available for the army and of the absence now of any provision for the lowest-paid members of the armed forces, discontent turned to action. This was not the result of any preconceived plan. Disgruntled soldiers simply seized control of the barrack gates in Jinja and refused to move. They were not armed and there was no further violence, but when Onama arrived on the scene he was put under pressure to grant a huge pay increase. After lengthy discussions he agreed to the soldier's demands and was released.

Without further delay Obote summoned a cabinet meeting and it was agreed that an appeal for help should be made to the British government. The *kabaka*, who as President of Uganda was also commander in chief of the armed forces, was not consulted and was highly critical of Obote for this omission. Obote, however, considered the matter to be one for the executive to decide. There was an emergency and he must act at once to deal with it. In similar circumstances he did not think a British prime minister would have sought the approval of the queen before taking action. The *kabaka*'s pride was hurt, however, and he did not easily forgive his prime minister. Nevertheless, Obote's immediate response to the situation proved effective. A battalion of the Staffordshire Regiment was airlifted from Kenya and quickly took control of the capital.

On 24 January Cuthbert Obwangor, minister for regional affairs, went to address the soldiers in Jinja barracks. They now added to their demand for a pay increase a call for the withdrawal of all British officers and NCOs. After Obwangor's departure the situation became tense until Major Idi Amin, one of the hastily promoted warrant officers, persuaded the troops to disperse to their billets. Obote then invited the Staffordshires to intervene, and in the early hours of 25 January they took over Jinja barracks without a shot being fired. While this was taking place Major Amin, accompanied by Major Katabarwa, called on Obote and presented the demands of the soldiers. Obote agreed to the pay increases and to the phased withdrawal of the British officers and NCOs. This was not a wise decision, but it was one which it was difficult to avoid. He also decided to appoint Amin commander of the battalion stationed in Jinja. Again this was a gamble, but at the time the outcome was wholly unforeseeable. Fortunately, the recently formed second battalion, stationed in remote Karamoja in the north-east, had not been involved in the revolt. On the advice of the retiring British commanding officer five hundred troops from the first battalion were dismissed from the army and later some of the ringleaders were imprisoned after trial by a military court.

The Staffordshires left early in February and the incident seemed to have been settled effectively and with a minimum of upheaval, but it had serious implications for the future of the government. The dispute between the president and the prime minister had seemed relatively insignificant but it proved to be the prelude to a more serious conflict between them. More immediately worrying, however, was the threat the army had been able to pose to the authority of the government, a threat which had been bought off by concessions. Even with the troublemakers removed from the scene there was every possibility that others might replace them. Disturbing, too, though not obviously so at the time, was the role played by Idi Amin. On the surface he had behaved impeccably. But his intervention could easily be represented, if he so wished, as a protest by the spokesman of the soldiers against a less than responsive government. There were rumours, too, that he had secretly promised the dismissed soldiers that he would recruit them again into the army when the opportunity arose. Whether or not Amin contemplated establishing a power-base for himself in the army at that point is not clear, but the stage was clearly set for him to do so. One factor stood in the way of any such development in the immediate future. Opolot, senior to Amin and with a considerable personal following in the army, was constantly wary of any bid for popularity by his rival.

There was an uneasiness in the air. In April three members of KY, Amos Sempa, the minister of finance and formerly a staunch supporter of Buganda separatism, J. S. Mayanja-Nkangi and J. S. Luyimbazi-Zake, published a pamphlet entitled *A Fresh Political Approach in Uganda* in which they called for a merger of the UPC and KY, arguing that Buganda was, after all, a part of Uganda and must forever remain so. Matching action to assertion they themselves joined the UPC, and with them went a number of others. While Obote did not doubt the sincerity of the three pamphleteers he was wary of the motives of some of the other defectors who, he feared, might be hoping to carry on the struggle for Bugandan separatism from inside the UPC. Other party members disapproved for a different reason. Their concern was that the new arrivals would tilt the scale in favour of a less radical approach to politics within the party.

These doubts proved to have been well founded when the national congress of the UPC was held in Gulu in April. The more conservative element within the party focused its campaign upon the election to the office of secretary-general, held hitherto by John Kakonge. Against him they put forward an alternative candidate, Grace Ibingira. Obote was in a quandary. Although he liked Kakonge, he was worried lest his decidedly radical political views might threaten to carry the UPC too far to the left. He was anxious, too, not to do anything which might provoke a wave of reaction in Buganda, and he had been secretly glad that his party had been defeated in the recent council elections in Kampala because he thought its candidates had lost touch with reality in their enthusiasm for radical ideologies. To the surprise of many of his closest associates, therefore, he urged them to support the candidature of Ibingira, while he himself pleaded an attack of malaria as an excuse to absent himself from the voting. The decision to support Ibingira was not a wholly wise move. In fact the UPC was in danger of becoming dominated by people who were distinctly more conservative in outlook than Obote was himself, rather than by its radical members, although any challenge to Obote's leadership still lay in the future. But the die was cast and Ibingira was elected as secretary-general. Leaving domestic problems temporarily behind, Obote had to turn his attention once more to issues outside Uganda.

In July 1964 he attended his first conference of commonwealth heads of government in London as prime minister of an independent Uganda. It was a measure of Obote's inexperience of the formality that could surround such occasions, as well as of his unpretentious nature, that he was unaware that dinner jackets were normally worn at the banquet attended by Her Majesty the Queen which preceded the deliberations. He did not in any case possess a dinner suit and wore a dark jacket over a long white robe as he might have done at an official occasion in Uganda. Seeing how the others diners were dressed he felt apprehensive lest his sartorial divergeance might give offence. He was both relieved and delighted when the queen, doubtless recognizing his unease, invited him to stand next to her for the official photograph of all the members.

The conference was chaired by the British prime minister, Sir Alec Douglas-Home, and concerned itself especially with the important role the commonwealth might play in inter-racial matters. From these discreet discussions Obote moved on, later in the month, to the more disputatious second meeting of the heads of state of the Organisation of African Unity, which was held in Cairo, where it was agreed that the permanent headquarters of the organization should be located in Addis Ababa. A foretaste of future problems for the OAU, and for Obote in particular, arose over the representation of the Congolese Republic, later Zaire. The conference permitted President Joseph Kasavubu to attend but flatly refused admission to Moise Tshombe, who had recently replaced Cyrille Adoula as the Congolese prime minister. Obote had earlier had contact with the republic, having been anxious to establish good relations with Uganda's western neighbour and having already been troubled by an influx of refugees into Uganda following upon the disturbances which marked the early years of independence in the Congolese Republic. He had liked Adoulà, with whom he had been able to get along satisfactorily, but Tshombe's record was not one to encourage undue optimism. Events were to show that his misgivings were not without foundation.

At this early stage in his public career Obote was still reticent about playing a prominent role in such a distinguished forum. Always preferring to settle matters by negotiation rather than by making a public pronouncement, he discussed with Nyerere, with whom he was developing an ever stronger friendship, the future of the national boundaries inherited from the colonial regimes, an issue to which he had given considerable thought. Sensing that Nyerere shared his concern, he urged the Tanzanian leader to propose that members should agree to recognize and respect the existing state boundaries. The arbitrary nature of those boundaries was generally accepted, but Obote was fully aware that any suggestion of change could have endless repercussions and would lead inevitably to disputes between member states.

It was, however, the problems posed by Israeli involvement in Africa that aroused the most vigorous debate. As soon as an African country achieved independence Israel tried to open an embassy there. The Arab members of the OAU wanted the embassies closed, but the other representatives resisted that proposal. In the various committees of ministers strong resolutions were adopted against Israel, but they were ignored by the heads of state in spite of considerable pressure from the Arab leaders who demanded to know if the other nations were truly their friends. Obote had no intention of closing the Israeli embassy in Uganda and he made an appointment to discuss the question with President Nasser of Egypt. Egypt, Obote knew, had close relations with Uganda's northern neighbour, the Sudan, and the Sudanese military government was anxious lest Uganda might become a base for covert Israeli activities in support of its internal opponents who were active in the southern part of the country. Obote assured the president that Uganda would act as an independent nation and would certainly not be the tool of a foreign power. In return Nasser admitted that Egypt had no right to try to impose a foreign policy upon Uganda. Nevertheless, Obote felt that the president's conciliatory manner was motivated less by Nasser's innate reasonableness than by his desire to remain on good terms with Uganda and Ethiopia, the countries from which came the water for the Aswan Dam.

At these conferences Obote made his first acquaintance with President Hastings Banda of Malawi. He travelled with him as far as Ethiopia on the return journey and spent a night in the same hotel. Over the years which followed he came to know Banda possibly better than did most of the other African heads of state. He thought he resembled Presidents Senghor and Houphouet-Boigny, in that he was as British – or South African – as they were French. He developed a considerable respect for the older man, accepting that he was honest according to his own standards. He was convinced that, at heart, Banda did not support apartheid, but had reached the conclusion that there was little the rest of Africa could do about it. Obote could not accept that view, but acknowledged that it was honestly held. He was amused that Banda always attended the opening ceremonies at commonwealth conferences and was also present at the official dinner, but took no further part in the proceedings, preferring to stay in his hotel, where Obote invariably made a point of calling on him.

Obote returned to deal with the issue which was to prove the turning point in his relations with the Baganda. He had always intended to carry out a referendum to determine the future administration of the Lost Counties within two years of independence as recommended by the British government. He knew that to do so would risk a clash with Buganda but he believed it was essential to go ahead. The *kabaka* had already made it clear that he would not give in without a struggle. More than a year earlier he had undertaken a hunting trip in the Lost Counties and had conceived the idea of changing the character of the electorate by encouraging Bugandan ex-servicemen to settle in the disputed area. By the latter half of 1964 several thousand new settlers had taken up residence there with strict instructions to vote in favour of a link with

Buganda. Obote countered by insisting that voting should be carried out on the basis of the electoral register compiled at the time of the 1962 elections. In the event, and despite vigorous protests about the electoral roll from Buganda, the result of the referendum proved to be a foregone conclusion. The overwhelming majority of the inhabitants of the two counties cherished their traditional attachment to Bunyoro and voted accordingly. Even then the Baganda did not give in. An action was brought in the high court to have the referendum declared illegal because the 1962 electoral roll had been used, but it failed.

After the referendum Sempa came to the conclusion that he could no longer support the government, so he crossed to the opposition benches in the assembly, taking with him Dr E. B. S. Lumu. He continued, nevertheless, to uphold the principle of a united Uganda. Zake remained loyal to the government, and Mayanja-Nkangi, the third member of the triumvirate, also backed the referendum. About the same time Obote gained further support when it was announced that Basil Bataringaya, the most effective member of the DP in the national assembly, had transferred his allegiance to the UPC together with five other members of his party. Before accepting Bataringaya's membership Obote insisted that he should publicly announce his decision to change sides, but there is little doubt that the transfer was undertaken in all sincerity. Bataringaya and his colleagues were anxious to make an effective contribution to the prosperity of Uganda and believed this could best be done by joining the governing party and criticizing policy where they felt they must instead of attacking the government on every issue as a formal duty. This approach accorded more closely with African traditions of democracy than did the more adversarial Westminster system of government, while the accession of strength was more than welcome to the UPC. With talent so thinly spread it was a pity to waste it upon routine criticism. It meant, too, that the UPC now had an overall majority in the national assembly and need no longer lean upon the rump of KY for support.

The result of the referendum had also led to the downfall of Buganda's chief minister, Michael Kintu, who had vigorously upheld the position of the kingdom and had sworn to resign rather than surrender any part of Bugandan territory. Now he found himself totally discredited by Buganda's abject failure at the polls. There remained the election of a successor, and it was with the strong support of Obote and the UPC leadership that Mayanja-Nkangi stood as a candidate for the post. Obote took this stance in the hope of being able to promote his main objective of preserving a link with Buganda more effectively while providing himself with a means of dealing more easily with potential opposition. He knew that Mayanja-Nkangi was in favour of a united Uganda, and he hoped that if his candidature was successful the new chief minister might be able to sway opinion within the *lukiiko* in favour of a more accommodating attitude towards the central government. He also knew that Mayanja-Nkangi was always ready to see every possible side to any question, with the result that he seemed unlikely to lead the sort of hard-line attack upon central government policy which his predecessor had espoused. This, Obote hoped, might prove advantageous in the event of a difference of opinion between the Baganda and his government. It was, however, more a measure of the temporary disarray of the Bugandan old guard than of Obote's cunning that Mayanja-Nkangi was elected chief minister.

It was fortunate for Obote that during this period of political turmoil he had few worries on the economic front. His government found external aid easy to come by on the limited scale for which it had been agreed to ask. In concert with Kenya and Tanzania, Uganda was able to get help from Britain for the development of their common services. The World Bank provided most of the resources for building schools and colleges, and the USA supplied funds to finance a big ranching project in Ankole. Israel, which had endeavoured to establish relations with the UPC even before independence, was quickly off the mark when Uganda threw off British tutelage. The Israelis offered no financial assistance, their prime contribution being to train airforce personnel to fly the planes which Uganda purchased from them. They also provided courses for soldiers while the officers were trained by Britain.

Although Obote played a prominent role in all the negotiations with foreign powers or their representatives he was careful not to impose his views upon unwilling subordinates. The officials of the party were elected by the party conference, not chosen by himself, and all important plans were formulated in cabinet meetings and then presented to the national assembly for its approval. The term 'a good diplomat' which was the highest accolade Obote gave to the foreign politicians and statesmen with whom he came into contact – men like John F. Kennedy and Harold Macmillan – was a measure of his own perception of the qualities required of a good leader. He admired men who could argue clearly and convincingly in preference to those who carried the day solely by force of personality.

In 1965 there was another meeting of commonwealth prime ministers in London in June, when the main topic under discussion was Southern Rhodesia, which was threatening to defy Britain by making a unilateral declaration of independence. The chief critics of this position were Presidents Nyerere of Tanzania and Kenneth Kaunda from Zambia, together with the prime minister of Sierra Leone. Obote said little, although he had strong feelings about the question, and the British prime minister, Harold Wilson, seemed reluctant to make any pronouncement. Following upon the conference Obote flew to Belgrade to discuss the extension of the Jinja dam and the supply of turbines. This was an undertaking which had been approved by the World Bank, not only because the quotation from Belgrade was the lowest Uganda had received, but also because Yugoslavia had broken with the USSR and the West was trying to woo President Tito.

From Yugoslavia Obote flew to India. Prime minister Nehru had died in May 1964 and Obote was able to meet his successor, Lal Bahadur Shastri, and also Indira Gandhi, who had been appointed minister of information and with whom he was later to be on very good terms. He also met Nehru's sister, Mrs Pandit, by whose graciousness and charm he was considerably impressed. This was his last visit to India for some time because trouble with the Indian community in Uganda made it inappropriate for him to return. From India he continued his journey to Hong Kong where he stayed with the governor, Sir David Trench, before going on to Canton by train. He then flew to Peking where he paid a courtesy call on the chairman of the Chinese Communist Party, Mao Tse-tung, before meeting the chairman of the state council, Chou En-lai. The latter was particularly interested to hear what had been said at the Commonwealth Conference about Vietnam. When Obote told him that it had been proposed to send observers from the commonwealth to see if there was any prospect of sorting out the situation Chou En-lai replied that China had no desire to see any imperial power on its doorstep, hence the support that had been given to the North Vietnamese.

Chou En-lai also talked at length about Africa and seemed to be well informed about the continent. He had visited ten African countries at the end of 1963 and in the early days of 1964, while earlier in 1965 President Nyerere had visited China and Chou En-lai himself had paid a reciprocal visit to Tanzania as recently as June. He believed, he said, that Africa was ripe for revolution. Obote was sceptical and replied that, with the possible exception of South Africa, the continent was certainly not, in his opinion, likely to produce the sort of revolution the other was contemplating. On a more practical level, Obote was able to discuss a scheme whereby China would assist in growing rice in a swampy area in the Eastern Province. This, in due course, proved a great success, although when Obote first announced what had been arranged his critics in Uganda were loud in their condemnation of what they conceived to be the establishment of a communist foothold in their country.

Accompanied by Chou En-lai Obote then flew to Shanghai, primarily on a sightseeing visit, before returning to Hong Kong by train. When he reached the latter destination he was besieged by the press who asked him what Chou En-lai had said about Hong Kong. Obote replied that the topic had not been raised. He was then asked what he himself thought about the colony. He said he had no informed opinion but that when the subject was discussed at the Commonwealth Conference the general view had been that, along with other colonies, it should be granted independence as soon as possible. This reply did not please his interlocutors, who were strongly opposed to independence. The next day Obote found that he was headline news in all the local papers, which accused him of having supported independence for Hong Kong. As he was a guest of the governor he found this sudden notoriety extremely embarrassing and hastened to explain to his host what he had really said. He also wrote to Harold Wilson to describe what had taken place in case he was misreported in Britain.

Leaving Hong Kong with some relief, Obote flew to Tokyo where he had discussions about some schools the Japanese had promised to open in Kampala. From there he went on to Moscow to talk about a mineral survey the USSR had carried out in Uganda but on which they had failed to submit a final report. In the event nothing came of the enterprise. In Moscow he was the guest of the prime minister, Aleksei Kosygin, whom he found to be extremely reserved in manner but of whose intellectual powers he had no doubt. Kosygin told him that the USSR was prepared to build an agricultural mechanical school in Eastern Uganda, between the towns of Tororo and Jinja. That promise was duly fulfilled and the school was a great success. Obote then flew to London where he had dinner with Harold Wilson with a view to letting the British prime minister know about Chou En-lai's fear of the presence of an imperial power in Vietnam. Also present at the dinner were George Brown and Richard Crossman, both of whom spoke loudly and almost continuously, which made it difficult for the diffident Obote to tell his story.

On the whole it had been a successful trip. Although most of his contacts had been with communist countries his travels had not had a political objective. His aim had been to get the assistance Uganda needed as economically and as effectively as he could, irrespective of the source. When Nyerere had visited China he had made it clear that Tanzania did not intend to become dependent upon any foreign power or to adopt any externally imposed ideology and Obote felt exactly the same about Uganda. Now, however, he came to the conclusion he had been away from Uganda far too long. It was time to see what had happened in his absence.

Events had moved quickly. After the Lost Counties referendum many of the Bugandan old guard had wanted all KY members to leave the cabinet in protest. They were unable to insist on this because the *kabaka* was president of Uganda and it would have been unseemly for the Bugandan leaders to have been overtly dissociating themselves from the government of which he was titular head. Abu Mayanja took the view that KY should be disbanded, but when he failed to convince the Bugandan establishment he joined the UPC, taking a number of other KY members with him. This was a further accession of strength to the UPC parliamentary party because Mayanja was already a member of the national assembly.

The rump of KY members then decided to pursue a new line, ostensibly joining the UPC themselves, but using Grace Ibingira as the leader of a movement to bring about a change of leadership from within the party. Although he did not possess strong leadership qualities himself, Ibingira was a clever negotiator, and he had come to the conclusion that Obote lacked the educational background to speak for his country. In Ibingira's opinion Obote had been chosen too hurriedly as leader, solely on the basis of his powerful attacks upon colonial rule in the legislative council. That he was mistaken in his assessment is clear. Because of the strength of his conviction that Uganda was ripe for independence Obote had indeed developed into an influential speaker in the legislative council. His election as leader of the UPC had, however, been the result more especially of the strong support he had had from within his own party and of his considerable skill in putting over his views to fellow members of the party executive. It was in intimate discussion rather than in dema-gogy that he excelled. Nevertheless, the shadow of a threat to Obote's leadership now made its appearance within the UPC itself, as the Bugan-dan hierarchy had planned. In December Ibingira, using as an excuse the need to attend to his ranch in Ankole, paid a secret visit to the USA. There he was able to raise funds, rumoured to amount to $1 million, to help check the spread of socialist ideas in Uganda. The money, whatever the true amount may have been, attracted a considerable following for Ibingira. The challenge to Obote was on foot.

With KY now nominally defunct and the UPC officially dominant in Buganda, it was necessary, in accordance with UPC rules, to hold elections to choose branch representatives and a leader of the Bugandan section of the party. Both issues were fraught with problems and with danger to the unity of the party. True to precedent in the kingdom, the elections were conducted in a less than democratic fashion. The UPC leadership was far from happy at the degree of interference by the chiefs, who appeared virtually to determine who was to be elected and who was not. But direct elections of a sort had taken place, so the result was accepted in preference to entering into open confrontation with the Baganda. Obote himself opened the conference of newly elected branch representa-tives which followed the elections, then left the meeting to go to Entebbe, where he hoped to find a quiet retreat in which he could prepare the speech he intended to deliver at the close of the conference. He was surprised, therefore, when, on meeting the *kabaka*, who by that time had virtually settled in Entebbe, Mutesa asked him who had been elected leader of Buganda's UPC. Obote immediately suspected that the Bugan-dan leadership must have been scheming once again, but replied that he had had no news. He was deeply disappointed when he learned that, although the party executive had, as he thought, prepared the ground carefully, Dr Lumu, formerly a prominent figure in KY, had been elected party leader for Buganda instead of the official candidate, Godfrey Binaisa, the attorney-general and a long-time member of the UPC. But that, after all, was the way things went in Buganda, and on reflection Obote concluded that the phasing out of KY had been a positive gain in spite of the setback over Lumu's election.

Ibingira now made his first, extremely tentative move to challenge the prime minister. On the strength of the new situation he called for structural changes in the UPC. Obote replied that this could not be done without the formal approval of a delegates' conference. He offered to summon such a conference, but Ibingira did not believe the time was ripe to test the strength of his support so he did not respond.

There were other consequences of Obote's recent visit to Europe and Asia which were also disturbing. In his absence Nadiope had paid an unauthorized visit to Europe in the hope of raising money for his own purposes, as Ibingira had done in the USA, and had become involved in a scandal over an attempt to claim that his traveller's cheques had been stolen after they had already been cashed. Meanwhile Ibingira had been trying to represent Obote's travels as a demonstration of the prime minister's communist leanings. Ibingira's US allies, deeply agitated by a fear of communist expansion, and his supporters in Buganda, worried about their own future, were not reluctant to accept his interpretation of events. In furtherance of this campaign he drew attention to the presence within the UPC of a number of young men who had been educated in India and who talked a lot about socialism. They did not, in practice, comprise a significant group within the party and certainly exerted no great influence upon the views of the party leaders. Nevertheless, coupled with concern, real or assumed, over the Chinese rice-growing project and over the plan for a technical school to be founded by the USSR, such ideas, as Obote was all too aware, helped to strengthen suspicions about the government's ideological position.

To promote this line of attack still more actively a rumour was spread to the effect that left-wing elements were plotting to overthrow both the central government and the *kabaka*'s government early in October. After a meeting of the executive of the UPC in Kampala in the same month, Ibingira remarked casually, as he was leaving, that he was going to be killed. Obote called him back and asked what he meant and who was likely to kill him. Ibingira replied that he believed some anti-KY members of the UPC planned to carry out the assassination. Obote immediately summoned the inspector-general of police and the minister for home affairs and called upon Ibingira to repeat his allegations. The inspector-general then investigated the people named by Ibingira but could find no case against them. Obote subsequently denied strongly any suggestion that the *kabaka* had called upon him to denounce the 'plot',[b] insisting that Mutesa would certainly have regarded such a request as unseemly. He also denied the *kabaka*'s own assertion[6] that, in spite of the latter's protest, he had addressed some troops in Kampala on 9 October.

From these internal wrangles Obote was called away at the beginning of 1966 to attend a meeting of the Commonwealth Conference held in Lagos, the first time the meeting had taken place outside London. The sole item for discussion was Rhodesia, which had featured prominently at the meeting of the OAU in December 1965. On that occasion a motion had been passed unanimously to sever relations with the UK unless the British government secured a satisfactory resolution of Rhodesia's unilateral declaration of independence within fifteen days. Since then more cautious councils had prevailed and only a limited number of countries had put the motion into effect, among them Tanzania. Obote had not felt that he could support his friend, Nyerere, in taking such a step, and at the Commonwealth Conference he refrained from making any comment when, in the face of considerable scepticism from many other members, Harold Wilson insisted that economic sanctions would soon put an end to Ian Smith's rebellion.

When the talks ended Obote was anxious to return to Uganda, but the chief justice of Uganda, a Nigerian, was on home leave and invited Obote to dine with him rather than taking the first plane back to Entebbe. The next day, when he was due to leave Nigeria, Obote learned that there had been a military coup. There had been no sound of fighting in Lagos, but Archbishop Makarios, who had been visiting Northern Nigeria, was flown to Lagos by helicopter and came to Obote's hotel. He brought news of the murder of Sir Ahmadu Bello, which had not yet been announced to the public. Obote also learned with sorrow of the assassination of Sir Abubakar Tafawa Balewa, whom he had held in high regard. These upheavals delayed Obote several days and when he returned to Uganda he was soon to be faced with a threat to his own position.

Chapter 7

President

The sequence of events which led to the total breakdown of relations between Obote's government and the Baganda arose from developments in neighbouring Zaire. However, these were only the catalyst for a rupture which, whatever Obote's hopes, had threatened to take place even before independence was achieved.[7] Obote had little liking for Moise Tshombe, the Zairean prime minister, whom he regarded as an agent of neo-imperialism. His sympathies lay with the National Liberation Committee, which opposed Tshombe's government. In January 1965 he arranged for one of the leaders of the Committee, Christophe Gbenye, to attend a secret meeting with Presidents Kenyatta and Nyerere and some of the UPC leaders in Mbale, a town in Eastern Uganda. Gbenye's audience was impressed by the case he made, but the rules of the OAU forbade interference in the internal affairs of member states. If, therefore, they wished to help him, they must do so clandestinely. Both Tanzania and Uganda shared their western border with Zaire, but the rebels were located in north-eastern Zaire so that Uganda was the obvious channel through which contact should be made.

The breach of the OAU charter was an act of disloyalty scarcely justified by the OAU's own refusal to admit Tshombe to its proceedings and was particularly surprising in view of the fact that that same body had appointed President Kenyatta to head a conciliation commission to try to sort out the Zaire problem. For Obote the situation was aggravated by the fact that the Buganda government was well disposed towards Tshombe and would certainly oppose assistance to the rebels if too much publicity were given to the plan. A measure of secrecy was called for. It was for that reason, as well as because Colonel Idi Amin's home was in the extreme north-west of Uganda, that Obote chose Amin, the second most senior officer and deputy commander of the army, to take charge of operations. Brigadier Shaban Opolot, the army commander, was too closely associated with Buganda to be trusted to carry out the task discreetly. After the meeting Gbenye stayed for three months, privately, in a house in Kampala rented for him by Obote.

The first overt evidence of friction between the president and the prime minister took place in February when the two attended a military function in Jinja. To Obote's surprise, the officers there took part in a ceremony in which, individually, they swore loyalty to Mutesa. They were followed by the NCOs, who took the oath as a group. The whole proceedings were unconstitutional and had certainly never been approved by the cabinet. Whoever had planned them must have intended to make it clear where the army's sympathies lay. Not wishing to put the matter to the test, the prime minister slipped quietly away during the dance that followed the official dinner, and slept that night at the home of a friend some ten miles from the barracks. The oath was cancelled by the government some time later and on 1 May the officers and NCOs took a new oath of allegiance to the government.

In March, while Gbenye was still living in Uganda, Daudi Ocheng, formerly secretary-general of *Kabaka Yekka*, drew the attention of the national assembly to the fact that Amin's account with the Ottoman Bank had recently increased so markedly as to suggest that some of the money had been gained improperly. Ocheng had an interesting background. His father, a Madi from the extreme north-west, had been brought up by Acholi foster parents and had met his future wife, a Langi, while the two were studying for baptism in Gulu. Their son, Daudi, had never felt himself to be fully accepted in Acholi and had happily gone to school at King's College, Budo, in Buganda. There he had met and become a friend of the *kabaka*, who was a fellow student. After Budo, the two went to Makerere. Then, while the *kabaka* went to Cambridge, Ocheng continued his own studies in Aberystwyth.

He returned to Uganda to become an agricultural officer and his ability was quickly recognized by the Protectorate authorities. In 1961 he was invited to become deputy finance minister in the Protectorate government as part of the campaign to involve Africans in the running of the country, but Ocheng did not shine in that role. In the elections to the legislative council later in the year he stood as a DP candidate in one of the Kampala constituencies, but was defeated by his UPC opponent. He became an agricultural officer again until, as a result of his friendship with the *kabaka*, he was summoned to work for the Bugandan government. It was in Buganda that, henceforth, he sought to establish his identity, and in 1964, with the backing of the *kabaka* and in company with Abu Mayanja, he was elected to the national assembly in a by-election as the representative of a Bugandan constituency.

Ocheng's raising of the Amin incident was his first significant intervention in the debates in the assembly. It was an important issue, which needed to be handled with care by the government because it was through his involvement in the undercover Zaire operation that Amin had acquired the money in question. At that stage Obote himself had no reason to believe that any dishonesty was involved and his support for Amin did not waver. The government therefore promised that the matter would be investigated, but procrastinated to such an extent that Ocheng tabled a motion calling for urgent action. Obote responded by summoning a secret session of the assembly and explained that the delay was due to the security implications of Amin's activities. He did, however, insist that he had every intention of taking the action needed to satisfy Ocheng's concern. Although this was sensitive ground, Obote still had little cause for concern about his own position as prime minister. Ocheng's accusations were, after all, levelled only against Amin, and solely on the grounds that he appeared to have acquired money improperly.

For a time the matter appeared to have receded into the background, but in October there was another unpleasant brush with the military. After the annual parade to celebrate the anniversary of Uganda's independence there was a reception at one of the *kabaka*'s official residences, Makindye Lodge. As the prime minister approached the house he was taken aback to see the route lined with tanks, armoured personnel carriers and troops in combat gear. Throughout the evening a number of officers followed the prime minister wherever he moved and at times completely surrounded him. They took no further action, but when Obote returned to his house in Kampala he summoned the minister of defence, Felix Onama, and ordered him to get all the troops away from the city immediately. This was done, but Obote was conscious of the potential threat to security offered by military leaders whose loyalty was suspect. He was shortly to have a closer view of that danger.

It was in January 1966 that Ocheng went over to the attack once again when he proposed a motion for discussion in the national assembly calling for the suspension of Amin pending investigations into his bank account. Obote summoned a meeting of the UPC parliamentary party on 23 January to discuss the attitude they should adopt towards the motion. At the meeting the prime minister explained the difficulties the government had encountered in carrying out the investigation it had promised, difficulties compounded by army regulations concerning the investigation of senior officers and by the impossibility of making regular contact with the Zairean rebel movement which had, in any case, recently split. He said that Amin had admitted having a large sum of money, but that he had received it from the supporters of Christophe Gbenye to pay for supplies. Obote reminded the meeting that the UPC had agreed to assist Gbenye, even though the government could not do so formally, and it was in fulfilment of that decision that Amin had acquired the money. In the circumstances the party agreed it would reject Ocheng's motion and urged Obote to honour the promise he had made two months earlier to visit West Nile District. He left, confident that no further problems would arise.

Obote discovered that something was amiss when he was in Moyo and received from the police the minutes of a cabinet meeting which had taken place in his absence. On 4 February, only minutes before Ocheng was due to introduce his motion into the assembly, an emergency meeting of the cabinet had been summoned. Obote himself was obviously unable to attend, and two of his strongest supporters, Adoko Nekyon, his kinsman, and Felix Onama, were also absent. Ibingira was the instigator of the move and he and his supporters, being in the majority at the meeting, reversed the decision taken by the parliamentary party. Cuthbert Obwangor who, as acting chairman of the cabinet had been left in charge by Obote, was taken aback by what was happening and made little effort to assert control.

The situation became still more confused in the ensuing debate in the assembly when Ocheng, having charged Amin with concealing his acquisition of the Zairean money from the government and also with looting gold, ivory and coffee, then enlarged the scope of his allegations by accusing Obote, Nekyon and Onama of being involved in corruption and other illegal acts which, he explained, was why there had been so long a delay in investigating Amin. Gaspar Oda, a member of the DP who had agreed to second the original motion, was taken aback by the new charges and said that, had he had prior knowledge of them, he would have insisted that the three ministers be present at the debate. One of them, Onama, was indeed at the meeting and challenged Ocheng to repeat the accusations outside the privileged confines of the assembly. Brushing aside the protest, Ocheng went on to accuse Amin, and by implication Obote, of being involved in a plot to train young men with a view to using them to overthrow the constitution and engineer a revolution.

In his own speech Ibingira virtually ignored the question of Amin's bank account and the whole question of Zaire. Instead, in an attempt to discredit Obote as much as possible, he concentrated upon the allegations of a plot to subvert the constitution. Having listened to Ibingira, Onama went upstairs to his parliamentary office and summoned Shafiq Arain and John Kakonge to discuss what should be done. Arain and Kakonge were known to be loyal supporters of Obote and Kakonge had become a specially elected member of the assembly with Obote's backing and against the wishes of Ibingira in a trial of strength between the two factions. Onama and his two colleagues recognised the gravity of the situation. The UPC members of the assembly had been totally confused by the reversal of their previous decision, apparently with the approval of the entire cabinet – or so they had been earnestly led to believe by Ibingira and his supporters in the lobby immediately before the debate. They were, of course, unaware that Onama and Nekyon had not been present at the cabinet meeting. It was agreed, therefore, that Onama should immediately acquaint Obote with what was going on, using the police radio. Kakonge, meanwhile, would return to the chamber and intervene in the debate at an appropriate moment to rebut the charges brought by Ocheng and Ibingira. Arain's role was to scour the lobbies and the tea room to brief as many back-benchers as possible and to canvass their support against the motion. He found this a difficult task. Most of the people to whom he spoke assured him of their loyalty to Obote as party leader and as prime minister, but, having heard Ibingira's speech and having been approached by such senior members of the party as Magezi, Kirya and Ngobi, they were not prepared to oppose Ocheng's motion outright. The participation of Magezi, Kirya and Ngobi is not easy to comprehend. Kirya had always been a strong supporter of Obote but probably did not understand the gravity of what he was doing. Magezi and Ngobi were men of a different calibre.

John Kakonge, as had been agreed, denounced the cabinet's reversal of the decision by the parliamentary party to reject Ocheng's motion and said that the whole proceedings were a plot concocted by Obote's opponents. In that he was not far from the truth, and Sam Odaka, minister of state for foreign affairs, gave him qualified support. Nevertheless, even Onama came to the conclusion that he must support the motion, if only to give himself and the other accused ministers an opportunity to clear themselves by accepting the call for a judicial enquiry. Many of the speakers, Abu Mayanja among them, insisted they were confident the ministers would be able to do so.

The inquiry having been agreed, Ocheng wound up the debate by perversely insisting that his motion had only been concerned with Amin's bank account. But he had achieved his objective of casting doubt upon the honesty of Obote and his immediate supporters, including Amin. In so doing he had prepared the ground for the implementation of another plot, engineered by Ibingira, Ocheng himself and Brigadier Opolot, with the possible collusion of the kabaka, to overthrow Obote's government by force, having first got Amin out of the way by suspending him from duty. The plotters next called upon Opolot to send a message to Obote requesting him, at the behest of the cabinet, to return at once to Kampala. In the meantime, troops loyal to Opolot were moved into the town and surrounded the building in which the national assembly met.

On receiving Opolot's message from the hand of a captain accompanied by a small detachment of troops whom the police had taken the precaution of disarming before permitting them to approach the prime minister, Obote replied that he would only return at the direct request of the cabinet itself. He had left Obwangor to deal with any matters which might arise, he went on, and he would certainly not return at the request of the army. He was, in fact, playing for time until he got a clearer idea of what was going on. Next, he sent messages by the police radio and by road to clarify the situation in Kampala. He quickly learned that Opolot had the support of only a section of the army and that the police remained solidly loyal to the government. He was told that it would be safe for him to return to Kampala provided he did not travel by too obvious a route.

This proved to be the case, but when he got back to the capital on 13 February Obote discovered that the *kabaka* had taken it upon himself to approach the British high commissioner to ask for military assistance. Twice he tried to telephone Mutesa to seek an explanation for his action, but the *kabaka* would not respond. Some time later, however, he admitted that the report was true, but explained in his own account of events that he feared a coup by Obote – the one referred to by Ibingira in the national assembly – and was simply making precautionary inquiries in case things got out of hand.[8] Two days later, on 15 February, Obote called a cabinet meeting and demanded that anyone who had lost confidence in him should resign. No-one did so. Nevertheless, the cabinet insisted that the inquiry called for by the assembly should be set in hand, in spite of Obote's denial of the allegations made against him by Ocheng. The prime minister accepted the cabinet's decision and appointed a distinguished panel of judges from Kenya and Tanzania, two of them British, to carry out the assembly's proposal. Obwangor, meanwhile, told Obote that he himself had been afraid to call a cabinet meeting in the prime minister's absence lest fighting should break out among the members. An honest man who was anxious to do what was right, he had been completely outmanoeuvred by Ibingira. In due course the judicial enquiry completely exonerated Obote of all the charges of corruption brought against him, while Ocheng's evidence, even against Amin, proved wafer thin.

The more Obote heard of the subterfuges that had taken place the more incensed he became. On 22 February he arrested Ibingira, Lumu, Kirya, Ngobi and Magezi, whom he believed to be the instigators of the plot to overthrow him. Opolot was suspended and his place taken by Amin. Obote also decided that the *kabaka*, because of his complicity with the plotters, could no longer be president. That decision was a matter of great regret to Obote, not only because of the difficulties he knew it would create in his relations with Buganda but because, through all his negotiations with the *kabaka*, he had been convinced that Mutesa was the agent of unscrupulous men rather than being himself the initiator of the conflict. After the arrests, Obote moved to Kampala, and stayed in the prime minister's official residence. Mutesa himself moved back to his palace at Mmengo.

The detention of Ibingira and Magezi was to mark the beginning of an estrangement between some of the western districts and the central government. In spite of Obote's high hopes the UPC had not become a popularly-based party in every district in the country. This was partly due to the origins of the party in the UPU/UNC merger and partly to the linguistic barriers that divided the peoples of Uganda one from another. At the time of the merger the UPU had been a parliamentary rather than a popular party and so it had remained. The loyalty of the electorate in some constituencies was still focused upon individual candidates rather than upon the party, and members of the assembly who had been elected on that basis had not sought to change it. The language barrier had always meant that canvassing in those constituencies had had to be left to the candidates who spoke the local language, without the presence of party luminaries from other districts who might have emphasized the role of the party rather than of the individual. Thus the arrest of Ibingira and Magezi was not seen by the voters in their constituencies as an example of a party taking disciplinary action against some of its members who were believed to have behaved dishonourably. Instead it was represented as an affront to the dignity of the electorate by an alien central government which was depriving the voters of the spokesmen they themselves had chosen. Fortunately for Obote, the same had not been true of the Eastern Province constituencies of Kirya and Ngobi. There the UPC had always had a strong, popular base, and the constituencies lacked the distinctive sense of identity engendered by the existence of the traditional kingdoms in the west.

The next step was to amend the constitution. A new draft was prepared by the attorney-general's department, led by Godfrey Binaisa, on the basis of principles agreed by the cabinet. Apart from an amendment to give more civil rights to women, the most significant change to the constitution of 1962 was the creation of the office of executive president. To reinforce the new arrangements constitutional heads of kingdoms and districts were barred from holding public office, which meant that the *kabaka* could no longer be president and Nadiope ceased to be vice-president. There was consequently no need to dismiss them formally. Chiefs, too, were forbidden to sit on kingdom or district councils, and the high court of Buganda, which had ensured subservience to the *kabaka*'s regime, was abolished. On 15 April the new constitution was presented to the national assembly. Although the members had had no time to peruse it in advance of the meeting, Obote insisted that it be adopted immediately. Obote himself, as leader of the ruling party, became president and John Babiiha vice-president. It was a dangerous road upon which Obote had embarked. Although the changes were endorsed by the high court in February 1967, they marked a serious divergence from Obote's avowed commitment to the principle of acting only in response to tested public opinion. Elections to the assembly were, of course, due not later than 1967, and Obote could argue that the voters would then have an opportunity to express their views on what had so precipitately taken place. Unfortunately for any such hopes, other events took place, which resulted in a constitutional appeal for public support being delayed indefinitely.

Inevitably the difficulty arose in Buganda. The Bugandan establishment responded vigorously to the changes. A number of Bugandan members of the national assembly refused to swear allegiance to the new constitution. The chiefs hung onto their seats in the *lukiiko* and the day after the meeting of the national assembly the *lukiiko* flatly rejected the new constitution. Disregarding this challenge to his authority, Obote, acting now as executive president, turned to other matters and announced a new five-year development plan aimed primarily at increasing agricultural production. The plan also contained proposals for reducing Uganda's dependence upon agricultural exports by encouraging industrial development.

Buganda was not so easily ignored. On 23 May the *kabaka*'s government issued an ultimatum ordering the Ugandan government to leave the kingdom before the end of the month. Obote's immediate reaction was to dismiss the threat, as Sir Frederick Crawford had done when Buganda declared its independence in 1961. But the position began to look more serious when an uncle of the *kabaka* called upon Obote the same evening. He said he was worried by the prospect of conflict between the kingdom and the central government and had spent all day trying, unsuccessfully, to convince his nephew that a clash should be avoided. Mutesa, he believed, had been badly advised by some of his supporters and was under great pressure from them. Bugandan chiefs had been ordered to stir up rebellion among their people who were pouring into the confines of the *kabaka*'s palace at Mmengo, anxious for a fight, and arms had been distributed among them. He was convinced there was a danger that an attack might be made upon the national assembly and its members.

The following morning there was trouble in the vicinity of the *kabaka*'s palace and the police intervened. In the afternoon Felix Onama, minister of defence, called on Obote who, since the adoption of the new constitution, had moved the presidential residence to Kampala. Onama said he was worried that things appeared to be getting out of hand and asked Obote to authorize the sending of troops to maintain order. The president, who had been in conversation with some of the Baganda who had retained their membership of the national assembly, asked their opinion about the request and they agreed that it would be wise to accede to it. Obote's view was that a small military presence should be able to restore order fairly quickly.

He was both surprised and shocked when, shortly after Onama's departure, he heard artillery fire. Amin, who was in charge of the military operation had, it transpired, ordered the use of heavy weapons. Obote immediately sent instructions to put a stop to what he was convinced must be excessive force. He subsequently accepted, however, that the presence of a large and hostile crowd, together with the rumour that there were thousands of arms in the *kabaka*'s palace, might reasonably have led to an error of judgement by Amin. In fact, when the palace was stormed all that was found were a number of hunting rifles.

The fighting around the palace was over by six o'clock in the evening, but there were troubles in other parts of the kingdom and the cabinet decided to declare a state of emergency in Buganda. Irreparable damage had been done to Obote's hopes of winning the co-operation of the Baganda. During the course of the fighting the *kabaka* had made his escape by climbing over the palace wall. Thence, concealed from time to time by his loyal subjects, he made his way to Rwanda and from there to England and exile. Buganda's hostility to Obote turned to hatred. The *katikkiro*, Mayanja-Nkangi, decided that his ultimate allegiance must lie with the *kabaka* and in turn sought exile in London. He was no bigot, and his anxiety to avoid any irrevocable act has already been noted. But when the choice was forced upon him it was his loyalty to the kingdom, and to the office he held in it, which overcame his intellectual commitment to a united Uganda. His behaviour demonstrated the virtual impossibility of reconciling even those Baganda anxious to see a united country to a central government, dominated by non-Baganda, which took precedence over the institutions of the kingdom.

There is little indication that the rest of the country was unduly disturbed by these events. For too long Buganda had seemed determined to distance itself from its neighbours, and it is scarcely to be expected that the people of the Northern and Eastern Provinces should have shed many tears for the Baganda in their predicament. The army, too, seemed, on the surface at least, to be a more loyal instrument of the government now that Amin had superseded Opolot as the army commander.

Hard on the heels of these internal problems Obote was forced to give his attention once again to wider issues. In September 1966 the Commonwealth Conference again assembled in London. President Nyerere did not attend because Tanzania had broken off diplomatic relations with Britain and Presisent Kaunda was represented by Zambia's foreign minister. In preparation for the meeting Obote travelled to Dar es Salaam to ensure that he understood the views of his two friends on the most contentious subject to be discussed at the conference, the behaviour of Rhodesia. The British prime minister, Harold Wilson, was quick to recognize the extent to which Obote now took the lead in debate. When Wilson proposed that he himself should vacate the chair after making his introductory speech about Rhodesia, Obote was the first to oppose the idea. Although the African leaders believed Wilson's aim was to avoid some of the obloquy he anticipated would come his way, Obote's remarks were made, as the British prime minister himself noted, in a polite and restrained manner. His reason for rejecting the suggestion, Obote said, was that he did not wish to give the impression that the conference feared Wilson might abuse his position where Britain's interests were directly involved.

When Wilson had made his statement it was again Obote who suggested that, before it was discussed, it should be circulated to all participants in written form to provide them with the opportunity to give it the detailed consideration it deserved, and this was agreed. The next three days, until Friday afternoon, were devoted exclusively to the Rhodesian issue. Obote's speech in the ensuing debate was patently intended to set out the general view of the African members, and again Wilson noted the restrained tone in which it was presented – 'more in sorrow than in anger'. Obote admitted he was in favour of using force to put an end to Rhodesia's unilateral declaration of independence, but conceded that the strategy and tactics must be determined by Britain. There must be no question of any settlement before majority rule had been accepted on the basis of one man one vote, but he refused to follow the more aggressive line of some members who demanded that Britain should take the lead in requesting the UN to impose sanctions on South Africa to discourage that country from sustaining Rhodesia. To go to those lengths would damage Britain's trade, Obote believed, and it would be foolish to weaken Britain and then demand results in the campaign against Rhodesia. If the African leaders' hopes were to be realized Britain must be strong.

Wilson was determined that the discussions on Rhodesia should be completed by Monday morning in order to provide time, however inadequate, to give consideration to the many other issues of importance to the conference. He therefore proposed that the customary meetings to take place at Chequers over the weekend should be devoted to hard work rather than to more social activities. Obote was in the third group of visitors to the prime minister's country residence, arriving on the Sunday. Whether because of some misunderstanding about the arrangements, or whether by design, he alone appeared to expect to stay overnight as had happened at previous conferences. As a result, when the other guests had departed after dinner, Obote had one of those long, late-night conversations with Wilson which the British prime minister so greatly enjoyed. It lasted until the early hours of Monday morning, and in the course of it Obote stressed his desire to help in any way possible towards reaching a satisfactory conclusion to the conference. Wilson himself confided that he was afraid the British governor in Rhodesia, Sir Humphrey Gibbs, might resign, leaving Britain with no foothold in the country. Obote responded with the suggestion that another person should be sent to Rhodesia secretly, with letters of appointment which would permit him to take over from Gibbs. He could not agree, there and then, to Wilson's proposal that Britain should make one last effort to reach accommodation with Ian Smith, even if the discussions took full account of the principles demanded by the conference, and were held only on the understanding that failure would be followed by a tougher approach. Wilson appreciated his reservations and did not press the point at that stage. Leaving Obote to consider the matter further he himself returned to London at 3.00 a.m. to prepare for the day ahead.

Later that day, in the course of private discussions, Obote's call for moderation failed to convert the more militant conference members, and it was only when Wilson had presented them with what was virtually an ultimatum that his plan was adopted.[9] Nevertheless, Obote had emerged from the conference as a significant figure on the commonwealth stage. He had shown statesmanship throughout the proceedings and had established a firm friendship, based upon mutual respect, with Harold Wilson. His performance had underlined his constant willingness to try to reach an accommodation with those whose views conflicted with his own.

On his return to Uganda Obote was faced with a range of pressing problems. The one which appeared to call for his immediate attention was the need to review the country's economic position. The vice-president, John Babiiha, had served for many years in the legislative council before independence. He had never been an impressive speaker, his contributions to debate being lengthy, convoluted and often confused. Since independence, however, he had been a very successful minister of agriculture. He understood his job and he got on well with the people, all of whom respected his practical ability. He had been particularly responsible for starting cattle ranching in Buganda, an innovation that had worked well. Thanks to his overall management, to the co-operation of the farmers who trusted him, and to the excellence of the soil and climate of Uganda, the country's economy had developed reassuringly in the early 1960s.

In the middle of the decade, however, there had been a slump in the prices offered for primary products on the world market. It became difficult to sell cotton and the prices offered for coffee, especially for robusta, which was used in the preparation of instant coffee, fell markedly. Cotton growers in the Northern Province, in the districts of Acholi and Lango, and in Teso, Bukedi and parts of Bugisu and Busoga Districts in the Eastern Province, were seriously affected, but were still able to produce enough food to supply their requirements. They also had just enough income from their market crops to purchase the immediate necessities of life such as paraffin and other types of fuel. At this time the Chinese rice scheme had not yet got under way, and the newly planted coffee in Busoga was not yet producing a saleable crop.

Looking at the prospects in the world market, and conscious of the fall in output of export crops due to the political upheaval in Buganda, the government concluded that cotton offered better long-term prospects than did coffee, and therefore tried to encourage cotton growing. The attempt was unsuccessful because the department of agriculture lacked the administrative infrastructure to put over its ideas effectively. Caution prevailed among the farmers who continued to grow coffee in areas where the conditions were suitable, preferring to accept a reduced income rather than risk a change of crop. So coffee still provided half Uganda's export earnings. With a view to increasing the income from coffee while trying to inculcate a clearer appreciation of economic realities, a committee of inquiry recommended in August 1967 that the emphasis should be upon quality of output rather than quantity. To that end robusta trees should be uprooted and only the finer arabica coffee should be grown. The committee also recommended that growers should be paid on the basis of the world market price. In the days of the Protectorate, agricultural experts had been firmly convinced that neither the climate nor the altitude of Uganda was suited to growing arabica coffee. A further recommendation, aimed at the government rather than the growers, was that export duty on coffee should be lowered. For too long the government had milked coffee profits in order to swell its revenue and to pay the salaries of a large bureaucracy.

While the country's main crops went through a difficult period, the production of tea increased by more than 30 per cent in 1966, with an output of 24.7 million lbs, compared with 18.4 million lbs in the previous year. There were increases, too, in the production of tobacco and sugar, and these, coupled with a significant growth in the manufacturing sector, meant that the favourable balance of trade was not only maintained but improved. Consequently, throughout the years of comparative recession, development projects were curtailed rather than jettisoned and the country never suffered from inflation because the government refused to print money and strove hard to maintain at least an even balance of payments.

From time to time Obote came under considerable pressure from financial experts from both India and the Sudan, whose advice he had sought, to cater for a deficit budget, but that he consistently refused to do. In taking that line he was supported by a financial adviser sent from Britain at his special request. Nevertheless, expenditure on medical services continued. New hospitals were built while older hospitals, inherited from the days of the Protectorate, were rehabilitated. By the end of the decade dispensaries had been opened in virtually every village in the country. The hoped for expansion in educational facilities had to be cut back to some extent, but in April 1967 the government was able to announce that it would spend £5 million on twenty-four new secondary schools to provide places for 14,000 children. Overall the 1960s was a decade of steady if not spectacular growth and all of it was achieved without overstepping the country's income. The one serious problem was the continuing gap between the incomes of a small core of highly paid government officials on the one hand and the large number of small farmers who produced Uganda's wealth on the other.

Overshadowing even the country's economic problems there remained the question of the government's relations with Buganda. Clearly a new start must be made. The basis of the problem, as Obote at last reluctantly admitted, was the impossibility of incorporating a hereditary, authoritarian, monarchical system within a democratic state. The obvious solution was to abolish the kingdom. But there were three other kingdoms, in addition to Buganda, and none of these had created any problem for the central government. Nevertheless, in the interests of consistency Obote decided they too must go. This was an unfortunate step, because it further emphasized the gap which had been developing between the central government and parts of the south-west since the arrest of Ibingira and Magezi.

On 9 June 1967 the government published constitutional proposals which would convert Uganda into a republic and the plan was debated in the national assembly on 22 June. In an endeavour to avoid undue hostility the amendments to the 1962 and 1966 constitutions were limited to those required to achieve the government's main objective, which was to bring the whole country under a unified constitution instead of having several different systems of government existing side by side. With the abolition of the kingdoms Buganda was divided into four administrative districts as it had been in practice for the convenience of British officials in colonial times, although in those days the kingdom had been retained as an overall umbrella. Each district corresponded more closely in size and importance to the districts in the rest of the country which, for want of a viable alternative, had remained the basis for local government even after independence and the division of the districts into a number of electoral constituencies. In this way the overshadowing bulk of Buganda was nominally, it not in fact, removed from the scene. The national assembly continued to sit, and there was still an official opposition in the House, a state of affairs which continued until Obote's overthrow.

Ibingira was later to claim that Obote boasted that he had made the *kabaka* president only in order to trap and destroy him,[10] but the *kabaka* himself never imputed any such motive to his rival. Although Mutesa did not warm to Obote, he did believe that the two of them, from very different standpoints, were trying sincerely to find an accommodation.[11] But accommodation was impossible. The tradition to which the *kabaka* subscribed was monarchical and authoritarian. Obote, in spite of recent events, was essentially a parliament man, attending sessions of the national assembly whenever he could. As head of state he presided at the official opening of a session, but during ordinary meetings he continued to sit on the front bench as leader of the governing party, listening closely to debates and being constantly aware of the feelings of the assembly.

Even now, when the UPC seemed stronger than ever before, new divisions began to appear. With Ibingira and his faction removed from the scene, Felix Onama's support for Obote began to wane for reasons that only emerged in January 1971, and their once close co-operation withered. It was both a source of strength and of weakness to Obote's rule that he had never had an inner circle of confidants. Because of his belief in the importance of party consultation and cabinet discussion he had hitherto always sought his advice from those elected by the party rather than from people of his own choosing. While this encouraged openness it did not necessarily promote loyalty to the person occupying the office of president. Onama felt no personal attachment to Obote, and when his own actions and aspirations proved to be at variance with the president's policy he felt under no obligation to stand by him.

Among the other casualties of this tumultuous year were the elections to the national assembly which, under the terms of the independence constitution, were due to be held not later than April 1967. The introduction of a new constitution should have provided an appropriate occasion on which to seek the approval of the electorate, but the existence of a state of emergency in Buganda, and the high profile adopted by the security forces made such a move difficult if not actually impossible. Yet it was during the political and economic turmoil of 1967 that the government achieved the major success which has already been mentioned. Throughout the year, representatives of the governments of Uganda, Kenya and Tanzania met every three months and their efforts were rewarded when, in December, the leaders of the three countries signed a treaty setting up the East African Community which was to serve the region so well until Obote's overthrow led to its gradual collapse. The treaty also provided for a common market among the three nations and an East African development bank was set up which opened in Kampala in July 1968.

In the mid-1960s, however, there was little time to savour the efforts made to overcome the difficulties facing Uganda's economy. While events in Buganda continued to impose a strain upon the country's security services, new problems were emerging in the north, where the civil war in the Sudan resulted in regular incursions of rebel forces over the border into Uganda in search of temporary respite. That border, which had, in any case, been moved southwards early in the century in order to give the boundaries of Uganda and the Sudan a superficially more logical form, had never taken into account the ethnic disposition of the inhabitants of the region. The local people had come to regard the border as an alien concept which, for most purposes, they could ignore. For the Sudanese rebels to take refuge with their fellow clansmen in Uganda when it suited them to do so seemed only reasonable. Although the Ugandan government was anxious to behave as a good neighbour to the Sudan, Obote could not help feeling some sympathy for the rebels because he believed that the Sudanese government had no policy for the southern region other than military conquest.

When Sayed Sadik al-Mahdi, a man of great ability, became prime minister of the Sudan in July 1966, however, Obote considered that an extra effort should be made. He visited Khartoum and came to an agreement with Sadik aimed at exerting every effort to restore peace in the troubled region. From this time Obote did all in his power to discourage the rebels from seeking to regroup and rearm in Uganda. But detection was difficult and, with a high proportion of Uganda's security forces recruited from the north, it was not easy to get wholehearted co-operation from the army or police.

What began as an administrative inconvenience took on a more serious meaning when Muhammad Ahmed Mahgoub, Sadik's predecessor, regained his former office as prime minister in May 1967 and returned to a policy of repression in the south. Onama, Uganda's defence minister, protested to the OAU that Sudanese troops, pursuing rebels over the border, had become involved in fighting with members of the Ugandan army. Then, following upon the six-day war in the Middle East in June, Obote became aware that the Israelis, who were playing a valuable role in training the Ugandan army, had begun to use their influence within the army as a channel through which to give encouragement to the dissidents in the Southern Suden. This was part of their overall strategy of harassing the Islamic states which, they believed, were committed to undermining and ultimately destroying the Israeli nation state. Much depended upon the reliability of Idi Amin, who had replaced Opolot as army commander when the latter had been suspended because of his complicity with those who had plotted against the government.

Since the 1964 mutiny, in which he had played a dubious role, Amin's loyalty to the government had seemed impeccable. He had, nevertheless, been recruiting into the army men from his own ethnic group and neighbouring peoples on both sides of the Uganda/Zaire and Uganda/Sudan borders. Had one questioned those recruits as to the focus of their loyalty, it would have been to their army commander rather than to a government of which they knew little and which, for many of them, was a wholly alien institution. That was scarcely cause for surprise. Few Ugandans identified strongly with the central government, even after several years of independence. Amin had also, to all appearances, carried out his liaison task with the rebels in Zaire in accordance with the wishes of his political masters. On the other hand, he had behaved with clumsy brutality in his handling of the siege of the *kabaka*'s palace, although once again he could have argued that he was carrying out the orders of his political superiors to the best of his ability in uncertain circumstances. In 1968 there were rumours of an army plot to overthrow the government, rumours which Amin vigorously denied, while Obote himself discountenanced the whole idea. What Obote did not know, until later, was that Amin had taken bribes from the Israelis to assist them with their campaign against the Sudan. When that did become known, disaster followed for the president. In the meantime, relations with the Sudan remained delicate, and care was needed to ensure that the border situation did not deteriorate still further.

One of the by-products of the Sudanese problem was Obote's 'good neighbourliness' campaign. Aimed at improving relations with all the countries with which Uganda shared a common border, the campaign was particularly intended to draw attention to the difficulties experienced with the Sudan. Kenyatta asked if the first meeting of the countries involved could be held in Nairobi and Obote agreed. This proved to be a mistake because the arrangements for the meeting were badly organized. The second encounter, which took place in Kampala in December 1967, was a much greater success. The leaders of twelve countries of Eastern and Central Africa agreed that, whenever possible, they would buy goods manufactured in Africa instead of trying to purchase them outside the continent. It was a matter of some interest to Obote that one of the leading protagonists of the campaign was Emperor Haile Selassie of Ethiopia who, although not a direct neighbour of Uganda, attended every meeting until the operation foundered after the overthrow of Obote's government in 1971.

In spite of more immediate worries, Obote still had to play his role in African and in commonwealth affairs. In both spheres the civil war in Nigeria had become the most urgent consideration, and the OAU was worried by the possibility that non-African countries, encouraged by appeals for aid from secessionist Biafra, might become involved. Even the member states of the OAU were themselves divided. Tanzania, Zambia, Ivory Coast and Gabon sympathized with and eventually recognized Biafra, in spite of the Nigerian federal government's claim that such recognition amounted to a gross breach of the OAU charter. Obote, characteristically, favoured negotiation. At the OAU summit in Zaire in 1968 a number of Nigerians led by Chief Awolowo, reproached him for, as they maintained, giving encouragement to the Biafrans by arguing that the only appropriate role for the OAU to play was for it to suggest that some of its senior members should bring pressure to bear upon the leaders of the two sides to hold discussions. They did not want to discuss the war, Awolowo said. All they wanted was victory. Obote replied that, even if the federal government were victorious, there would still have to be talks in order to reach any sort of accommodation. His view prevailed. On 23 May 1968 the first of a series of meetings to discuss the main issues for which the war was being fought was held, appropriately, in Kampala. But with Biafra demanding a cease-fire and the withdrawal of federal troops from its territory, and the federal government insisting that Biafra should renounce its claim to secession, no progress was made.

The Soviet intervention in Czechoslovakia in August 1968 presented a challenge to those countries of the Third World, Uganda among them, which had insisted upon their non-aligned position *vis à vis* the Western Powers and the Eastern Bloc. By a large majority the UN Security Council condemned the Soviets' action and Uganda was among those commonwealth countries which, over this issue, openly abandoned their non-aligned role and came out against the USSR.

In January 1969 the first Commonwealth Conference since 1966 took place in London. On that occasion Obote played a far less prominent role than he had done at the previous meeting, the lead being taken by Nyerere, who had re-established diplomatic relations with Britain in July and whom Obote regarded with considerable respect for his wisdom and his wholehearted devotion to the interests of all the peoples of Africa. Nyerere, speaking with power and restraint, did not insist upon the use of force as the only solution to the Rhodesian impasse, although on this point Kaunda took a different view and made his opinion clear in another impressive speech. The atmosphere at the conference was much less tense than it had been in 1966 and Obote's only significant contribution to the debate was to warn against too dilatory an approach to achieving a settlement lest this should encourage intransigence on Smith's part. The continuation of sanctions, which were proving particularly burdensome to the African population, might then encourage the latter to accept an unsatisfactory settlement.[12]

Even with all those issues to occupy him Obote's attention could not for long be diverted from Buganda. There did, however, seem to have been some reduction of the tension in that quarter, and early in October 1968 there was considerable satisfaction when a brother of the *kabaka* and three Bugandan chiefs, all of whom had been held in detention since Mutesa's overthrow, were eventually released. But the sense of relief was short lived. Later in the month Abu Mayanja, still a member of the national assembly although sitting now on the opposition benches, was arrested, together with Daniel Nelson, who for three years had edited the *People*, the newspaper which represented the views of the Uganda Peoples Congress. Nelson was beaten and detained for five hours before being released on the personal intervention of Obote. His arrest had been a case of mistaken identity and Nelson was magnanimous enough to admit that although Obote was, in his view, a man to be respected rather than liked, the president was unquestionably concerned about legal niceties. The whole incident, however, underlined both the inefficiency and the brutality of the newly formed security unit which had, in fact, been instructed to arrest Rajat Neogy, editor of *Transition*, a cultural journal held in high regard in the intellectual world.

In due course Neogy was arrested and he and Mayanja were charged with sedition. Although they were released on bail, they were immediately detained under emergency regulations. The charge against them related to a letter written by Mayanja to, and published in, *Transition*, in which he deplored the fact that there was still no Ugandan member of the high court. He added that he could not believe the rumour, heard in legal circles, that a number of recommendations made by the judicial services commission had been rejected, for the most part on tribal grounds. Mayanja's readiness to repeat the rumour, while apparently dissociating himself from it, might have been brushed aside by an administration more confident of popular support, more particularly in view of Mayanja's well-known delight in indulging an anarchic sense of humour.

Obote, committed to unifying the country, was in no mood to be lenient. He had already verbally attacked intellectual critics of the government for the subversive impact their pronouncements made upon a country struggling to establish its identity. Recently, too, a group of people in Buganda had fired upon the president's car under the impression that Obote was travelling in it. Fortunately the attack had merely startled the vice-president, John Babiiha, who was the sole passenger in the vehicle, but this was only one of a number of manifestations of unrest.

Coincidentally the police claimed to have discovered letters which, they believed, had come from supporters of the *kabaka* in Britain, urging Mayanja to foment trouble for the government. Obote concluded that the letter to *Transition* was Mayanja's first attempt to carry out his instructions. The letters were signed in code and could not be traced to their originator, but their provenance was thought by the government to be beyond doubt. In the circumstances they could scarcely be used as evidence and the police did not wish to reveal the fact that they were aware of the letters' existence. The attorney-general, Godfrey Binaisa, therefore advised the government that it was unlikely Mayanja and Neogy would be convicted on the charges brought against them, and his prognostication proved to be correct. When the two were brought to trial in February 1969 they were acquitted but were again detained under emergency powers. The government did not think Mayanja himself constituted any serious threat but saw him as the agent of a malign faction in Buganda. Although the *kabaka*'s government had been dissolved, and the *lukiiko* with it, after the introduction of the new constitution of 1967, there was still a diehard clique of the *kabaka*'s supporters, both in Britain and in Buganda, who kept in close touch with each other and who were committed to the overthrow of Obote. Nevertheless, the use of emergency powers in the situation as it was known to the public could only undermine Obote's reputation as a ruler who respected the law.

The role of Neogy in these events was to have considerable implications for the future. When he was detained after his acquittal the British government protested that he was a British subject and must be released. The Ugandan government replied that he had renounced his British citizenship after independence and had taken Ugandan nationality. Neogy had indeed intended to renounce British citizenship, as had many other Asians who felt committed to Uganda. They had gone to the British high commission to announce their intention and had signed a document to that effect for which they were given a receipt. The high commission should have sent their documents to London because only the Home Office had the authority to cancel British citizenship, even though the action was being taken at the request of the person concerned. For some reason, possibly because officials were unaware of the ruling, the high commission had never despatched the documents, so that all those involved were still British citizens. Retrospective action could not be taken because, under the Independence Act passed by the British parliament, an application ceased to be valid three months after the Ugandan government had approved a request for citizenship unless confirmed by the Home Office in London. Moreover, under Ugandan law Ugandans were not allowed to have dual nationality. Clearly, Neogy was a British citizen, and he was duly released in March 1969.

This finding created turmoil in Uganda's Asian community because, not long before, Kenya had begun to expel large numbers of Asians, and the British home secretary, James Callaghan, had become worried by the prospect of their claiming British citizenship and demanding residence in Britain. The British government had therefore introduced a quota system to control immigration by non-white holders of British passports. The concern of Uganda's Asians had been further exacerbated when, during a conference of commonwealth leaders in London on 5 January 1969, Obote had made a statement to clarify Uganda's position *vis à vis* the quota system and to alert the British government to the problems it threatened to create. There were 40,000 Asians, he had said, mainly small tradesmen, who held British passports, and who would have to leave Uganda at some stage. His government had no intention of pushing people around, but it was ultimately wrong that a vital aspect of the economy should be controlled by foreigners.

Obote certainly did not underestimate the important contribution Asians had made and were still making to the economy of his country and he was fully aware that the vast majority of Uganda's African population had, hitherto, shown minimal interest in business at any level. He had no intention of acting precipitately and was simply stating a principle. His remarks were levelled not so much against the Asians in Uganda as against the British government. The latter body, by introducing restrictions on the immigration of non-white passport-holders, had, in Obote's opinion, devalued the passports themselves and had discriminated against some of its citizens. In Uganda, however, the statement was not read with such detachment.

Later in January the Ugandan government announced plans to hasten the Africanization of commerce, trade and industry, but rejected a proposal to replace all non-Ugandans within five years. Its recommendation was that Ugandans of African descent should have preference in any appointment to jobs for which they were qualified and that non-Ugandans should be required to have work permits and licences for trading. The jobs of non-Ugandans should be considered on merit, and changes should be made as soon as qualified Ugandans became available. The unease to which this plan gave rise among the members of Uganda's Asian community was heightened by a new Immigration Act, scheduled to take effect on 1 May 1970. Under its provisions non-Ugandan Asians would be required to possess one of a variety of entry permits if they wished to remain in the country. The principal one would be valid for only a limited period, and would not be issued if to do so appeared to be to the disadvantage of the inhabitants of Uganda in general. If it were issued it could be withdrawn after one year, unless the immigration control board was satisfied that no Ugandan was qualified to fill the post.

In vain did the Ugandan high commissioner in London insist that there was no time limit by which Asians must leave Uganda, or the government repeat that the new legislation did not apply to Asians who had taken out Ugandan nationality. The Neogy incident had all too clearly alerted thousands of Asians to the fact that they were not, after all, firmly established as citizens of Uganda, as they had reasonably assumed, and that they were consequently liable to expulsion without any guarantee of being accepted in Britain. The proposed legislation appeared to make that prospect even more imminent. Whole areas of towns were abandoned by nervous shopkeepers. In Jinja, for example, Uganda's second largest town, some 60 per cent of the 145 shops owned by Asians in the two main streets were the property of British passport-holders. Within weeks of the new law being promulgated all of them had been closed. The shops owned by naturalized Ugandan Asians remained open and a few of the empty properties were rented by Africans, but business remained uneasy.

The demand for permits to enter Britain increased rapidly and culminated, when the response of the British authorities in Uganda seemed too slow, in demonstrations at the British high commission building in Kampala. This, in turn, led to a bizarre series of incidents. The consular official responsible for issuing the permits, Brian Lea, came under considerable pressure, not least from wealthy Asians wishing to expedite arrangements for their admission to Britain, and he may well have feared that his dealings with them would become known to the high commissioner if he was not already aware of them. He therefore connived with some of the Asians to disappear and to let it be known that he had been kidnapped. The news of the disappearance was conveyed to Harold Wilson while he was attending a theatre. He at once left the performance and sent an urgent message to Uganda demanding that Scotland Yard be allowed to investigate. Obote refused firmly, stressing that the incident did not, as yet, appear to be important. No-one had been killed, and there was no proof that any kidnap had taken place. Shortly afterwards Lea reappeared and Obote at once ordered that an inquiry be instituted, presided over by a British judge. The manner of Lea's disappearance was clearly established and it was suggested that he had been involved in some form of corruption and hoped that if he staged his own kidnap the truth might not emerge and he would be sent home as a minor hero.

The Lea incident was, in itself, of little significance, but the sequence of events which led up to it was deeply damaging to Obote. A policy that had not been intentionally oppressive had aroused immense disquiet among an economically invaluable element in Ugandan society, and had lost the president the trust of a significant group of people. The arrest of Neogy and Mayanja had also stirred up lively dissent among the students at Makerere. Obote responded by addressing a seminar for East and Central African students in Kampala in April 1969. The exercise of student power, he said, was commendable, but it should manifest itself not simply in condemnation but in endeavouring to create a world order capable of satisfying the rational needs of the people. The speech typified Obote's concern for a constructive, sympathetic approach to his country's problems, and it certainly helped to neutralize the opposition that had been developing among some of the better educated sections of Uganda's population.

In July 1969 Obote suffered a blow of a more personal nature. He had been invited by President Kaunda to open an agricultural show in Lusaka, and while Kaunda was making his introductory remarks to the people in attendance he was handed a message which he read at once. He went on to conclude his speech before announcing that he had just been notified of the assassination of Tom Mboya in Kenya. Obote was deeply distressed. Since the time of his own campaign to promote Mboya's candidature for election to the Kenyan legislative council his friendship for the able Luo politician had grown steadily. He admired his ability and, like many others, he saw him as the natural successor to Kenyatta as president of Kenya. Mboya's death only underlined the instability lurking within African society.

The visit of Pope Paul VI to Uganda in July and August 1969, the first ever made by a pope to the African continent, gave Obote a more favourable opportunity to strengthen his position. His leading political opponents, the members of the Democratic Party, had, from the party's inception, been closely associated with the Roman Catholic Church, while the UPC, in so far as it had any religious affiliation, was assumed to be linked with the Church of Uganda, the heir to the Anglican Church Missionary Society in Uganda. The Pope's visit was intended primarily to enable him to dedicate a shrine to Ugandan Catholics martyred in the late nineteenth century and to consecrate a number of bishops. Nevertheless, he made a point of visiting a shrine dedicated to Anglican martyrs, and in public addresses he stressed the need for peace and for the rejection of violence to achieve political ends. Obote took the opportunity to offer a friendly hand to his Roman Catholic fellow countrymen by acknowledging the honour conferred upon Uganda by the Pope's visit. Echoing the Pope's remarks he called for co-operation while deploring tribal and racial conflict. No less an organ than Le Monde newspaper commented favourably upon the excellence of the organization, 'flexible, discreet and effective', provided by Uganda to make the papal visit a success, but less sensitively qualified its encomium by adding that it was clear Uganda had fully assimilated its British heritage.[13]

Among his other aims the Pope expressed a wish to meet leaders of Nigeria and Biafra while he was in Uganda. This was arranged, but it was not papal mediation which brought the war to an end. That was the result of the military defeat of the Biafrans early in 1970. Nevertheless, the contending parties had yet another opportunity for discussion and Obote did not consider the Pope's efforts had been wholly wasted. Later, in September 1970, Obote invited General Gowan, the Nigerian leader, to call on him in Kampala en route to the OAU summit meeting in Addis Ababa. Gowan did so and the friendly relationship Obote had established by his endeavours to promote a settlement in Nigeria was reflected in the opportunity he was later to have to seek asylum in Nigeria after his overthrow. He did not accept the offer because he thought he would be too far away to influence events in Uganda. At the OAU summit it was proposed that the next meeting, in 1971, should take place in Kampala. Obote was reluctant to agree because of the expense his country would incur. He submitted to general pressure, however, but because of the turmoil which was to overwhelm Uganda the conference did not assemble in Kampala until 1975.

Any goodwill Obote may have won among his political opponents by the welcome he had given to the Pope was quickly dispelled. Just before setting out for a meeting of the heads of state of the OAU in Addis Ababa in September he ordered the arrest of Benedicto Kiwanuka, president of the DP, and of Paulo Ssemogerere, the party's secretary. Charges of sedition were preferred against the two in connection with the publication of a pamphlet in March 1969. Worse was to follow. In November the exiled kabaka, Sir Edward Mutesa, died in London. Since he had fled from Uganda he had been living in near poverty in England, and his presence there, and the circumstances of it, acted as a permanent reminder to the Baganda of the part played by Obote in their ruler's overthrow. The *kabaka*'s death simply accentuated the hostility felt by the Baganda towards Obote. Rumours that Mutesa had been poisoned, although flatly denied by the findings of the inquest held in Britain, persisted among the late ruler's supporters. Buganda seethed with hatred for the president, and although the government offered to pay the cost of transporting the *kabaka*'s body to Uganda for burial the offer was not accepted. It was claimed that in the prevailing situation it would be impossible to carry out the appropriate burial rites and there would be no guarantee of safe conduct for those wishing to accompany the coffin to Uganda.

The result of this upsurge of feeling was to be seen in an attempt on the life of Obote in Kampala on 19 December 1969 as he was leaving Lugogo Stadium at the end of the annual delegates' conference of the UPC. It had been a lively meeting, at which plans to hold elections became involved in a demand for a one-party state. The protagonists of the latter idea were mainly young radicals who had been educated in India, but they had the support of Basil Bataringaya and other former DP members who had defected to the UPC. One-party states were fashionable in Africa at that time. Tanzania had recently adopted such a system and Kenya had become a *de facto* if not a *de jure* one-party state through the absorption of the Kenya African Democratic Union by the Kenya African National Union. Obote himself vigorously opposed the idea, but was outvoted by those who felt they wished to keep up with the modern trend in Africa. He had no intention of accepting the proposal until it had been debated in the national assembly, and in the light of the views expressed by the members of the assembly who were present at the conference he had little doubt that it would be defeated. He was firmly of the opinion that a one-party state was contrary to democratic principles and he believed that his opinion was shared by an overwhelming majority of the cabinet. It was significant, in the light of later events, that in the course of the meeting, Idi Amin had pledged full support to Obote.

As Obote left the stadium he was fired upon from the crowd and wounded in the face. He was whisked away to hospital in his car but something akin to panic seized the crowd. Many who were leaving tried to force their way back into the stadium in the hope of avoiding further shooting, while those trying to get out were unaware of what had taken place. The vice-president, John Babiiha, at once declared a state of emergency. Road blocks were set up around the capital and the security forces frequently acted with unprovoked brutality in checking those who were called upon to halt at the check points. It was some time before it was known that the president was alive and would recover, and in the period of uncertainty a pattern of repression was quickly established by the army, particularly in Buganda, which was to continue through the months of suspicion which followed. On 20 December the Democratic Party was banned as 'a danger to peace and order', a measure Obote himself would not have approved in spite of the detention of the party leaders, but it was characteristic of the panic which had seized the country that such hasty steps were taken.

The distrust felt for the Baganda in particular was in no way dispelled by the arrest of five men and their conviction for the attempted murder of the president. All were Baganda, but none of them held any significant appointment; one was a taxi driver, three were farm workers and one was a motor mechanic. However, police intelligence suggested that they had been paid by leading members of the former Bugandan hierarchy, working in conjunction with supporters of the late *kabaka* who had shared his exile in London. Once again, as in the case of Abu Mayanja, no proof could be produced at the trial. The five were sentenced to death but Obote refused to sign their death warrants because he was convinced he had no right to deprive anyone of life.

Writing in the *Guardian* of 22 December 1969 that shrewd commentator on African affairs, Patrick Keatley, discussed the long history of ethnic conflict in Uganda. Of Obote and the part he was playing in Uganda's affairs he concluded, 'It is very doubtful, indeed, if any more effective national leader exists to lead his nation out of tribalism.' An equally acute observer, Colin Legum, had stated in the *Observer* the previous day that the neighbouring states of Kenya, Tanzania, Sudan and Zaire were all relieved that Obote had survived because they regarded him as 'the stabilising force in a country that has slowly been putting its house in order after the dramatic crisis in 1966.'

Obote had a further narrow escape from attack while in hospital receiving treatment for his bullet wound. He had been prescribed a course of injections, and his wife and her sister, who was a qualified nurse, took turns in keeping a watch on him. One night, Miria, who was sleeping in the next room, was awakened by a commotion in her husband's room. She rushed in, to find her sister struggling on the floor with the night nurse who, either not knowing the sister was herself a nurse or thinking she was asleep, had tried to inject the patient with water instead of with his medicine. The nurse broke the syringe, but security guards who appeared on the scene discovered the bottle containing the medication in her pocket. Ever resilient, Obote was back in his office on 30 December and was soon observing his regular schedule of working until after midnight and starting out again the following morning at eight o'clock. He himself had survived, but there was another casualty of the assassination attempt which was to have serious repercussions – the plan to hold elections, which were again postponed, until 1971.

Chapter 8

Amin's coup

The work to which Obote now devoted himself was the implementation of the *Common Man's Charter*, published under his name in December 1969 after it had been submitted for the approval of the annual delegates's conference of the UPC on 24 October. Although it professed to be no more than an attempt to set down in writing a number of far-reaching proposals adopted by the annual delegates's conference of the party held in June 1968, it bore all the hallmarks of Obote's authorship. One commentator, Mahmood Mamdani, was of the opinion that what the pamphlet describes as a 'move to the left' was nothing more than a move against the petty bourgeoisie of Buganda, the landowners and traders who were in a position to stir up tribal opposition to the government. Far from introducing socialism, Mamdani argues, Obote was cynically exploiting the idea while deliberately centralizing economic power in the hands of his own governing bureaucracy and converting it into an economic bureaucracy.[14] The pamphlet's vehement condemnation of tribalism and feudalism undoubtedly supports Mamdani's contention that Obote was, if only in part, criticizing the record of Buganda. It is clear, however, that Obote had no intention of creating an undiluted socialist system or even of making a pretence of doing so. He was fully aware that, in the circumstances in which Uganda found itself in 1969, such a programme might well have caused a total breakdown in the economy. Moreover, the fact that the implementation of the Charter did not live up to the high moral stand taken in it by the author is not incontrovertible proof of cynicism on Obote's part. Time did not permit him to put more than a limited number of the provisions of the Charter into effect.

Resounding rhetoric is a well-tried tool of politicians and is not always an indication of insincerity. The *Common Man's Charter* was a target Obote set for his country, the ideal on which it should set its sights. Obote was not, in any case, a doctrinaire socialist. He was by nature a pragmatist. Although his personal inclination was towards a society in which socialist principles were observed, he had been made aware by his experiences overseas, but even more by his recognition of the limited resources of ability as well as of wealth at Uganda's disposal, that an unswerving adherence to political or economic dogma would be disastrous for his country. It was not for nothing that he quoted in the Charter the aims and objectives of the UPC, including its economic aim which was 'To plan Uganda's Economic Development in such a way that the Government, through Parastatal Bodies, the Cooperative Movements, Private Companies, Individuals in Industry, Commerce and Agriculture, will effectively contribute to increased production to raise the standard of living in the Country.' This was not socialism; it was a mixed economy that was being proposed.

Nor is there any conclusive evidence to suggest that Obote was trying, belatedly, to appease the masses of the people who felt they had not benefited from independence to the extent they had hoped while an elite minority was creaming off the wealth which should have been more widely distributed. Whatever dissatisfaction might have been felt on those grounds posed little threat to the government. There was, after all, no real hardship in a country so naturally fertile and in which land was plentiful. Any protest was far more likely to come from a still more recently educated elite, excluded from the opportunities that independence had opened so generously to its predecessors and with the ability to publicize its disappointment vigorously.

What the Charter illustrated most clearly was that Obote was, above all, concerned with the rights of Africans and in practical terms this meant he was a Ugandan nationalist. It did not mean that he was xenophobic, although his condemnation of colonialism, neo-colonialism and imperialism was genuine enough. He hated unsolicited foreign intervention in his country. He disliked, too, the legacy of dependence upon an economic system designed to meet the needs of an imperial age. But he recognised that no country, especially a relatively small African country, could rely exclusively upon its own resources in the complex circumstances of the twentieth century. He was aware that Uganda's heavy dependence upon agriculture, and particularly upon the production of coffee and cotton for export, was unsatisfactory. But if that was the best way to earn foreign exchange, then for the time being it must be accepted. At the same time, every effort must be made to ensure that those foreign earnings were not squandered upon the purchase of foreign-made luxury goods for the few. Admirable sentiments, but, as Obote was aware, not easy to enforce.

One of the obstacles to the achievement of those aims was frankly acknowledged in the Charter itself. Uganda's educational system, the still influential legacy of the Protectorate era, had produced a relatively small elite who were capable either of serving the country or, equally effectively, of promoting their own interests or those of their families or ethnic groups. In circumstances where wealth was still limited there was not only a natural disposition to look after one's immediate circle; it was also traditionally incumbent upon any who succeeded to assist those who may well have made considerable sacrifices to help them towards success. While the political horizons of many of the elite may have extended even beyond the bounds of Uganda itself, their social and economic outlook was far more circumscribed, rarely extending beyond their tribal community, if it even stretched that far. For Obote, Buganda typified the extreme version of this limitation, a limitation which confined the political as well as the other aspects of life. While he deplored any subservience to external powers, he was also vigorously opposed to internal divisions which put the part before the whole country. That his main criticism in this connection should have been directed towards Buganda was not wholly surprising in the light of events since independence. To rid the country of those divisions would, he frankly admitted, call for the generation of a new attitude towards the whole of life.

Bearing in mind the restrictions under which Obote was forced to operate, it was only to be expected that, in practice, the blueprint contained in the Charter had to be amended in a variety of ways without invoking cynicism to explain what happened. Uganda's main foreign-exchange-earning export crops had been highly susceptible to fluctuations in market prices. Nor had it always been possible to provide encouragement to growers in the shape of the higher incomes for which they hoped after independence. While, therefore, stressing the importance of the domestic contribution to Uganda's development and uttering a warning against capitalism, Obote accepted that foreign investment was essential to the country's development. The aim should be to avoid becoming too entangled in the strings which would almost certainly be attached. One way to do that was to look for as many different sources of aid as possible. Nor should the search be limited to countries of the Eastern Bloc.

It was unfortunate that the programme should have been designated a 'move to the left'. In the eyes of many Western observers this meant a shift towards communism, of which Obote's opponents had always been ready to accuse him. In the same way, his advocacy of African rights, especially as manifested in his opposition to the British proposal to supply arms to the South African government, was interpreted by the West as tantamount to the rejection of non-alignment in favour of a rapprochement with the Eastern Bloc. The new Conservative government in Britain, elected in June 1970 and led by Edward Heath, was exasperated by the way in which African leaders whose countries – for sound economic reasons – continued to trade with South Africa, refused to accept that Britain was acting in good faith, as well as in its own economic interests, in offering to send arms for what was believed to be the defence of South Africa against external, probably communist, aggression. In such an atmosphere of mutual disapproval it was not surprising that the British government was liable to make facile misjudgements when contemplating the statements of men like Obote.

A more detached assessment might have revealed that what was happening was less terrible than Obote's critics were inclined to assume. Two measures might help to demonstrate what the Charter looked like in action. In October 1969 legislation was enacted requiring banks operating in Uganda to incorporate locally with a capital of Ugandan £1 million each. Six foreign banks responded positively without any feelings of apprehension, and the country's foreign reserves benefitted accordingly. At the same time, another measure, the national service plan was announced. This did not imply military service but was intended as a means to make the most of Uganda's internal resources. Boys and girls leaving primary school without any prospect of further academic education were to go for a period of one or two years to one of four camps, one in each province. There they would be taught farming and a variety of other useful skills. It was not a popular proposal and was immediately seized upon by opponents of the government who claimed that it would break up family life. The plan was never put into practice because Obote's government was overthrown. If it had been implemented it might have provided opportunities for a large number of young people to realize more of their potential.

Many overseas investors in Uganda – including the leading banking concerns, Barclays DCO, National and Grindlays and the Standard Bank – were greatly relieved by the terms of the Charter. Neighbouring Tanzania had recently taken far more drastic steps. It had, for example, nationalized the whole of the sisal industry. Uganda's plan did not envisage anything of that sort. The Europeans and Asians who had businesses in Uganda also recognized that they were not so strongly based there as were their opposite numbers in Kenya whose investment was very much greater, so much so that the Kenyan government could not ignore their views. Consequently, foreign investors in Uganda had felt in a precarious position until the Charter gave them new confidence. They accepted 60 per cent participation by the government because they were reassured that this meant their activities would not be nationalized and they themselves would not be driven out of the country. From Obote's point of view the arrangement had a number of advantages. First, it meant that Uganda would retain foreign expertise. Second, since it was the government that was gaining a holding in the foreign companies, private individuals would, he hoped, be prevented from accumulating too much wealth. The government's profits could then be used for the benefit of the whole population.

To pass judgement upon the Charter would only be to speculate since it had too little time to demonstrate its long-term effects. For example, the government had acquired a share in only seven British companies, including the National and Grindlays Bank, Brooke Bond-Liebig and Shell-BP, by the time Obote was overthrown. That any attempt to implement the Charter would have encountered difficulties there can be no doubt. Many feared that it would only benefit those who had already been fortunate enough to gain office after independence, while newer aspirants to a share in the good things the country had to offer would be for ever excluded. This view was certainly encouraged by Obote's opponents. Equally, there can be little doubt that there were those in positions of authority who would have exploited to the limit any opportunities which might have been available to them. But that that was any part of Obote's plan is certainly not true. Nor did the opportunities occur, much to the disappointment of some of his closest associates. For his own part, Obote had no longing for personal wealth, but he had a burning desire to promote social justice. What he lacked was the strength, both personal and material, to realize his dreams. By his very nature he relied upon persuasion rather than coercion, and when others acted contrary to his plan he was not ruthless enough in checking them.

It was economic reality rather than personal cupidity that created the first problems for the Charter. The desire to treat foreign companies fairly in order to retain their confidence came up against financial obstacles. In May 1970 it became necessary to change the agreement to pay 'adequate' compensation by substituting the word 'reasonable', and to delete the promise to pay promptly. Companies became worried when they saw the prospect of receiving compensation within six months recede into an indefinite future. They were even more concerned when it was made clear that any payments must come from working profits in a situation where instability was making profits problematical. Obote had obviously underestimated the difficulties the Charter would create, but they were difficulties of a practical rather than of an ideological nature.

There was concern in another quarter when it was reported in July that the labour minister, E. Y. Lakidi, had said that the government intended to dismiss 80,000 Kenyan and Tanzanian workers to make way for Ugandans in skilled and semi-skilled employment. This was wholly contrary to Obote's professed desire to keep on good terms with his country's neighbours and provided another example of the way in which economic necessity undermined his best intentions. Kenya responded by claiming that such an act would be in breach of an agreement made as recently as March, which guaranteed to citizens of the East African Community freedom to find employment in any of the three member countries without special permits. There was talk of closing the port of Mombasa to Ugandan trade by way of reprisal and EAC opinion hardened further when, in October, a stream of refugees, deprived of their work, reached the port of Kisumu from Uganda, complaining that Ugandan officials had refused to allow them to take their savings out of the country.

Although the security situation in Uganda as a whole was good, along some main roads which gave an easy means both of access and escape to wrongdoers, especially in Buganda, conditions had deteriorated markedly. The repercussions from the attempted assassination had led to increasing violence, both on the part of the opponents of the government and of the security forces which responded to the violence in kind. Gangs armed with weapons, which they had probably acquired from Zaire, held up cars travelling along main roads, ejected the occupants and seized the vehicles, which they then sold, also in Zaire. The motives behind these acts of pillage were mixed. In some cases the aim was simply to satisfy greed. In others there was a direct political element that simply sought to cause disruption and create difficulties for the government. More frequently the actions were the result of a breakdown of respect for law and order enforced by an unpopular government, hence the high concentration of crime in Buganda as compared with the peaceful conditions obtaining in the rest of the country. In these circumstances, the harsh response of the security forces, taking advantage of the state of emergency imposed after the assassination attempt, only aggravated the situation. Road blocks, set up by the army, not only caused inconvenience to innocent travellers, but also led them to look upon the security forces with distaste or even hostility. Obote himself did not think that the violence, disconcerting though it was, warranted the continuation of the state of emergency, but he allowed it to remain in force as a check upon possible attempts by ill-wishers who had fled to Britain to stir up more trouble. His decision aggravated the situation. Relieved of the necessity to search for evidence to justify arrests the police adopted the easier option of seizing anyone against whom they might have a real or imaginary grudge, or who just happened to be in the wrong place at the wrong time.

Among the main contributors to the growing disillusionment with the government were the activities of the General Service Unit (GSU), set up with the aim of making Obote's position more secure and commanded by his kinsman, Akena Adoko. The GSU occupies a prominent position in the demonology of Obote's first presidency, yet an observer well positioned and well equipped by experience to pass judgement has written that the sins of the GSU were to be attributed primarily to amateurish gullibility. In an era of rampant suspicion, Gerald Murphy, a former senior colonial police officer, who was head of the Ugandan CID under Obote and who, after Obote's overthrow, was recalled to Uganda to investigate the GSU, remarked upon the propensity in Africa to believe that members of other tribes are capable of any villainy. The members of the GSU were untrained for their anti-subversion role and, in Murphy's opinion, could well have been tempted from time to time, 'to proffer dubious items of information as evidence of their diligence.' Consequently, although not a single death could be laid at the door of the GSU, and its behaviour never began to approximate to that of Amin's death squads, the wrongful arrests that frequently resulted from its unscrupulous endeavours converted many who formerly had felt only goodwill towards the government into its sworn enemies. At the same time, and in order to fortify their own uneasy position, the members of the GSU used their privileged relationship with Obote to undermine the standing of the police, who were called upon to make the arrests resulting from the false accusations levelled by the GSU. In those ways, if not in the grisly manner attributed to it by its critics, the GSU contributed significantly to the country's instability.[15]

Another problem for the government sprang from the delay in sending well-educated young men for training as army officers. Obote had never liked the *effendi* system and had made a point of despatching suitable young men to Sandhurst as soon as the opportunity presented itself after independence. That meant that the first of them returned to take up their appointments in Uganda only in the mid-1960s, and it took them some time to gain the experience of command necessary before the *effendi* system could be phased out. It was Obote's hope that the phasing out process would be accomplished by 1972. In 1967 he introduced a scheme to encourage early retirement among the *effendi* and senior NCOs who might hope to reach that rank by offering them a course which, if they completed it successfully, would enable them to become short-service commissioned officers. They would then retire two years later with the rank of captain and with the pension appropriate to that rank. In the meantime, Obote had no grounds for doubting the army commander, Idi Amin's loyalty, even if that officer's mode of operation was becoming increasingly open to question. Evidence that Amin himself had a guilty conscience, however, came to light at the time of the assassination attempt upon Obote in December 1969. Although there was nothing to suggest that Amin was in any way connected with the shooting, he went into hiding. The reaction of most of his fellow officers on his re-emergence was not one of suspicion but rather of contempt for what they saw as cowardice, although it was more probably blind panic. His second-in-command, Brigadier Pierino Yere Okaya, openly accused him of desertion.

When Okaya and his wife were shot dead in the northern town of Gulu in January 1970 the finger pointed clearly at Amin. Although Obote instituted an inquiry into what had taken place, evidence was difficult to come by because of Amin's hold over the army. Even the General Service Unit, created by Obote as a special bodyguard distinct from the army, was gradually, like the army, being infiltrated by recruits loyal to Amin.

Gradually, however, and in spite of Amin's efforts to block the investigation, evidence began to accumulate which indicated that he had been at least an accomplice to the murder of Okaya. Obote at last turned to seek means to disembarrass himself of his association with a man whose professional reputation, although still not, Obote believed, his personal loyalty to the government, was so much in doubt. Many of the army officers, and particularly those trained at Sandhurst, increasingly disapproved of Amin's methods. Among the non-commissioned ranks, the Langi, Obote's own people, supported the president, while the Acholi, who formed a large proportion of the army's personnel and who still adhered to the traditions of a professional force, were also loyal to the government rather than to Amin. In September therefore, with Amin in Cairo, Obote sought to round off the Okaya enquiry. To strengthen his position he promoted Amin to chief of defence in order to remove him from direct contact with the army. At the same time he appointed as army commander Brigadier Suleiman Hussein, a man upon whom he believed he could rely, and he made Lieut.-Colonel David Oyite Ojok, a fellow Langi, adjutant and quartermaster-general.

Obote had never doubted Amin's shrewdness, and he knew he had a network of informants at his command. On this occasion both factors joined to help Amin to escape the trap laid for him. Learning what was going on in his absence, Amin returned from Egypt unexpectedly and the plan to put him to the test fell through. But he did not forget, and when he later seized power, all the police officers involved in the investigation, as well as those enquiring into the assassination attempt against Obote, were murdered. Among them was Mohammed Hassan, head of the CID.

It was the report of the public accounts committee which provided the grounds for questioning Amin's actions more closely. In the course of its annual investigation into government expenditure the committee drew attention to a £1 million deficit in the defence budget. Immediately upon hearing the news Obote wrote to Felix Onama, the defence minister, insisting that the matter be cleared up as soon as possible. The report, he said, would be debated in the national assembly in March and he needed a full explanation of what had taken place. It later transpired that, with the knowledge of Onama and of the permanent secretary for defence, Amin, at the request of Israel, had been channelling money from the defence budget and arms from his country's reserves to the Southern Sudanese rebels. In the light of his later promotion of Islam it may seem surprising that Amin was prepared to assist people rebelling against an Islamic government. It was not, however, until his visit to Libya in 1972, whence he returned, it was said, with a briefcase containing $2 million, that he openly espoused the Islamic faith. Of the truth about the contents of the briefcase there can be no proof, but it was noted that he held the case firmly in his left hand while taking the salute at a parade in Khartoum during his return journey to Uganda.

The extent of the charges against Amin only emerged in January 1971, at a time when Obote was under considerable pressure from his friends, Nyerere and Kaunda, to attend a conference of leaders of the commonwealth in Singapore. The reason for their importunity was their desire to present a united front in criticising Edward Heath's government for insisting upon its right to supply arms to South Africa for defence purposes. In July 1970 Obote had issued a statement accusing Britain of offering the hand of friendship as well as moral support to the government of South Africa while it still pursued its policy of apartheid. This followed hard on the heels of a request from the Confederation of British Industry to the British government calling for a protest to Uganda on behalf of British companies likely to be affected by a change in the law regarding compensation.

Thus, on two grounds, Obote was at loggerheads with Britain. For that reason he was less sanguine than his friends about the likelihood of their being able, albeit jointly, to influence British policy, and he was anxious to avoid provoking more serious conflict. He had other, more immediately pressing, reasons for wishing to absent himself from the Singapore meeting. He was deeply involved, for example, in preparing a new five-year development plan which had to be completed by March and he felt he should be on hand to keep up the momentum of the work. Still more important, he was determined, in spite of the turmoil in Uganda, to hold elections for the national assembly in April. He believed they had been postponed for far too long, even if there were understandable reasons for the delay. He was reluctant to leave the country at a time when political rivalries would be coming to the boil and a steadying hand would be needed to ensure that satisfactory plans were made and put into effect.

His friends persisted, however, so he called a cabinet meeting to discuss what should be done. At the same time he summoned Amin to see him, intending to warn him that he would be called to account for the deficit in the defence budget. The cabinet meeting was a lengthy one and a message was brought to Obote to say that Amin was waiting in the anteroom. Obote saw no reason why the general should not be given time to reflect upon his misdeeds, so he did not see him until the meeting was ended and it had been agreed that he should go to Singapore after all. He then told Amin that, on his return, he would require a full explanation of the financial transactions to which the public accounts committee had drawn attention. Far from showing resentment, Amin was utterly obsequious, as he had always been when in the presence of authority, and he even withdrew from the encounter backwards, bowing as he went. Obote still regarded the whole issue as no more than a deplorable administrative problem for which he would be answerable to the national

assembly. He had certainly no reason to think that it would lead to a
serious clash with Onama and Amin. It is possible, too, that, even at this
late stage, Amin, if not Onama, was concerned with exculpating himself
rather than with planning to subvert a system under cover of which he
had been able to build up considerable influence.

It was at this point that more subtle minds than Amin's own sought to
use him to protect their interests. Onama almost certainly recognized the
threat to his own position which would result from an enquiry into
defence expenditure. The Israeli government must also have seen the
challenge to its role in the Sudan implicit in Obote's statement. Dispo-
sitions began to be made accordingly. Soon after Obote's departure for
Singapore, half of the officer corps, all of them loyal to Obote, were sent
on leave by Onama. Although leave was due to them the fact that they
were all sent at the same time can be seen, in retrospect, as a preparation
for the coup which followed. This and other actions by Onama did not
go unnoticed. The minister of internal affairs, Basil Bataringaya, formerly
a prominent member of the Democratic Party but for some years a
staunch supporter of Obote, heard from the inspector-general of police,
Erinayo Oryema, a report of a plot to assassinate Obote at Entebbe
airport on his return to Uganda. Bataringaya at once summoned an anti-
assassination committee, consisting of people he believed to be loyal to
the president, and it was decided to send Christopher Ntende, the minister's permanent secretary, to Singapore to appraise Obote of what was
happening. Obote could not believe the report and insisted that the
information be checked. As a precautionary measure, however, he sent
instructions that a number of strategic points should be guarded and
that care should be taken to see that all army units were commanded by
reliable officers.

In the meantime events in Uganda had moved quickly. Ojok, visiting
Entebbe airport with a view to making security arrangements for Obote's
return, met Amin there, apparently doing his own reconnaissance. Ojok
also reported that he saw an Israeli officer, Colonel Bar-Lev, who warned
him not to get himself killed. Ojok's encounter with Amin appeared to
confirm the rumour of an assassination plot, and Bar-Lev's reported
remark seemed to indicate Israeli complicity. At the same time, Ojok's
presence in Entebbe must have alerted Amin to the fact that steps were
being taken to counter his efforts. Obote was kept informed by Bataringaya of what was happening and the day after the events in Entebbe
Brigadier Hussein summoned the senior officers in the army to Kampala
for a briefing on the anti-assassination plans. Amin, however, now took
the initiative. Two important factors were in his favour; first, the absence
on leave of half the officer corps, and second, the officers attending
Hussein's briefing were still in conference and had not yet returned to
their commands. Troops supporting Amin were consequently able to take

control of all the regimental centres and to seize the armouries because the units loyal to the government were virtually leaderless. The parliament building, where the anti-assassination committee was still meeting, was surrounded by Amin's troops and the members fled in confusion. Brigadier Hussein was captured a few days later and died in prison from the injuries he received. Several other officers were arrested.

The civilian population learned of the coup on the afternoon of 25 January 1971 when it was announced over Uganda radio that the army had taken control because of the deficiencies of Obote's government. An anonymous broadcaster accused the government of corruption, of giving preferential treatment to the Langi, of introducing economic policies that benefited the rich at the expense of the poor and of creating a private army (the GSU) which was not answerable to the normal military authorities. He also said that Obote himself had recently taken overall control of defence while reducing the role of Amin – which as executive president he was, of course entitled to do.

Shortly afterwards, it was claimed that the army had asked Amin to take charge. It was not the army, however, but only that part of it, mainly Nubi and members of related ethnic groups recruited by Amin, which had been responsible for the coup. Equally clearly, Amin had not responded to a general demand that he should take upon himself the leadership of the country. Indeed, it is unlikely that he himself had ever foreseen the consequences of his action. He had simply got rid of Obote to protect himself. What happened next was sheer chance as far as Amin himself was concerned, although in time he came to revel in his unexpected acquisition of power. The jubilation of the people in Kampala, which was certainly not shared by the inhabitants of the Northern and Eastern Provinces and only by some in the Western Province, is explicable only in the context of the Bugandan leaders' hatred for Obote. So strong were their feelings that they even welcomed the elevation of the president's hitherto apparently loyal henchman, the man directly responsible for the attack on the *kabaka*'s palace, if it meant an end to rule by the man they detested. It is clear that when they came to think more carefully about the new situation the Bugandan leaders took Amin at his face value and were confident they could manipulate him to suit their ends. They were yet to appreciate that power can beget a lust for power in people suddenly raised to positions they had never dreamed of occupying. They were to learn, too, that Amin, whatever his other limitations, possessed a more than average measure of cunning, and that he had at his disposal an armed force against which the combined intellectual resources of Buganda, or even of the whole country, could do little other than to make the best of the situation by supporting him, as some prominent people did.

Before those events had taken place Obote had been active in Singapore. He was aware that few people in Uganda were deeply concerned about the South African arms question, even if they knew about it, so that what he said in Singapore on that score – indeed his very presence there – would bring him little credit at home. But he was deeply committed to the OAU's policy of fighting apartheid and, having agreed to attend the Commonwealth Conference, he felt he should stand by his convictions. In a statement to the press on 18 September he accused Edward Heath of having made no attempt to find an alternative to the naval facilities provided in Simonstown in return for which he was prepared to send arms to South Africa. If Heath went ahead with his plan, he said, there might be outbreaks of violence against Europeans in Uganda. Furthermore, such a deal would be an open invitation to the USSR to replace Britain as the most influential power in many parts of Africa.[16] Uganda might even leave the commonwealth. It was an unduly aggressive statement, springing from the depths of Obote's feelings about apartheid, but it was intended to startle rather than to be taken at its face value. The beleaguered Heath did not, however, see it in that light, and his dislike for the Ugandan leader was further strengthened.

Confirmation of the news of Amin's coup interrupted Obote's campaign and he hastened back to East Africa. Arriving at Nairobi airport on 25 January he was conducted to a hotel in the city. Friends in Kampala made numerous attempts to contact him by telephone to urge him to return because they believed all was not yet lost, but their messages did not get through to him. One supporter made his way to Nairobi and told Obote that the troops in Karamoja and in other parts of the Eastern Province were still loyal, as too were those in the Western Province. Those in the west were too far away to be of immediate assistance, but Obote was sufficiently heartened to urge his informant to arrange transport to get him back to Eastern Uganda. News of his plan leaked out, however, and his hotel was surrounded by police.

Nyerere was in India at the time, but he instructed his vice-president, Rashidi Kawawa, to summon a cabinet meeting which should invite Obote to Dar es Salaam. Another Tanzanian minister, Amir Jamal, then flew to Nairobi to extend his government's invitation. Seeing that his hopes of returning to Uganda immediately were unrealizable, Obote accepted, and was given a warm welcome by the Tanzanian government on his arrival in Dar es Salaam. At the end of the month, he flew to Mombasa to have talks with Kenyatta and then went on to Addis Ababa, where he briefed Emperor Haile Selassie on what had taken place before flying back to Tanzania. Cutting short his visit to India, Nyerere himself returned to Dar es Salaam and discussed with Obote the possibility of an invasion of Uganda to restore him to office. Obote advised against it because, he said, too many countries had already expressed their sympathy for Amin's coup.

Tanzania, Zambia, the Sudan and Nigeria were among the countries which remained loyal to Obote. The British government, however, recognized Amin's regime on 5 February, no doubt relieved that it had no longer to contend with such a severe critic of British policy – one, moreover, who was thought to be tainted with left-wing sympathies. It derived encouragement, too, from the fact that Amin had begun to release the political prisoners detained by Obote. Among these were the five ministers Obote had accused of plotting against him, and also Abu Mayanja, Benedicto Kiwanuka and Brigadier Opolot. All were in good health and said they had not been subjected to harsh conditions while they were in prison. It was not without significance, however, that the crowd which assembled in Kampala to witness the official release of the detainees carried more emblems indicating support for the late *kabaka* than for Amin himself. Nevertheless, on 20 February Amin was promoted to the rank of full general and appointed president of Uganda by those officers and men of the army and airforce who had remained loyal to him. He then revoked the state of emergency which had been in force since the attempted assassination of Obote in 1969, but announced that elections to the national assembly could not take place for five years and that in the meantime his government would remain in power.

The benevolent face Amin presented in his early days in power was soon replaced by a sterner countenance. Basil Bataringaya had been arrested immediately after the coup on suspicion of having tried to enlist the support of part of the army in an attempt to kill Amin. Shortly afterwards he was murdered. By March there were reports of excessive brutality by soldiers manning road-blocks and of nightly shootings of prisoners at the Karuma Falls on the Nile in the north-west.[17] Roy Lewis, writing in *The Times* on 31 March, however, reflected the British government's satisfaction at Amin's success when he said that the new president had shown skill 'in surviving the paranoid period of Obote's dictatorship.' It is interesting that such criticism of Obote by the British press (the *Observer* excepted) emerged only after his overthrow, and after his attacks on Britain's proposed arms deals with South Africa. As late as 30 January *The Times* itself had admitted that, in spite of a recent deterioration in the economy, Amin had not inherited a load of debt.

The evidence of Amin's cruelty steadily accumulated, in parallel with his own accusations against Obote. On 15 April Amin claimed that 80 men and been seized near the Kenyan border en route for Tanzania to be trained as guerrillas by Obote. They had not, in fact, been travelling together, or with any ulterior motive, but had been taken from ordinary public service buses. A few days later Amin protested to the Sudanese government that 500 Ugandans loyal to Obote had crossed over from the Sudan into Uganda and had clashed with some of his own soldiers. More detached observers were later to claim that any border skirmishes were more likely to be the result of ethnic clashes within the Ugandan army than any attempted assault by Obote's forces. This would hardly have been surprising in view of Amin's calculated campaign to annihilate all pro-Obote sympathizers within the armed forces, a campaign which began almost immediately after his seizure of power. Martin Meredith, writing in the *Observer* on 30 May 1971, claimed that nearly all senior and middle-ranking officers in the army had been killed or imprisoned if they had not already fled.

Earlier in the month Amin had offered 1 million Ugandan shillings (£56,000) for Obote, dead or alive, and 500,000 shillings each for Sam Odaka, Obote's foreign minister, and Akena Odoko, a kinsman of Obote, both of whom were in Dar es Salaam. On 7 June Amin told the press that he had encouraged volunteers to kidnap Obote,[18] and speaking in Paris in September, he said that if Obote were brought to Uganda alive he would face charges of corruption. This he later changed to a charge of murder.

Among others to suffer at Amin's hand were the members of Obote's immediate family, who were subjected to harassment. Soldiers were sent to Mrs Obote to demand an inventory of all the items in her house. The value of the records with which her husband had supplied her soon after their marriage, and of a similar collection of receipts she herself had subsequently accumulated, soon became evident. She did not hand over the evidence immediately. Instead, making an excuse that the files were probably in the garage, she slipped away and had photocopies made of all the material and it was those copies she handed to the soldiers who then left. In the nights that followed Mrs Obote heard shooting in the neighbourhood and began to think of leaving Kampala with her two sons. It was suggested to her that she might go to Lira, in Lango District, but, after considerable thought she came to the conclusion that she would be safer in Kampala.

Mrs Obote spent the whole of 1971 in the capital, but early the following year friends advised her she was in grave danger and should leave and try to make her way to Tanzania. Her flight had to be planned with great care. She sent the children to Nairobi by bus, accompanied by one of her sisters. She herself followed, in disguise, with a companion, in their family car, which was not registered in her name. By good fortune they were able to pass a number of road-blocks and crossed the border safely. In Nairobi she joined her children at the house of friends.

The plan was that they should stay there for a week while arrangements were made for their onward journey to Dar es Salaam. It was a mistake. At Amin's request they were returned to Uganda where they were handed over to a Ugandan police officer in the eastern town of Tororo. Amin's intention, they were later to learn, was that they should be sent to Lango where arrangements would be made for their murder and the Langi would be accused of turning against their former leader. Fortunately, the police officer in charge of Tororo had previously worked for Obote and he refused to take action until he had firm instructions. He telephoned to Kampala, but the man who took the call did not know of Amin's plan so he said the captives should be sent to the capital.

Obote, who was visiting Khartoum, learned what was happening from his friends in Nairobi who made contact with him through the Sudanese embassy. He immediately got in touch with President Nyerere who telephoned Kenyatta urging him to ensure that no harm came to the family. The Archbishop of Uganda also intervened, with the result that Mrs Obote and her children were taken from Kampala central police station to see Amin. The latter asked Mrs Obote why she had run away. She replied that she had intended to take her children on holiday. Turning to the boys Amin asked them individually if they had really wanted to join their father. When they said that they had, Mrs Obote, knowing nothing of Kenyatta's involvement, thought their reply had sealed their death warrant. Instead they were sent home, their departure being covered by television cameras invited by Amin to witness his clemency.

Mrs Obote could not feel safe, suspecting that Amin, having been thwarted in his plan, would try again to have her and her children killed. She began at once to plan another escape, considering all the possible routes out of Uganda but eventually deciding that they must follow the road they had previously taken to the Kenya border. Once again she sent the children ahead by bus and followed by car the next day, driven by a friend who pretended to be her husband. They explained at the roadblocks they encountered that they were going to visit the man's sick mother in Tororo. Once over the border Mrs Obote was met by another friend who took her with all speed to Nairobi airport where she was reunited with her children. All three were immediately flown to Dar es Salaam. There they were taken to a house on the beach where President and Mrs Nyerere awaited them. Mrs Obote wept with relief.

While these events had been taking place Obote had been thinking how best to enlist troops with a view to invading Uganda at some future date. He discussed his proposal with Nyerere and the two agreed that the best place to recruit and train them would be in the Sudan. By agreement with the chairman of the Sudanese Revolutionary Council, Gaafar Nimeiry, from October 1971 President of the Sudan, Obote moved to Khartoum in April 1971 and from there sent messages into Uganda calling for support. Already there were a considerable number of refugees in the Sudan, who had fled from Amin's cruelty. They were now joined by others who responded to Obote's call from as far afield as Tororo, as well as from Acholi and Lango. Not all of those who set out reached Khartoum, but about 2,000 did, and were trained intensively by the Sudanese army. Among those who now joined Obote was his old ally,

Lieut. Colonel David Oyite Ojok. It was while Obote was in the Sudan that *The Times* reported that Nyerere was no longer providing him with hospitality.[19] It was not clear whether this was intended merely as a statement of fact or whether it carried the implication that hospitality had been deliberately withdrawn.

The plan to invade Uganda from the north had to be dropped in 1972 after a settlement was reached between the Sudanese government and the rebels in the southern part of the country. Obote decided to transfer his troops to Tanzania in June, they travelling by sea while he went ahead by air. In Dar es Salaam he was joyfully reunited with his family and they joined together in a prayer of thanksgiving, a practice they were subsequently to follow whenever one or other of them had been away for any period. The Tanzanian government generously allotted the troops a plot of fertile land near Handeni on which they immediately got to work. Later in the year it was taken into use as a camp for Tanzanian national servicemen after the Ugandans had been called away.

The reason for their departure was that in August Amin claimed that God had spoken to him and called upon him to eject all British Asians from Uganda. Orders were given accordingly and caused grave alarm, not only in Uganda but also in Britain, where disillusionment with the government's erstwhile hero quickly set in at the prospect of having to accommodate thousands of exiles. Sensing that there could be trouble for Amin, Obote and Nyerere decided that it might be an auspicious moment for the exiled Ugandan forces to launch an attack across the border. Soundings were taken with the British foreign office in the hope of enlisting support. Sir Alec Douglas-Home, the British foreign secretary, merely replied that Britain would give any help possible, other than material assistance. Although this amounted to little more than a covert declaration of moral support, Obote looked upon it as a benison indeed, coming from the government of Edward Heath, who, until recently, had been so markedly hostile.

The invasion force was transported hastily to Tabora where the troops were armed. They had no time, however, to familiarize themselves with their weapons before being hurried to Tanzania's north-western frontier. They were to be commanded by Colonel Tito Okello, the most senior among the officers of the Ugandan army to make their escape to Tanzania. Okello, an Acholi, was utterly loyal to Obote, but having been one of those who had gained promotion through the *effendi* system was not the ideal leader for such an expedition.

Two pieces of news encouraged Obote. First, he learned that a young man, Yoweri Museveni, who had previously been a student in Dar es Salaam and had fled to Tanzania when Amin seized power, had claimed to have irrefutable evidence that, as soon as the forces advanced on Mbarara in South-western Uganda, many of the garrison of the town would come over to them and would accept him as their leader. Museveni had a number of friends in the Tanzanian government and his statement was accepted without question. Second, Obote received a report to the effect that a considerable number of soldiers from Amin's army were prepared to defect and assemble in Entebbe, ready to march on Kampala if leadership could be provided. It was arranged, therefore, that this should be the main strike force and that it should be commanded by the much more able Lieut.-Colonel Ojok, who would fly to Entebbe in secret with one hundred NCOs and other troops to provide a nucleus around which to create an effective army.

This latter operation was a failure. Because of the secrecy with which Ojok's side of the venture had to be conducted a succession of problems arose. His plane took off from Dar es Salaam with only a pilot as crew, the other crew member, a flight engineer, having been delayed on his way to the airport. The plane was scheduled to land in Arusha to pick up the support troops who had been moved there to conceal their ultimate destination. Again, because of the need for secrecy, no landing lights were turned on at Arusha airport and the plane damaged a wheel on landing. Without anyone on board or on the airfield to help with repairs the aircraft was unable to take off and the operation had to be aborted. On learning of this, Obote immediately telephoned to Entebbe, an extremely risky undertaking from a security point of view, and ordered the waiting soldiers to disperse unobtrusively. This they were able to do without much difficulty. More hazardous was the removal of the numerous vehicles which had been assembled to transport them to Kampala. It was a measure of the secrecy with which the whole arrangements had been made, or of Amin's lack of vigilance, that this latter operation was carried out successfully.

In the meantime the other force, under Okello, had crossed the Kagera River which marked the boundary between Tanzania and Uganda, and advanced against minimal resistance to Mbarara, which was seized. Museveni's promise was not, however, fulfilled. Amin's troops did not desert in large numbers to join the invading forces. Instead, after an initial hesitation on the part of the Ugandan army which had made the successful advance of Obote's troops possible, Amin mustered his forces and attacked the invaders with overwhelming strength. Obote's troops, lacking both the numbers and the equipment to resist, had to withdraw, leaving behind their wounded, who were killed by Amin's men.

Back in Tanzania the defeated soldiers were allotted a patch of land, some twenty or thirty miles from Tabora, which had been intended as a camp for national servicemen. The plan had been abandoned because the area was considered too dry. There, Obote addressed his men, stressing that they were all farmers or the sons of farmers; he would get them some hoes and they must clear and cultivate the soil. For the first six months the Tanzanian government supplied the soldiers with food, but they were so successful in cultivating the land, and even in finding water, that it was not long before a farm, five miles square, was producing a variety of crops, including maize, cassava, beans and tobacco. Ugandan methods of cultivation came as something of a revelation to the Tanzanians in the vicinity, who learned, for example, that cassava grew far more strongly if the shoots were planted horizontally rather than vertically, and that sweet potatoes should not be planted in holes but in mounds of soil. While clearing the bush the Ugandans also made charcoal and in so doing developed a thriving, small-scale industry.

Obote himself spent most of his time in Dar es Salaam. He and his family were penniless, dependent upon the kindness of the Tanzanian government for their accommodation and food. Friends from Kenya sent money to buy clothes for the children and with what was left over Obote bought three cows. Fortunately, education was free. Obote met Nyerere frequently and the two discussed a wide range of issues. This regular contact, and the friendship shown to the whole family, counted for almost as much as the material assistance that was so generously proferred. The sense of being in exile, although acute, was softened by the companionship and sympathy which they had from President and Mrs Nyerere. Obote himself became extremely interested in what was going on in Tanzania, and from time to time he visited Lusaka to have discussions with his friend, President Kaunda, his airfare being paid either by Kaunda or Nyerere. And whenever Kaunda visited Tanzania he called on Obote. The latter also maintained regular contact with envoys from Uganda who kept him informed about what was going on there, and he remained the focus of loyalty for all those who wished to see the overthrow of Amin. An agreement signed between Nyerere and Amin after the failure of Obote's invasion, under the terms of which each party promised not to harbour people plotting against the other, meant, however, that Nyerere himself was unable to offer any assistance in promoting that aim.

In 1976 a somewhat bizarre event took place. A conference of Ugandans in exile in Eastern and Central Africa was summoned to meet in Lusaka. There is considerable doubt as to where the idea originated, but the organizers were young men who had had little political experience. There appeared to be a feeling abroad, however, that if all those who were opposed to Amin could organize themselves there was a lively prospect that he might be overthrown. Obote received an invitation to the conference but could not afford to travel to Lusaka and did not wish to ask either Nyerere or Kaunda for money for the airfare. In any case, he believed the convenors carried no political weight and that the plan would prove ineffective. The meeting set up the Uganda National Movement (UNM) and elected Prince John Barigye, the eldest son of the

Mugabe of Ankole, as chairman. Yoweri Museveni was chosen to be minister for defence, based in Tanzania.

Obote believed that someone in the Tanzanian government must be behind the scheme, if only covertly, an opinion which was reinforced when the Tanzanian minister for intelligence and security called on him and exclaimed excitedly that this was what everyone had been waiting for and Amin would be overthrown. Obote remained sceptical, arguing that those involved in the UNM were unknown in Uganda and would get no support. In fact, nothing did happen, but the UNM continued in existence, Edward Rugumayo succeeding Prince John Barigye as leader, and there was a branch in Nairobi where other exiles were based. The whole episode had about it an air of fantasy, dreamed up by people who were willing to respond to any rumour which offered a hope that their exile might come to an end. The covert involvement of the Tanzanian security ministry was real enough, as was to be demonstrated only a short time later.

In February 1977 Obote learned from a broadcast made by Uganda Radio that Archbishop Janani Luwum was dead, as a result, it was said, of a car accident in which the archbishop and two other passengers had been killed. Seeking further information Obote telephoned several numbers in Uganda before accidentally making contact with his old friend, Tucker Nabeta, with whom he had not spoken for ten years. From Nabeta he learned that Luwum had been arrested the day before his death and confronted with two men who were accused of hiding arms in the archbishop's house. Obote knew the two, one of them having been a friend since his schooldays in Gulu, and he was confident that neither they nor the archbishop would have had any dealings with arms. Although he himself had had no contact with any member of the clergy of Uganda since going into exile he feared that Amin may have suspected the archbishop and the other two dead men of having been in league with him.

His fears increased perceptibly when he heard from Nabeta that Amin's troops were searching for another old friend from his days in Gulu, Yona Okoth, Bishop of Bukedi diocese in Eastern Uganda. Nabeta did not know the whereabouts of Okoth, so Obote tried several other numbers before locating the bishop at the home of a civil servant. The man and his wife, together with Okoth, were anxious to make their escape to Kenya, but soldiers were manning a road block on the Nile Bridge near Jinja. Obote took it upon himself to find an alternative route. His plan was to make contact with a friend who owned canoes which plied on Lake Kyoga. With difficulty he tracked the man down at his home in Kampala and, over the telephone, arranged for Okoth and his two companions to travel to the county of Bugerere, in Eastern Buganda, and from there to cross over to Busoga by canoe. From Busoga they would be in relatively friendly territory right up to the Kenyan border. In this way Okoth made good his escape and later became archbishop of Uganda himself.

Chapter 9

Return from exile

Nyerere's determination to abide by his agreement with Amin to refrain from giving any support to movements aimed at subverting the government of Uganda was shaken in October 1978 when Ugandan troops crossed the Kagera River and seized more than 700 square miles of Tanzanian territory – ostensibly as a reprisal for a Tanzanian attack on Uganda. The real reason for the invasion was to distract attention within the Ugandan army from the divisions that had occurred even within a body which had been consistently loyal to Amin. The president's idiosyncratic and frequently cruel dominion had gradually alienated virtually the whole country. His ministers had found it impossible to fulfil their responsibilities when all decisions were taken, often on the basis of a transient whim, by Amin himself, and without any prior consultation. His critics, particularly among the intelligentsia, had been murdered or had fled without waiting to be attacked. Prominent among those killed in the early days of Amin's regime were Benedicto Kiwanuka, Uganda's first prime minister and subsequently chief justice under Amin, and Frank Kalimuzo, vice-chancellor of Makerere University. At a later stage Archbishop Janani Luwum of the Church of Uganda was also murdered, as has already been seen, and many others were to suffer in like manner.

Even those who had remained silent had not escaped the death squads if it was thought they presented some, probably imaginary, threat to Amin's rule. Ordinary people living near roads which gave access to marauders were pillaged by the troops who, without professionally trained officers and purged of the more experienced soldiers who had been loyal to Obote, were little more than an armed rabble. Administration at all levels had broken down, and attempts by Amin to replace the former district administration with his own officers only led to further oppression and a consequent disrespect for authority, although such feelings could not be openly expressed.

The expulsion of the Asians in 1972 had marked the beginning of a decline in the economy, which, by 1978, was in ruins. Formerly thriving businesses had been handed over to officers in Amin's so-called army who had simply sold off any realizable assets and had then left the business to rot. In the towns, people survived only because of a thriving black market. Country-dwellers in remoter areas were better off because, thanks to Uganda's universally fertile soil, they could at least grow their own food, even if they were unable to buy any imported or other manufactured goods. Widespread discontent in its most acute form was thus avoided, and the armed forces could contain any trouble which might threaten.

This enforced equilibrium was disturbed when Amin's arbitrary cruelty was turned against his own military leaders. Jealousy of any potential rival led him to attack even some of his most senior officers, the very men who had benefited most from his extravagant gifts of goods and property sequestered from the Asians and others who had inadvertently aroused Amin's displeasure or cupidity. Insecurity bred hostility, until Amin could never be sure upon which sections of the security forces he could rely. All that was left for him was to create an external threat against which to rally his troops. It was this unstable situation which led to the invasion of Tanzania.

President Nyerere took his case to the OAU, seeking for support in demanding the withdrawal of the Ugandan troops. Although he disliked Amin intensely he did not plan to indulge in reprisals, only to clear Tanzania of the invaders. He was deeply shocked, therefore, when the other members of the OAU failed to respond, even in some cases appearing to favour Amin. It is possible that some of the African leaders had been shamed by Nyerere's uncompromising stand over South Africa while they themselves had havered, or else had been angered by his support for Biafra, and so were not wholly sorry to see the man who seemed consistently to claim the high moral ground himself discomfited.

Returning to Dar es Salaam, Nyerere confided in Obote, whom he had summoned back from a holiday in Zambia, that he had no option but to launch a counter-attack, but that he did not wish to penetrate deeply into Uganda. If the campaign were to be prosecuted further, with the overthrow of Amin as its objective, the last stages must be undertaken by Ugandan troops. He asked Obote what should be done if the invading force did ultimately reach Kampala. Conscious of the continuing hostility of some of the Bugandan former hierarchy, Obote replied that this should be left to the decision of the Ugandan people. The best way of getting things going would be to assemble in Tanzania representatives of the areas which would be liberated in South-western Uganda, together with any other responsible people who might have made their escape, and let them draw up a plan. This was the germ of the idea which, in different circumstances, Nyerere was to adopt in March 1979.

Before any military action was undertaken the Tanzanian security ministry again intervened, in an attempt to stir up the Ugandan troops living near Tabora against Obote. The aim was probably to promote the interests of the more radical exiles who had convened the meeting in Lusaka in 1976, and the action was certainly taken without the knowledge of Nyerere. Whatever the motive, the attempt on this occasion was unsuccessful. Tanzanian troops began their counter-attack, aided by about one thousand Ugandan soldiers from Tabora. These latter were under the nominal command of Colonel Tito Okello but were effectively led by Lieut.-Colonel Ojok. Additionally, a small, rival force of Ugandan exiles, about three hundred strong, was provided by Yoweri Museveni. Once again there were reports of large numbers of dissident troops waiting to turn against Amin if leadership were forthcoming from outside. On this occasion they were said to be located in the Eastern Province and would muster in Tororo. The prospect of starting a second front against Amin with a minimum of resources seemed attractive. A small force of about one hundred Ugandan soldiers who had been left behind when the others moved out of Tabora was sent across Lake Victoria in January 1979 to Kisumu, where they spent a week. From thence they went on to seize the barracks in Tororo, proclaiming themselves to be supporters of Obote. The expected rising did not take place, however, and the troops had to withdraw.

The advance of the main invading force from the south-west proceeded apace, and in January, with the approval of Nyerere, Obote sent two teams to follow the troops. Their objective was to encourage the revival of local bodies which could take responsibility for organizing a peaceful and orderly society in Western Uganda and Buganda and restore the local government which had been dislocated by Amin. The plan was to assemble village committees to deal with immediate problems. They, in turn, would elect representatives to sit on district committees which would handle wider issues.

The leader of one of Obote's committees was Paulo Muwanga, who was to play a very important role in future events. Muwanga had had little formal education but he had been one of the founder members of the UNC in 1952. Later he had been rusticated in the eastern town of Soroti by the Protectorate government. Obote, who was then a member of the legislative council, had had to pass through Soroti when travelling to and from Kampala, and had called on Muwanga frequently. The two had got to know each other quite well, on a superficial level, and Obote believed Muwanga to be a dedicated supporter of the Ugandan independence movement. Later still, Muwanga joined the UPC, and during Obote's presidency had been his country's ambassador in Cairo before being recalled to be put in charge of protocol in Uganda itself. Under Amin he had accepted an appointment as ambassador in Paris, partly because he was afraid to refuse and partly because it gave him an excuse to get out of Uganda with a well-paid job. When Amin charged him with embezzling the funds of the Paris embassy he fled to London.

He was recalled to Tanzania by Obote as soon as the invasion of Uganda was agreed upon because, as a Muganda, it was hoped he would be acceptable to the people of Masaka District where it was intended that the team of which he was put in charge should operate. Museveni, whose opposition to Obote was already beginning to show itself, disapproved of the whole undertaking, claiming that in a revolutionary situation only military control was necessary. His views carried little weight at that stage because his small contribution to the invasion entitled him to only a modest voice in the determination of policy. Rather than being involved in the main battle he had busied himself in Western Uganda in the wake of the Tanzanian army which bore the brunt of the fighting. There he assembled support from his kinsmen among the Banyaruanda refugees who were located in Ankole. These men were armed by Tanzania in the hope that they would join in the campaign to overthrow Amin, but they were used by Museveni to strengthen his own position in the west where he claimed they were rooting out Amin's supporters.

The Tanzanian president's next move was to suggest that Obote should fly with Vice-President Rashidi Kawawa to Masaka and be ready to move into Kampala with the victorious invaders. Obote was not enthusiastic about returning to Uganda in such an exalted fashion lest his doing so should arouse hostility among his old enemies and destroy the hope of unity in Uganda. He had already stated publicly in Dar es Salaam in January that he did not regard himself as having any personal office in Uganda to gain or regain. Now, pressed by Nyerere, he agreed to act as president until elections could be held to confirm or reject his candidature. Although he was anxious to have parliamentary support if he were indeed to become president again, he was not oblivious to the fact that a sitting incumbent would be in a strong position, and he was confident that the basic organization of the UPC would re-emerge from wherever it had been concealed to support his cause. The Ugandan people, uniformly sick of Amin's excesses and tired of war, would almost certainly have welcomed wholeheartedly anyone who could restore order. In those circumstances Obote was astonished when, having reached Bukoba on the western shore of Lake Victoria in company with Kawawa, he was recalled by Nyerere to Dar es Salaam, as were the two political teams he had despatched ahead of him.

What had happened, although Obote was not to be sure of it for many years until he read David Owen's autobiography, was that the Tanzanian government had approached Britain for logistical help because the campaign was placing an intolerable strain on the country's resources. While the fighting was in progress, supporters of the late *kabaka* in London had impressed upon the British government, and upon the Tanzanian high commissioner in Britain, that Obote would be totally unacceptable in Buganda as president of the country and that for Tanzania to seek British help for such a plan would be disastrous. In the light of this information David Owen, foreign secretary in James Callaghan's Labour government, offered assistance only on condition that Obote played no part in the scheme of things. Instead, as the Baganda in London suggested, he insisted that Yusufu Lule should become president. By some quirk of memory Owen, writing in his autobiography, described Lule as 'a mild, decent, former children's doctor', which is perhaps an indication of how little attention he had been able to give to Ugandan affairs.[20]

It was a tragic miscalculation on Owen's part. It is impossible to say with certainty what might have happened if Nyerere's original plan had been put into effect. There were still some of the old guard of Baganda who would never willingly accept Obote as president, but amid the widespread horror aroused by Amin's tyrannical rule, and in view of the general desire for a return to stability, their voices would scarcely have been heard. The overwhelming majority of the people of Uganda yearned for Amin's overthrow, and even among those who had no great liking for Obote there was considerable agreement that he was probably the only person who could head a government capable of restoring law and order in the wake of a Tanzanian victory. Had he returned, as Nyerere had originally intended that he should, there was at least a chance that the divisions which later arose might have been averted. The British intervention made such an outcome virtually impossible.

Owen's stipulation was conveyed to Nyerere who, although at a loss to understand what pattern would now emerge, was forced to accept it. He was uncomfortable about jettisoning his old friend, but recalled him to Dar es Salaam and invited him to a meeting in February with Yoweri Museveni, whom he had also recalled. To Obote's astonishment, Nyerere announced that Museveni would become military commissar, effectively in overall control of Ugandan soldiers operating against Amin. Obote's supporters, Okello and Oyite-Ojok, were to be relegated to a subordinate position, but the Tanzanian president seemed prepared to accept the arrangement because he believed his decision would ensure that overall control of the Ugandan forces would remain in the hands of a known political radical. In practice, Ojok's presence at the head of the troops in action meant that he alone, and not Museveni – or even Okello, who was also recalled to Dar es Salaam – was really in command, although that may or may not have been Nyerere's intention. Obote certainly derived little pleasure from what Nyerere had done. For once his rigid self control almost gave way under the power of his anger. He could think of no reason why his friend should apparently have sidelined him, and the idea that the troops he had fostered for so long should be handed over to Museveni, with whose views on the future conduct of affairs in Uganda he strongly disagreed, hurt him deeply. With great restraint, he kept his counsel, knowing he was in no position to act decisively.

The Tanzanian president next summoned a conference, in Moshi, which aimed to be as representative as possible of all shades of Ugandan opinion, but with the assurance that the overall direction of the proceedings should be in the hands of people with a radical outlook on government. He intended to make sure that Lule was elected president, in accordance with Britain's instructions, but he was anxious to prevent the conference from falling under the sway of men who, like Lule, would be unsympathetic to Tanzania's political philosophy. He therefore named as convenors four men whose political views were unquestionably radical but who, again to avoid conflict with Britain, were not known supporters of Obote. They were: Dan Nabudere, Edward Rugumayo, Yash Tandon and Omwony Ojwok. The first two, from the point of view of age, bridged the gap between the old political leaders and the new radically-minded nationalists upon whose support they relied and who wanted power for themselves.

The way had been prepared for such a conference by the hitherto unproductive Uganda Freedom Movement, the convenors among them, one group of them based in Dar es Salaam and the other in Nairobi. They had called a meeting of Ugandan exiles in Nairobi on 1 January 1979 at which they had agreed to set up an organizing committee to pave the way for more extensive discussions. News of the proposed conference in Moshi spread rapidly, and Ugandan exiles began to converge on Tanzania from all over the world. Shafiq Arain, a former minister in the East African Community and a loyal supporter of Obote, had just returned to London when he was summoned back by Obote in order to be present at the meeting. In the airport in Geneva he was surprised to see many more Ugandans, some of whom were unknown to him, but all of whom were clearly heading for Tanzania. One man whom he knew well, Paulo Ssemogerere, formerly a close colleague of the DP leader, Benedicto Kiwanuka, who had been murdered by Amin, joined him and talked excitedly about the prospect of a return to Uganda. According to Arain, Ssemogerere automatically assumed that Obote would head the new government, as was only appropriate in view of the manner in which he had sustained the opposition to Amin in association with Nyerere. He said, however, that he hoped Obote would think in terms of forming a broadly based government so as to ensure unity among all the peoples of Uganda. With that view Arain, and, indeed, Obote himself, were in total agreement.

In Dar es Salaam Arain found things were not so clear cut. The convenors who had taken it upon themselves to determine who should and who should not attend the conference, did, indeed, invite Obote.

Although they said he could bring five associates, they insisted that he must be present in an individual capacity and not as leader of the UPC and putative president. Obote sought the advice of Nyerere who told him both orally and in writing that it would be wiser if he did not attend. Puzzled, Obote accepted Nyerere's opinion but, as he had been asked to do, named five supporters to attend. The five were not, however, admitted to the conference, nor were many other eminently worthy Ugandans who represented a wide range of valid interests. These included the Rt. Revd. Yona Okoth, university students in exile, and women whose husbands were currently fighting against Amin and who had formed an anti-Amin association in Tanzania as early as 1973. While members of both the UPC and the DP were present they were outnumbered by representatives of the various pressure groups which flocked to the meeting. Many of these latter groups had been conjured up solely for the purpose of attending the conference.

The anxiety of the convenors to ensure that the old political parties should not dominate the proceedings meant that the conference could lay little claim to speak for the unrepresented millions of the country it now proposed to rule. Such an arbitrary collection of individuals could have little prospect of creating a credible government, but the convenors had no intention that it should. The conference, they believed, would provide the facade behind which they themselves, and others of a similar political persuasion, could take control.

There were a number of obstacles in their way. First, in spite of their attempts to limit the role of the old parties, there were among those present several men, like Paulo Muwanga, admitted on the strength of his recent contact with Uganda, who were still loyal to the UPC. Next, they could not ignore the role of Nyerere who, to their surprise, insisted that the conservative Yusufu Lule must become head of state. Nor could they overlook the importance of the military who were represented at the conference, against the wishes of the convenors but on Nyerere's insistence, by Colonel Okello. The latter was a known follower of Obote, but had been briefed by Nyerere to support Lule's appointment. In spite of the convenors' attempts to determine who should attend the conference there were also present a number of people who positively welcomed Lule as leader and who hoped for a political future for Uganda very different from that conceived by the radicals. This meant that if the latter group were to retain any hold upon power they must institute a dual system of authority so that the influence of Lule and his supporters should not be paramount. As a result, friction among the future leaders of Uganda was endemic from the outset. To make matters worse, two accounts of the proceedings were later circulated, each claiming authenticity.

The conference transformed itself into the Uganda National Liberation

Front (UNLF) and Lule was named president of the front and chairman of an executive council, a body consisting of eleven men who were given the task of guiding the activities of the Front. It was also agreed that the president of the UNLF should, in due course, become president of Uganda. Unfortunately, the council had no time to make preparations before the UNLF was called upon to take over the government of Uganda and, not surprisingly, it proved ineffective.

More important for the future was another body set up by the conference, the National Consultative Council (NCC), originally called the Advisory Council, which, although it was supposed to consist of one representative of each of the groups present, in practice was dominated by the radicals and was chaired by Edward Rugumayo, who had been the left-wingers' candidate for the presidency.[21] In the radicals' version of the conference minutes, published later after Lule had begun to act too independently for their liking, it was to be claimed that, in the absence of a delegates' conference, the NCC should be supreme and should supervise and control the executive and the administration. Any temporary administrative arrangements made by the executive must be ratified by the NCC. At the conference itself this relationship was certainly not made clear, and a recipe which made the prospect of a clash with the government almost unavoidable may actually have been invented after the conference had dispersed. But the existence of what were virtually two governments, one led by Lule and one by Rugumayo, was the natural outcome of a conflict of interests and intentions at Moshi. That Lule was not the man to overcome this conflict was soon revealed when he compiled a list of members of his prospective cabinet. The list demonstrated all too clearly that he was out of touch with the situation in Uganda and knew few of the people who could wield influence. Nyerere sought the help of Obote who, in consultation with the leaders of the UNLF, excluding Lule, compiled an alternative, coalition list.

Meanwhile, the Tanzanian army was advancing steadily upon Kampala, accompanied by Ojok's force of exiles, and they were received everywhere with jubilation by the Ugandan population, including the Baganda. To ensure that there should be no problem when victory was won, a message was sent secretly by the Tanzanian government asking Ojok if he was prepared to accept the Moshi conference's decision that Lule should be president. While the fighting for Kampala was still raging Ojok had induced an engineer to muster a number of technicians who proceeded to re-open telephone contact with Dar es Salaam on the morning of 11 April, the day on which Kampala fell to the invading forces. Ojok had then telephoned Obote to ask what he should say when announcing the capture of the capital. Obote told him he should call upon all his fellow countrymen to accept a national government. He must, however, make no reference to the UPC or to Obote himself. Consequently, when Ojok received the message from the Tanzanian government, he assumed it came with the approval of Obote and made no demur about accepting it.

The fall of Kampala came before the UNLF had had time to make any detailed plans for the government of Uganda. On 11 April Lule, ignoring the list compiled by Obote at Nyerere's request, hastily named a cabinet which was intended to reflect the ethnic composition of Uganda's population. Unfortunately for any hopes of a smooth assumption of power, only four of those nominated were simultaneously members of the NCC. This underlined the deep division between Lule and his self-styled supervisors. After a hurried flight to Uganda, Lule was sworn in as president on 13 April 1979. For the Baganda it was a popular move. Without belonging to the old hierarchy, Lule had never spoken against the *kabaka*. He was quiet in manner, he had had considerable experience in diplomatic circles and, of course, he was a Muganda. Moreover, when he was sworn in as president he had spoken first in English and then in Luganda, the language of the kingdom. He had said, 'This is our opportunity', which the Bugandan old guard, pricking up their ears, had interpreted as meaning that this was the moment for Buganda to assert that supremacy in Ugandan affairs for which they had fought so long. Herein lay the beginnings of the revival of old divisions. Yet even outside Buganda Lule's appointment was not unpopular, because his reputation suggested he would act with moderation, a pleasing prospect after so many years of violence.

Unfortunately, intelligent, polite and polished though he was, Lule was no politician, as his timid performance as a minister under the Protectorate government had clearly demonstrated. Although of a dignified appearance, he lacked a commanding presence. Nor had he read the omens at the Moshi conference. He assumed that he had come to office with all the powers of an executive president appointed under the 1967 republican constitution. He proposed to rule through his cabinet, with the NCC, as its name suggested, acting only in a consultative capacity. This approach did not appeal to the NCC. Differences of opinion soon arose over almost every aspect of policy. Lule's attempt to restore the provincial administration, with Buganda once more united, led to fears that old conflicts would be revived. His desire to rid the country as quickly as possible of Tanzanian troops did not meet with the approval even of some members of his own cabinet. Further, his use of what he deemed to be his executive powers to arrange an emergency aid programme of £100 million worried those of a more radical outlook, Nyerere among them, who disliked the implied reliance upon a capitalist economy and who feared Uganda might soon be at the mercy of foreign speculators. According to Lule, Nyerere's disapproval of what was taking place was made plain at a meeting held in Mwanza on 2 May. There, Lule was later to claim, the Tanzanian president stated that he wanted his troops to remain in Uganda in order to create a climate in which the country could evolve as a socialist state. He was anxious to integrate the communications systems of Tanzania and Uganda and was prepared to offer Tanga as an outlet for Ugandan goods in transit in the hope of weaning Uganda from its reliance upon its link with Mombasa through Kenya. He also stressed the importance he attached to Obote's return to Uganda.[22] Privately, he already had doubts about the wisdom of Lule's appointment.

Those doubts surfaced in a conversation Nyerere had with Obote in the first week of June. Because of the divisions that had rapidly emerged among the leadership in Uganda, Nyerere said, Lule's administration existed in name only. He proposed to summon Lule to another meeting in Mwanza and he wanted Obote to be present to prove to the Ugandan president that he, Nyerere, and Obote were at one on all matters relating to Uganda. Obote, who had been understandably angry at being forced to stay in Tanzania lest his presence in Uganda should prove disruptive, at first demurred, arguing with some bitterness that this was to be a meeting of governments. As a refugee he had no *locus standi* in such an assembly. He added that he was deeply grateful for the manner in which he and his family had been cared for, but he would be an outsider at Mwanza. He could not sustain his anger for long in the presence of a man he so much admired and respected, however, and at length he agreed to attend.

Lule, meanwhile, persisted with his own line of action. On 7 June, the day before he was summoned, with his cabinet, to the meeting with Nyerere in Mwanza, he dismissed or demoted, without consulting anyone, a number of his critics and replaced them with ministers more in sympathy with his own views. Among the latter was Grace Ibingira, Obote's old opponent. When challenged by the NCC Lule claimed that, from the outset, he had appointed his cabinet and made promotions within the army without consultation and no-one had protested because he was simply exercising his valid powers under the 1967 constitution. His critics, led by Rugumayo, said that the Moshi conference had been the constitution-making body for post-Amin Uganda and that in making those appointments Lule had acted contrary to the rules which had been adopted at the conference. However, they went on, because the minutes of the conference had not been available at the time, no exception had been taken to what Lule had previously done, but he had no authority to act in a similar manner subsequently. Here, then, was a total clash of opinion to which there appeared to be no amicable solution and which the meeting in Mwanza could do little to dispel.

In the course of the discussions it became clear that Lule's position in Uganda was extremely precarious. To strengthen that position he had secretly planned to appoint the popular Festo Kivengere, Bishop of Kigezi, in South-western Uganda, as vice-president. His plan, however, had become known to Nyerere and to Obote, and Nyerere, referring first to his surprise that only Obote should seem unwelcome in Uganda, went on to suggest that Obote should become vice-president. Unaware that the Tanzanian president knew of his plan, Lule hastened to say that there was no office of vice-president and, in any event, although Obote had friends in Uganda, he also had enemies, and his return would create a security problem. Nyerere replied that the politician who had no enemies did not exist. Lule was adamant, but went so far as to offer Obote the post of ambassador to the United Nations on condition that he went straight to New York without visiting Uganda.

As the delegates were leaving, Obote called Muwanga aside and urged him to activate the UPC because he felt sure an election was imminent. Muwanga, who was a member of Lule's cabinet, was in no sense Obote's man, but he had always appeared to be a loyal member of the UPC and Obote did not doubt that he would like to see the UPC in power again through the electoral process. In any case, Obote was convinced that the only way to give the government a firm basis of authority, and the only hope of putting an end to the divisions which had already begun to tear the country apart, lay in consulting the electorate as quickly as possible.

In the event, more drastic action was taken by the NCC, which had no urgent desire to put its authority to the test of an election but disliked Lule's use of what it regarded as dictatorial powers. Charging the president with having made fundamental changes to the composition of his cabinet without consultation, the NCC passed a vote of no confidence in him. The council, with Rugumayo and his fellow radicals to the fore, then called upon the cabinet to intervene. Many members of that body had also turned against Lule, fearing that the changes he had made had been intended to strengthen the influence of Buganda and the other kingdoms against the representatives of other ethnic groups. A cabinet meeting in Entebbe on 19 June dissolved into a lengthy wrangle. Lule himself, unaccustomed to the hurly-burly of politics, and criticized it seemed on every side, felt his pride wounded and his integrity questioned. He therefore withdrew from the meeting in order to telephone to Kampala to ask for a police detachment to be sent to arrest his critics. Pending its arrival he invited the Tanzanian troops on guard at state house to intervene. They refused on the ground that they took orders only from Tanzania, and when the police detachment arrived the soldiers turned it away.

By this time the cabinet, having concluded that Lule could no longer continue as president, had set about choosing a successor. There was no consensus among those present and three candidates were considered, two of them being Rugumayo and Muwanga. On the first vote Rugumayo gained most support but did not have an overall majority. Muwanga, who won the least number of votes, dropped out, and at that point the name of Godfrey Binaisa was mentioned. Binaisa had been attorney-general in

Obote's government until ill-health had forced him to retire. The third candidate then dropped out and the decision rested between Rugumayo and Binaisa. In the voting which followed Binaisa won a slender majority, a clear indication that within the cabinet at least the young radicals were not in control. An emissary was immediately sent to Kampala to summon Binaisa to Entebbe. Awakened in the early hours of the morning he was convinced that he was to be arrested. Instead, and to his considerable relief, he was told on his arrival in Entebbe that he was to be president. The news was signalled to Nyerere, who told Obote what had happened. The latter gave it as his opinion that, with an unelected president, dissension would still remain, but Nyerere said he thought Binaisa was a much shrewder politician than Lule and would be able to control his subordinates.

From this point all Obote's efforts were concentrated upon returning to Uganda. Even based in Dar es Salaam he had done all he could to reactivate the UPC and it was at that time he coined the slogan that all Uganda's politicans must be subjected to 'the verdict of the high court of the electorate.' Binaisa was duly sworn in as president on 20 June. Lule, meanwhile, was conducted to Dar es Salaam under armed guard where, he was later to claim, Nyerere urged him to recognize Binaisa's appointment.[23] Although he was a Muganda, Binaisa had no foothold in the kingdom. His earlier association with Obote's government had cut him off from his fellow Baganda, by whom his present assumption of office in the wake of Lule's overthrow was seen as a further betrayal. There were demonstrations against him in Kampala which were dispersed, with a considerable show of force, on the order of Museveni, minister of state for defence.

Although Binaisa appointed ten members of the UPC in his cabinet of thirty, he was in no sense keeping the presidential seat warm for Obote. Having been taken by surprise by his appointment he had, nevertheless, every intention of remaining in office. He saw no reason to resist the pressure from the young radicals who had played a dominant role in ousting Lule when they called for a two-year ban on political parties. At the same time, he tried to create a balance of interests in his cabinet, retaining Yoweri Museveni, a known opponent of Obote, as minister of state for defence, while restoring Paulo Muwanga, a Muganda but also a supporter of the UPC, who had been demoted by Lule, to the ministry of internal affairs.

In November, a meeting of the Commonwealth Conference was due to take place in Lusaka. Obote sought the approval of Nyerere to attend the meeting so as to have a word with Binaisa. Nyerere agreed, and when they met Obote told Binaisa that he would like to celebrate Christmas in Uganda and then to stay there. To Obote's astonishment and dismay, Binaisa collapsed in front of him, and Obote was afraid he would be accused of assassinating the president. Before a doctor could arrive, however, Binaisa recovered, and when Obote repeated his request the president said he thought it would be unwise for him to return and even more so to stay in the country. Obote reluctantly accepted the advice, but subsequently importuned Nyerere at regular intervals to be allowed to return home as a private citizen.

In spite of Nyerere's optimistic forecast Binaisa proved unable to keep a firm hold on his subordinates and he met with considerable difficulty in maintaining law and order. One of the reasons for this was the rapid and unco-ordinated growth of the army. In view of Okello's support for Lule's presidency and Ojok's agreement to it, the UNLF had appointed them as commander and chief of staff respectively of the Uganda National Liberation Army (UNLA). They had an unenviable, perhaps an impossible task. The small, disciplined force which Ojok had originally commanded during the invasion had grown rapidly during the pursuit of Amin's forces as they withdrew eastward to take refuge in Kenya, or northward, via Teso, Lango and Acholi, to cross the Sudanese border. Arms and uniforms were easily acquired by anyone who was prepared to use them. They had been jettisoned or sold by Amin's defeated troops or were seized from stores abandoned by the retreating army.

Museveni, with his Banyaruanda recruits in Western Uganda, was not the only one to muster supporters under arms and to attach them nominally to the UNLA. Nevertheless, Museveni's action might seem particularly open to question since he was minister of state for defence under both Lule and Binaisa and thus effectively in control of the defence portfolio which was only nominally supervised in each case by the president. In the east and in the north other members of the NCC and of the cabinet sought to strengthen their own hands in similar fashion. Former NCOs, who had been retired on captains' pensions by Obote's government when it tried to rid the country of the *effendi* system, were now recalled to the colours as commissioned officers by different factions within the UNLF, while officers and NCOs who had fought in the liberation army were given rapid promotion. In this way the UNLA ceased to be a tightly controlled unit. Instead it became an armed rabble, with each component part inadequately officered and owing loyalty to different political leaders, while all were prepared to use their arms to loot or to take reprisals against anyone they or their sponsors deemed to be their enemies.

In Kampala itself there were numerous cases of brutality but there was little prospect of redress because no-one, apart from the perpetrators, knew who was responsible for them. In May 1979 Museveni's levies accompanied the Tanzanian army to the West Nile District, in the extreme north-west of the country, in pursuit of Amin's men. The Tanzanian forces withdrew in September and thereafter Museveni's troops undertook a campaign of reprisals against anyone in the region whom they deemed to have been sympathetic to Amin. Their actions left a legacy of resentment against the UNLA and the central government which was to last for many years and which made it easy for Amin's supporters to filter back over the border and foment trouble. A measure of retribution was, in this instance, meted out against the aggressors when Binaisa removed Museveni from the ministry of defence in the course of a cabinet reshuffle in November. There was an ironical aspect to this move in that Museveni had himself been urging that Ojok be relieved of his appointment as chief of staff.

Binaisa, it should be remarked, made his cabinet changes without consulting the NCC, the very act which had led to Lule's downfall. The NCC did, in fact, debate the matter angrily for two days, but Binaisa survived. Whatever the reason for this it can scarcely have been a result of the enlargement of the council a month earlier, because the change had not led to any noticeable alteration in the character of the membership. The intention behind the enlargement had been to incorporate people who had remained in Uganda throughout Amin's regime into a body which, hitherto, had consisted entirely of exiles. This was a response, in part at least, to pressure from the general public for greater representation in the country's central policy-making body. There had been a widespread demand for the elections which it had been agreed at Moshi should be held within eighteen months from the final defeat of Amin, and that had occurred on 3 June when the last vestiges of Amin's army were driven from the country. Binaisa, however, was as reluctant as the members of the NCC to jeopardize the existing distribution of authority by seeking popular approval. It was decided, therefore, that the district councils, which had themselves been nominated by the government, should submit the names of possible candidates for consideration by the NCC. That body would then select three or four names of people deemed to be suitable to stand for election in each district. Finally, the district councils would act as electoral colleges to choose the successful candidates. In this way the NCC ensured that any increase in numbers would not result in the introduction of too many hostile elements into their midst.

Although a nominal tribute had been paid to the idea of greater representation of the people, it did little to increase Binaisa's personal popularity. This was particularly the case among the erstwhile supporters of the UPC who, remembering him as a former party member, saw him now as something of a usurper. Nor had the original object of the measure been wholly achieved. A considerable number of the newly elected members were themselves, like the original members of the NCC, returned exiles rather than people in more immediate touch with the population at large.[24] The UNLF, in consequence, had little popular support now that the euphoria following upon Amin's defeat had begun to fade and it was clear that little had been done to improve the lot of those who had suffered materially from his rule. Suspicion grew that the members of the new government were using their power for their own financial benefit. The whole society had become so demoralized by Amin's arbitrary tyranny that corruption was accepted as essential to survival and was no longer condemned, except by those who were unfortunate enough to be unable to profit from it. The black market was the norm in virtually every aspect of commercial life. But envy of those who too blatantly abused their positions of authority for their own profit still created deep divisions in the country.[25]

Some of the leading Baganda had survived Amin's regime without serious damage to their material prosperity, but the precariousness of their good fortune had imposed a strain upon them which they were glad to shrug off when Amin was overthrown. While prepared to accept almost any saviour, they had been particularly pleased by the appointment of Lule as president. His overthrow had blighted their hopes of Buganda's ascendancy, and the competition for the fruits of victory made them wary of any leader who might appear to threaten the strong economic position which they had built for themselves through the good fortune of inheritance, by their own hard work, and, more recently, by the judicious use of corruption and an appropriate measure of collaboration. They had been in the forefront of those who protested at Lule's overthrow and now they viewed with apprehension the continuing uncertainty in the relations between the president and the NCC. The inability of the government to maintain order provided further grounds for doubting whether the regime of Binaisa could survive.

Thus it was that the spectre of Obote's return began to cast its shadow over them. Whereas in April they might have accepted him as president, provided he could have brought peace and unity, now there were so many divisive factors at work and so little prospect of stability that Obote began, once again, to appear as the great enemy in the eyes of the more prosperous Baganda. It was in November 1979 that he was first spoken of as the progenitor, even if only indirectly, of Amin's tyranny.[26] Before then, whatever the degree of his unpopularity, he had been seen as Amin's victim, even if there had been rejoicing at his discomfiture. From this time his opponents increasingly echoed the new accusation until many people forgot that Obote, since the coup, had consistently campaigned against Amin. Instead they came to regard him as having deliberately paved the way for the atrocities of Amin's rule.

That Binaisa retained office as long as he did was due to the divisions among the other groups within the government rather than to his popularity or achievements. After his disagreement with the NCC in November over his cabinet changes his position was constantly open to challenge. But there was neither a united voice raised against him nor yet a potential usurper who could command sufficient allegiance to provide a threat. In February 1980, however, Binaisa took the first step which would lead to his downfall. He removed Paulo Muwanga from the office of minister of the interior because he had banned three newspapers. Nyerere, who had been watching the disputes in the Ugandan government with grave concern, insisted on Muwanga's reinstatement. He was less than pleased when Muwanga then began a campaign within the NCC to oust Binaisa, so he sent his foreign minister to Uganda to bring pressure to bear on Binaisa to resolve the crisis which was developing.

Early in March Nyerere summoned Binaisa to Dar es Salaam to tell him of his dissatisfaction with the reports he was receiving of factionalism and corruption in the Ugandan government. Binaisa could scarcely be held responsible for what was taking place, except in so far as he had been unable to salvage anything from the post-Amin chaos which had only been exacerbated by the unhappy interlude provided by Lule's feeble presidency. Resentfully he started back for Uganda, and the warm welcome he received from President Moi as he passed through Nairobi could have been no more than a temporary alleviation of his sufferings. He knew full well that Moi's sentiments resulted less from any respect the Kenyan president might have had for him personally than from Moi's concern about the influence Nyerere was able to exert upon Uganda's affairs.

It was not long after Binaisa's visit to Dar es Salaam that Obote announced his intention of returning to Uganda and competing in the elections as soon as they were introduced. He said it was clear that the various office-holders had failed to achieve any sort of reconciliation among themselves and that they had made no progress towards reconstructing the country. By way of a riposte, Binaisa announced on 19 March that elections might, indeed, be held as early as October, but that anyone wishing to stand as a candidate must do so under the umbrella of the UNLF because political parties were divisive. Former members of the UPC and the DP protested vigorously against what they thought to be both a denial of political freedom and an attempt by those in office to perpetuate their hold on power. Supporters of the political parties must still have been in a minority in the NCC, however, because the council endorsed Binaisa's proposal. Shortly afterwards, it was agreed that elections should take place in December. Early in May, the government formally banned political parties from campaigning in preparation for the elections. Obote responded that he would defy the ban, which he said was unconstitutional, and that he would return to Uganda on 27 May to begin his campaign.

Obote's return was timely, for in the middle of May Binaisa was overthrown. The cause of his downfall was a clash with Brigadier Ojok, whom he dismissed in an attempt, as he claimed, to improve relations between the public and the armed forces, which had taken over security duties in Kampala from the Tanzanian army in March. It was a dangerous move, for Ojok had a powerful following within the army and the support of the armed forces was vital in a country so disturbed and ill-governed. Ojok refused both to accept the post of ambassador to Algeria, which Binaisa offered him, or to surrender his position as chief of staff. Muwanga, who had been waiting his moment to attack Binaisa, spoke up in Ojok's defence, claiming that the president had no authority to dismiss the chief of staff without consulting the NCC. Binaisa, speaking as president and commander in chief of the armed forces, disagreed.

This was Muwanga's moment. Many of his leading rivals in the UNLF were out of the country. Nabudere was in Yugoslavia, attending the funeral of President Tito. Rugumayo was in Tanzania, as, too, was Museveni, while Tandon was also away from Uganda. In his role as chairman of the military commission of the UNLF, Muwanga decided to trust to the support of the army in a bid to overthrow Binaisa. Museveni was, it is true, vice-chairman of the military commission, but his absence from the country, coupled with his dislike for the president, ensured that he would cause no trouble. Muwanga therefore signed a statement accusing Binaisa of betraying the Ugandans and Tanzanians who had died in the fight to overthrow Amin, and claiming that the military commission had taken charge of the country and was committed to holding elections in which political parties would be free to sponsor candidates. Museveni was opposed to this latter proviso but was outvoted by the other members of the commission, comprising Muwanga, Ojok and two other army officers, Zed Maruru and William Omaria.

The success of the coup would entirely depend upon the support of President Nyerere who, although critical of Binaisa, was worried by this new upheaval. Nyerere held a meeting in Arusha with President Moi of Kenya and President Nimeiry of the Sudan to discuss what had taken place in Uganda. They agreed to accept the new government on the understanding that, pending elections, the NCC should be retained as the country's law-making body. Nimeiry, who had been surrounded by Soviet advisers when Obote was in Khartoum in 1972, was now less attracted by socialism and was not a little concerned lest Nyerere might try to impose a Tanzanian-style socialist government upon Uganda. Under the mistaken impression that Rugumayo was less left-wing than Nyerere, he took the former, who was still in Tanzania, back to Nairobi on his return journey to the Sudan, in the hope that he might be able to exercise a moderating influence in Uganda. But Rugumayo, like most of the radicals with the exception of Museveni, refused Muwanga's invitation to return home, preferring to remain at a distance from events there. Museveni returned at the instance of Nyerere, with whom he had maintained relatively close contact for many years since he had first gone to Tanzania as a student.

Meanwhile, a new cabinet was named, in which supporters of Obote replaced seven of Binaisa's appointees. John Luwuliza Kirunda, one of the new members, typified this change of emphasis. Kirunda, a Musoga and leader of the pro-Obote faction in the NCC, became minister of labour. Obote had first got to know Kirunda when the latter was a medical student at Makerere and had helped the UPC in the 1961 elections. When Amin seized power Kirunda was studying gynaecology in England, but had returned to Uganda at the end of his course and had worked for a time in Masaka and then at Mulago hospital in Kampala. He disliked what was happening in the country, however, and fled to Nairobi. He wanted to go to England, but Obote persuaded him that his skill was needed in Africa and he agreed to work in Lusaka. He had been present at the Moshi conference and had been elected to the NCC. Returning to Uganda with Lule, he had been active in reviving the UPC there. Later in 1980, he was to become secretary-general of the party and subsequently minister for the interior.

Muwanga presided over the proceedings of this new cabinet in which four army officers served as ministers without portfolio. Now that he was in power, however, his intentions were far from clear. But Obote's return to Uganda on 27 May 1980 meant that elections could not be long delayed, and if the UPC was victorious, Muwanga would have to hand over authority to the man whom the UPC members accepted without question as their leader. Of Muwanga's willingness to do that Obote may have had some slight doubt, but any such uncertainty was almost certainly without justification at that time. Muwanga's defection six years later may well have been due less to any long-concealed disloyalty to Obote than to a growing conviction that his leader no longer trusted him. That, however, lay in the future, and to all intents and purposes Muwanga behaved for the time being as a committed member of the UPC, so much so that he was to be accused of treating other political parties unfairly.

Obote's deep concern was about the role the army may have played in supporting the military commission in the overthrow of Binaisa and about Museveni's influence over the army. On both counts his doubts were confirmed when the military commission rejected the proposal to reintroduce at once a presidential form of government similar to that which had existed before Amin's coup, a proposal he had submitted at Nyerere's request. Obote was later to discover that the men urging Muwanga to pursue this negative line were those former members of the UPC whose extreme radical views had done the party grave disservice during Obote's prime ministership and who now had the support of Museveni. Change would have to be postponed until the elections were held, a compromise which Obote considered to be wholly unsatisfactory, although it appeared to be the only basis upon which any co-operation was possible.

Thousands of well-wishers greeted Obote on his return to Uganda, including some of the members of the new government. He had taken great care over preparing the speech he would make on his arrival and had made sure of Nyerere's support by submitting it to him for his approval and by discussing its contents with him at great length. Before leaving Dar es Salaam, he had given a dinner party for President and Mrs Nyerere and for a number of leading figures in Tanzania as a gesture of thanks for all the kindness that had been shown to him and his family. He handed over his cows to the ruling political party and Mrs Obote gave a piece of land which she had cultivated to a special friend.

In the course of his prepared speech to the people of Uganda, Obote took the opportunity offered by the presence of so many influential persons to deny that he was hostile to the former kingdoms and that he had been in any way responsible for the excesses committed by Amin. It was a popular declaration. Recognizing the powerful challenge which Obote was certain to offer in the forthcoming elections, Museveni decided to form his own party. The leader of the party, he said, must have two qualifications. First, he must not be a Muganda because the DP was led by a Muganda, nor should he be a northerner because the UPC had a northern leader. The relevance of the condition stated is difficult to see because the DP was not exclusively a Bugandan party, nor was UPC support confined to the north. The argument left open a place for a leader from the west or the east, however, and Museveni certainly came from the west. Second, the leader must have an army to support him, and Museveni was making sure that he could meet that qualification. His recruits already numbered several thousand, while the UNLA, of which Museveni's force was nominally a part, now totalled something in the order of 25,000 men under arms – they could scarcely be described as soldiers. Finally, Museveni declared, the new party must resist any attempt by a dictator to seize power by military force, an ironical comment in the light of his own subsequent path to office.

The outcome of Museveni's efforts was the formation of the Uganda Patriotic Movement (UPM), which was launched on 14 June at a rally in Kampala attended by about 4,000 people. In the same month the DP also announced that it proposed to elect a leader. Yusufu Lule declared his intention of returning to Uganda to seek election as soon as he received written assurances of his safety. He reached Nairobi, but the DP did not welcome his offer and his supporters were not allowed to take part in the party conference. Paulo Ssemogerere was virtually assured of the leadership. He had worked closely with the former leader, Benedicto Kiwanuka, and when the latter was assassinated by order of Amin he had been a constant source of help to Kiwanuka's widow. She now accompanied Ssemogerere as he attempted to rally the support of his party and her presence gave him the appearance of being heir apparent to the leadership.

Lule's challenge was finally dissipated when Muwanga, as chairman of the ruling military commission and acting on the advice of President Nyerere, refused him permission to re-enter Uganda unless he withdrew some of the accusations he had made after being ousted from the presidency. Although this pleased the DP, they did not publicize their satisfaction. Instead, it was Muwanga who incurred the wrath of the crowds of Baganda who lined the route between Entebbe airport and Kampala along which they expected Lule to travel on 17 June, and who had to return to their homes disappointed. Obote, too, was unhappy with the decision to prevent Lule from returning, but when he approached Muwanga on the subject the latter insisted that the final word had lain with Nyerere. Obote also raised the question of the continuing detention of Binaisa, but was told that the Tanzanian army was adamant.

Soon after his return, Obote undertook an extensive tour of the country. Everywhere he was greeted by delighted crowds. In Moroto, the main town of Karamoja, the people insisted upon dancing all day long, claiming that they had not danced since Amin's coup in 1971. Obote was presented with a sack of old Ugandan money which the Karamojong leaders said they had kept until the day of the return of the UPC. Unfortunately, the money was of no value, because the currency had been changed by both Amin and Binaisa, but the gift was a sincere token of Karamojong support for the party. In Sebei, also in Eastern Uganda, the people similarly demonstrated their jubilation with dancing. In Lira, the main town of Obote's home district, teams of choirs sang until after midnight. In Acholi, in the north-west, both Obote and his wife were brought near to tears when they saw the large numbers of orphans who attended the rallies by which they were greeted. Further west still, in West Nile District, their advance party was ambushed by remnants of Amin's army which had crossed back into Uganda from the Sudan, but that was the only opposition they encountered. Even in Masaka, a Muganda county chief appealed to Obote to urge the military commission to send supplies of maize meal and beans to combat the famine that was overwhelming his people. This was a very serious indication of the extent to which drought was ravaging the country, for the Baganda would not normally have deigned to eat maize.

It was not only the threat of famine which cast a cloud over the rejoicing which marked Obote's return. He was deeply disturbed by all the indications he saw of the reappearance of the divisions to which Uganda had formerly been prey. In a speech in Mbale he warned politicians to be wary of encouraging faction. Towards the end of June, in an effort to avert the revival of tribalism presaged by the reaction of the

Baganda to the exclusion of Lule, he called for a government of national unity irrespective of which party was successful in the elections. To promote his scheme he stressed that the UPC was not a communist party, as its opponents had often maintained, and that its members were in no way committed to the continuing presence of Tanzanian troops in Uganda.

His detractors remained unconvinced. An approach to Ssemogerere with the proposal that the UPC and the DP should form a coalition government was rejected, although Ssemogerere said he would be willing to offer seats in a DP cabinet to a number of UPC members if his party was victorious. Obote demurred, pointing out that this fell some distance short of a coalition. Already, however, ancient prejudices had taken hold, and were strengthened by an increase in violence in Kampala, which was thought by many to be motivated by political rivalry. The murder of Leonard Mugwanya, a DP politician and son of one of the party's founders, gave credence to that belief among those who saw Muwanga as the agent of the UPC and the murderers as his henchmen. The fact that some of the acts of violence were committed by men in uniform had little significance. Uniforms were easily come by, and even if the perpetrators of the violence were members of the UNLA it would be difficult to know to whom they owed allegiance, or whether they were not simply acting individually to pay off old scores. Lacking sufficient numbers of trained officers and NCOs, Okello and Ojok could not hope to discipline the ill-assorted troops under their nominal command.

These problems were echoed in other parts of the country where they could not readily be attributed to electioneering. In the north-east, where Obote had been so rapturously received, a number of Karamojong who had acquired weapons from Amin's retreating troops carried out several raids. The response of the UNLA was heavy-handed and badly co-ordinated. As a result, considerable damage was inflicted upon innocent people, many of whom had already suffered at the hands of the raiders. Then, in October, former members of Amin's forces who had taken refuge in the Sudan and Zaire recrossed the border into Amin's former home district of West Nile, and its main town, Arua. Ugandan and Tanzanian troops quickly recaptured the lost territory and then seized the opportunity to take reprisals against the civilian population, whom they accused of siding with the invaders. There can be little doubt that some of the UNLA forces who had formerly served in the army and who had suffered under Amin brought an added zest to their attack upon the tyrant's fellow tribesmen.

It should not be forgotten, however, that at this stage the UNLA was not, in any sense, Obote's army, nor yet the army of the UPC. Officially it was the instrument of the military commission, but its members owed their loyalty to a variety of sponsors rather than to the government. Accusations that meetings of the DP were subjected to harassment by the army, and thus by Muwanga acting on behalf of the UPC, were also open to question. That troublemakers tried to break up party meetings was beyond doubt. But who the troublemakers were, and what their motives, cannot be determined. Obote, meanwhile, carried out a second tour of Uganda as part of his electioneering programme, on a platform of peace, unity and prosperity. Again he was well received everywhere, including Buganda, where no-one even went so far as to enquire about his views on any future role for the traditional rulers.

Chapter 10

President again

The approach to the elections was bedevilled by suspicion and wild accusations, the chief target being Muwanga, whom his critics constantly accused of favouring the UPC. Obote himself was wary about Muwanga's motives for a different reason in view of his association as chairman of the military commission with Museveni, the deputy chairman. His main concern was that the two might try to subvert the election process in order to retain power in the hands of the military commission. His doubts, however, seemed daily less well founded as Muwanga pursued his idiosyncratic but apparently enthusiastic road towards elections at the end of 1980.

At the outset, Muwanga rejected the proposal that there should be an all-party commission to make recommendations regarding the elections, arguing that this would delay what was already an urgent necessity. In spite of there being eleven dissenting votes from DP, UPM and Conservative Party (Bugandan traditionalist) members of the cabinet, the government decided that the new parliament should consist of 126 members. Yusufu Lule was to claim that this gave 'the North', with a smaller population, more seats than were allocated to the more populous Buganda. His argument was flawed on a number of counts. In the first place, he did not define the north, but appears to have lumped together both the Northern and Eastern Provinces while ignoring the Western Province. But the population of the Northern and Eastern Provinces together certainly outnumbered that of Buganda, while the Northern Province itself was awarded considerably fewer seats than was Buganda. Moreover, not all the north, or even the east, was exclusively UPC country. Acholi and Busoga, for example, could reasonably be expected to return some DP members. The intention, it is true, was that constituencies should be roughly equal in population, but because some of the northern constituencies were mainly inhabited by pastoralists who ranged over a large area where communications were difficult it was accepted that population numbers in such constituencies might be smaller. For different reasons some of the less populous constituencies were also to be found in

Buganda. In fact the overall electoral profile was similar to that of 1961, although Kampala now had four constituencies, rather than three, and instead of being almost exclusively urban they each embraced some of the surrounding countryside in an attempt to raise the population to something approaching that of the other constituencies.

Lule's criticism marked the beginning of a campaign to suggest that the elections were not conducted fairly. It also inaugurated the concept of a north/south division in Uganda, a claim which had certainly had little previous justification – unless Buganda is to be equated with 'the South'. It was a concept which, once aired, was to become a regrettable reality under the pressure of later civil strife, when skilful use was made of the accusation that 'the North' was victimizing 'the South' in order to justify whatever was done against the new government by its opponents. The claim that the elections were unfair was also widely used as a justification for all the acts of rebellion which were soon to revive some of the worst features of Amin's period of misrule. It must, therefore, be examined fully.

It is particularly important to look at the role of Muwanga, whose influence was paramount during the crucial period leading up to the elections. If the argument about the size of constituencies was largely unfounded, Muwanga's insistence that the eleven who had disagreed with his decision to limit the number of constituencies to 126 should either accept cabinet solidarity or resign was more open to question. He withdrew his demand two days later, after talks with Ssemogerere, but the eleven did agree to abide by majority decisions in the future, so that he gained his point, whether rightly or wrongly. The motive for his behaviour on this occasion is not clear. His action could not have helped the UPC, unless he hoped thereby to remove all members of other parties from the cabinet so as to allow himself greater freedom to promote the cause of the UPC without overt criticism. It is not a convincing argument.

The dispute did not end there. Members of the Democratic Party and of the Uganda Patriotic Movement began to boycott meetings of the NCC because, they still maintained, the military commission was favouring the UPC. The leaders of the DP nevertheless continued to urge their candidates to register for the elections which were to be held on 10 December. Museveni's UPM took a more hostile line and sought a high court injunction to prevent registration from taking place. The petition was rejected, whereupon the UPM, too, began to register its candidates. The incidence of violence in and around Kampala caused grave disquiet, however, and the DP leadership accused Ojok of ordering the arrest and harassment of its members, a claim which Ojok stoutly denied. In other parts of the country, violence more clearly unconnected with the elections continued to create difficulties both for the general public and for those charged with maintaining order. Since May there had been reports that Karamojong, armed with weapons taken from Amin's retreating forces, had once more been raiding parts of their own district as well as the neighbouring district of Teso. The troops of the UNLA proved ineffective in putting a stop to these attacks and their heavy-handed methods again caused almost as much suffering to the peasantry as did the raiders themselves.

In October, former members of Amin's army who had taken refuge in Zaire and the Sudan recrossed the border and seized part of West Nile District. As before, Tanzanian and UNLA forces recaptured the lost territory and then took the opportunity to inflict heavy casualties on the civilian population. This incident provided a further occasion for accusations of election-rigging to be made against Muwanga. It was claimed that he took advantage of the troubles in West Nile to suspend elections in the district and that the electoral commission appointed by the government then declared the six seats in the district to have been won by the UPC unopposed because it was the only party to present candidates in accordance with the regulations. The latter part of the statement was, indeed, correct. The superior organization of the UPC enabled it to overcome the serious difficulties which candidates encountered in trying to meet the conditions for registration laid down in the more peaceful circumstances of 1961/2. Some of the prospective DP candidates were especially handicapped because they had fled into Zaire to escape the attentions of the vengeful security forces. When they returned they were unable to sort themselves out with sufficient speed to meet the deadline for registration. Doubtless Muwanga was less than distressed by the DP candidates' failure to meet the rules laid down for them and had no hesitation over enforcing the regulations to the letter, but the nature of the charges levelled against him were clearly false. Similarly, the claim that the disturbed state of Karamoja District also gave unopposed seats to the UPC in dubious circumstances had even less justification. Only one seat in that district was uncontested.

Far from deriving satisfaction from this wrangling and the discomfiture of his political opponents, Obote himself was deeply disturbed because he was all too aware of the threat the confusion presented to any hope of unity. In a further attempt to create a community of interest he closed a conference of the UPC in Kampala on 6 November by stressing the non-tribal character of the party and went on to appeal to the Baganda to support him and not to pursue a separatist line. He admitted that, during his former presidency, mistakes had been made and that his government had sometimes overreacted to events in the kingdom. But he insisted that he had no personal quarrel with the Baganda. The Bugandan leadership was unimpressed. Having had their hopes of power raised during Lule's brief presidency, they were not easily reconciled to a role which denied them even the prospect of being first among equals, and they still believed all was not lost for them. The Conservative Party was intended to represent the interests of the kingdom, but the Bugandan leaders could not be confident of victory through that channel. Instead, they brought their influence to bear upon the Bugandan electorate to support their former opponents in the Democratic Party, who had more widespread support and with whom they hoped at least to be able to make a deal if they failed to dominate them.

The Democratic Party, however, lacked the organizational skills of the UPC and the experience of Obote. The latter toured the country intensively to win support. Although in the run-up to the elections all parties were given equal time for broadcasting their views over Uganda Radio, the UPC seemed to enjoy a preponderant share of publicity. This was because the party organizers submitted detailed accounts of their rallies and other electioneering activities for inclusion in the news bulletins. By contrast, the DP waited for reporters from Uganda Radio to attend its meetings, but because there were few reporters available for that task the coverage, except in the vicinity of Kampala, was limited. Nevertheless, this disparity was attributed by the disgruntled opponents of the UPC to the bias of the military commission and of Muwanga in particular, and it was listed among the examples of the unfair practices which obtained during the elections.

Muwanga seemed determined to assume responsibility for whatever was to happen. He cut short further debate over electoral procedure by dissolving the NCC. Furthermore, angered by the view of the chief justice, William Wambuzi, who stated that there had been no constitutional grounds for the overthrow of President Lule, Muwanga dismissed him, appointing in his place a man he believed would be more compliant. From the point of view of establishing his impartiality in electoral matters it was a badly chosen moment for Muwanga to get rid of a judge of known integrity and independence of outlook because it would be the responsibility of the chief justice to call upon the leader of the party winning the elections to form a government. Muwanga's action was immediately claimed by his detractors to have been motivated by his anxiety to ensure that if anything occurred to thwart the victory of the UPC a man of independent mind did not hold such a crucial position.

On learning what Muwanga had done Obote protested that a chief justice could not be summarily dismissed, but his intervention came too late. Constitutional niceties made little impression upon Muwanga, who proceeded to announce that ballot papers should not be marked but that there should be separate ballot boxes for each candidate. These proposals fuelled the fear that the voting would be manipulated, and even the hitherto co-operative DP threatened to boycott the elections. On the intervention of President Nyerere, who still had 10,000 troops in Uganda to bolster his argument, Ssemogerere agreed to withdraw his threat, after being promised that measures would be taken to ensure that counting would be fairly carried out.

In the hope of guaranteeing fair play, all four political parties agreed to the appointment of a nine-man commonwealth monitoring team under the chairmanship of Ebenezer Debrah, who had recently been Ghanaian high commissioner in London. The other members came from Australia, Barbados, Botswana, Canada, Cyprus, India, Sierra Leone and the UK. The appointment came too late to avert some of Muwanga's alleged malpractices, but in its interim report the team commented, 'It is unique in the annals of democracy for a sovereign nation to invite an international group to observe its national elections and to report whether they were free and fair.'

Nevertheless, the observers had much to criticize in the conduct of the elections, but it was inefficiency rather than dishonesty that incurred their disapproval. Many polling stations opened hours late and were permitted to stay open long after the official closing time to make up for the delay. When Obote arrived at a polling station in Kampala at 9 a.m. it was not open, and the officials did not appear until an hour later. They were followed, after a further lapse of time, by the DP candidate, who brought with him the ballot boxes, voting papers and the register of electors. Elsewhere, too, ballot boxes and voting papers failed to arrive at their destinations at the scheduled hour, and the observers were unhappy with Muwanga's decision to declare that some of the constituencies were uncontested. But it was the DP and UPM, not the commonwealth observers, who brought accusations of jerrymandering and election-rigging, and they were ably assisted by foreign journalists in publicizing their complaints.

The first results to emerge came from Buganda, where counting could take place immediately the polling stations closed. On the eve of the poll Shafiq Arain had warned journalists that this would be the case, and that in most instances DP candidates would be successful. Arain was particularly knowledgeable about the situation in Uganda, having played a leading role in the UPC's election campaigns in 1961 and 1962. He had also been appointed by Obote to oversee the party's campaign in 1980. He added that, in his opinion, the pattern would not be the same in the rest of the country and that reporters would be wise to await the outcome of the counting elsewhere before venturing any prediction about the overall result. His advice was not followed, and the BBC predicted a landslide victory for the DP on the evidence of the first results to be announced.

Jubilant supporters of the DP assembled in Kampala, and there were some clashes with UPC members which the police brought under control without much difficulty. Elated by their early successes, some DP supporters claimed victory in constituencies where the counting had not even begun because of the delays in opening the polling booths. Muwanga, in a panic, tried to regain control of the situation by issuing a proclamation that no results should be announced until they had been forwarded to him by the returning officers. He himself would then determine whether the elections had been free and fair or whether new elections should be held. Obote, who had not stood for election because as leader of the UPC he would automatically become president if his party were victorious, was in Kampala, as has been seen, and he immediately protested to Muwanga that his action was a grave disservice to the UPC. Further delay in announcing the results, especially those from areas where the UPC was likely to be successful, would only suggest to the DP that it had been victorious but that its success was being concealed. In an attempt to offset that possibility, the commonwealth observers were called to Kampala from the outlying constituencies and freely admitted that their own observations did not substantiate the DP's claims to victory in a number of districts.

Muwanga never did announce any results, and he withdrew his claim to do so completely, but the damage had been done. In spite of the observers' assurance that, bearing in mind the criticisms they had made on grounds of inefficiency, they believed the elections had been valid and would broadly reflect the 'freely expressed choice of the people of Uganda', any result which favoured the UPC was almost certain to be challenged. When it became clear that the UPC had achieved overall victory the DP called for a new election. The Baganda leaders in particular were convinced they had been cheated. Museveni, who had himself been defeated by a DP (not a UPC) candidate in his home constituency, claimed that the boundaries of the constituency had not been clearly defined. Neither his successful DP rival nor the defeated UPC candidate registered any protest on the score. In fact Museveni's UPM won only one seat in the whole country, in spite of having fielded eighty-two candidates, a crushing defeat that certainly could not be attributed to dishonest practices. The battle had been almost exclusively between the UPC and the DP. Yet, although it claimed that many of the results had been inaccurately recorded, the DP proceeded with only one of the many petitions it filed in the high court. This could scarcely be attributed to any fear that justice would not be done, because the court had no hesitation in rejecting a number of the petitions brought by the UPC.

It was as a result of Obote's second term of office as president that the case against him gained credence outside Uganda, and for that reason his performance during this period must be looked at most critically. He began auspiciously. On his installation on 15 December he at once ordered the release of Binaisa who, three weeks later, left with his family for Kenya. Obote then went on to pledge that the government would respect the rule of law. The greatest challenge to the people of Uganda, he said, was to regenerate the country morally and to rehabilitate the economy. As an earnest of his own good intentions he stated that he intended to form a government of national reconciliation. However, an approach to Ssemogerere with the offer of the post of either minister of foreign affairs or of finance, together with a number of other cabinet appointments for members of the DP, was turned down after some reflection. Obote formed the opinion that Ssemogerere himself was not averse to the idea but was dissuaded by others, possibly by the leaders of the Catholic Church, who wanted a DP government and who still had hopes of reversing the outcome of the elections. But even without the backing of the DP, Obote was able to appoint a cabinet which comprised a useful blend of experience and ethnic diversity. The nomination of ten army officers to the national assembly, which had been determined before the elections, was less reassuring.

President Nyerere sent immediate congratulations on Obote's appointment, but the latter was far from happy with the situation in which he now found himself. The governments which had held office during the previous eighteen months had met with little success in trying to alleviate the problems created by Amin's regime. Only the fertility of the soil and the excellence of the climate had enabled the people at large to survive the collapse of trade and the breakdown of communications with the outside world and even within the country itself, which had resulted from nine years of misrule. Items such as sugar and salt were unobtainable, while the acute shortage of petrol and other types of fuel had reduced transport to a minimum so that the export of coffee, the one ready source of foreign exchange, had almost come to a halt. It was vital that Uganda should seek external assistance, particularly, Obote concluded, from the IMF, to start things moving. Nyerere was opposed to any such action on principle, but accepted that Obote was now in office and must reach his own decisions.

Pending the receipt of external help, the new president made it his main priority to revive the coffee export trade. To do this he enlisted the assistance of the army to load onto trains and trucks the stocks that had accumulated either through the unwillingness of growers to publish the fact of their existence to the rapacious Amin or through the inability of Amin's government to move them. That vital task Obote put under the control of his most competent military officer, Ojok, the army chief of staff, whom he also appointed as chairman of the coffee marketing board in an attempt to improve the overall efficiency of the industry. It was also necessary to renegotiate arrangements with Kenya to make possible the onward transit of the coffee to the port of Mombasa. Before the end of the year, a deputation led by Erifasi Otema Allimadi, the new prime minister, who had served in all three civilian governments since the overthrow of Amin, opened discussions in Nakuru.

This was a hopeful beginning in view of President Moi's suspicions of

Nyerere's role in Uganda, and early in 1981 further meetings led to the re-opening of trade with Kenya and of the transit trade to the coast. Obote was surprised by Moi's insistence that the greater part of the coffee should be moved by road when the railway seemed the most appropriate means of handling such a bulk cargo. He learned later that important Kenyan financial interests were involved in road transport. It was in the course of those meetings that Kenya's brilliant vice-president and minister of finance, Mwai Kibaki, again met Obote with whom he had at one time had numerous contacts. Seeing him afresh, Kibaki was greatly impressed by the Ugandan president, not least by his obvious willingness to listen to the criticisms brought by the DP, so long as the party conducted its opposition along constitutional lines.

The black market, which had become a normal feature of life under Amin, had spawned a social class that thrived on the opportunities for profit-making to which the scarcity of almost everything had given rise. An attempt to curb the soaring cost of such basic commodities as meat, milk, plantains and vegetables by introducing fixed prices only led to their disappearing from the markets because traders refused to sell their goods for less than had become customary. When police confiscated the traders' stock the traders themselves complained that they would never get replacements because the farmers would not sell their produce for such low prices. Faced with what appeared to be an intractable problem the government weakly claimed that it had never endorsed price fixing, which, it said, had been introduced on the initiative of a local branch of the UPC. The traders could scarcely have been convinced by that assertion, but they were happy enough to recommence their activities now that the government had backed down. The whole sequence of events illustrated the magnitude of the government's task in trying to restore morality and fair dealing, and the inadequacy of the means at its disposal to achieve that goal. Nevertheless, the British government was prepared to accept Obote's assurance that foreign investments would be safeguarded and that there would be no nationalization of foreign holdings.

Paulo Muwanga's role in the new regime might well have given rise to serious difficulties. Many of his actions before and during the elections had brought not only him, but the UPC too, into disfavour. He might also have laid claim, in the circumstances, to having been the kingmaker who had been responsible for restoring Obote to office and have sought to make capital out of it. In the event, no difficulties arose. Muwanga was shrewd enough to realize that, as a renegade in the eyes of his fellow Baganda, his only hope of hanging onto power would have been to rely on a very unreliable army, so he readily agreed to serve the new government as vice-president and minister of defence, in which capacities he worked loyally, at least for some time.

The difficulties created for Obote by the ill-disciplined force he had inherited were sharply illustrated early in February 1981. In an attempt to place Kampala under the control of the police rather than the army, orders had been given for all troops to be withdrawn from the capital. Incensed, it was said, by the fear of being despatched to some less salubrious part of the country, some soldiers went on the rampage. Their choice of Rubaga, the area round the Roman Catholic cathedral, as their target may or may not have been deliberate, but critics of the government were quick to bring accusations that the violence had been directed against the DP in general and against Catholics in particular. Four days later, evidence of another problem for the government was provided by a series of attacks launched against police stations in the suburbs of Kampala by heavily armed men claiming to be members of the Uganda Freedom Movement. Arms and ammunition were stolen. The movement, said to have been formed soon after the overthrow of President Lule, was mainly composed of Roman Catholics and was led by Andrew Kayiira. Kayiira was a former prison officer who had been sent to the US for further training during Obote's first presidency and was there when Amin's coup took place. He became minister of the interior under Lule and was the man Lule had asked to send police to Entebbe to arrest the cabinet which was about to overthrow him. The force he then began to build up was never very large and its subversive activities reached their peak in the middle of 1981. The following year it was defeated by the UNLA and Kayiira fled, returning to renew his campaign against Obote in 1985.

There was sporadic trouble, too, in the West Nile District where, after the elections, supporters of Amin again crossed the border and clashed with the UNLA. There was heavy fighting and Amin's men took refuge in a school. The children were not in residence but many of the staff were there, and in the ensuing battle the civilians suffered heavy casualties. The blame for this was laid on the UNLA by the missionaries in charge of the school, although Amin's forces had initiated the fighting. The crude methods of the UNLA were no different from those they had employed under Binaisa and Lule, but they reflected badly upon the new government which, as yet, had had little time to create order in the armed forces. They also supplied fuel for the propaganda of those who wished to see the overthrow of Obote and the UPC. Additionally, the fighting in the West Nile District encouraged more refugees to seek security in the Sudan, and that, too, was used as evidence of the failure of Obote's administration to maintain order.

Still more serious for the reputation of the government were the activities of a body calling itself the People's Resistance Army and led by Yoweri Museveni. After the crushing defeat of all but one of his party's candidates in the December elections, Museveni soon collected, not the handful of followers he later claimed to have had at his disposal, but the large military force he had been recruiting under the umbrella of the UNLA while he was in the defence ministry. These he took to the bush in Luwero District, to the north of Kampala, in February 1981, and before the end of the month a spokesman for the movement claimed that 5,000 men were under arms. With that force Museveni immediately launched a guerrilla war. He sought to justify his actions by claiming that the elections had been rigged, but the abysmal performance of his own party gave little ground for his complaint, more particularly since the DP, the only party which might conceivably have felt aggrieved, was apparently prepared to act as a constitutional opposition. That was a state of affairs which has been consistently ignored in subsequent assessments of Museveni's behaviour, although it was wholly in accordance with his freely expressed opinion that military rule was the only way open to Uganda.

Part of Luwero had been incorporated into Buganda since its annexation from Bunyoro in the nineteenth century, and although it was not one of the two 'Lost Counties' in which a referendum had been held, its population comprised a greater ethnic mix than any other district in the former kingdom. Museveni's first step, therefore, was to launch a campaign of terror against those he believed might be loyal to the government. Thousands fled southwards in search of safety, and the government lacked the organization either to make adequate provision for their accommodation or to move a sufficiently large military force to crush the rebellion at the outset. Hampered by the shortage of fuel for transport, and with the army involved in the struggles in the north-west and in the urgent task of loading coffee in Kampala and the eastern districts, the government sought international help in handling the refugees. In the meantime, makeshift arrangements were made to house them in camps which soon became overcrowded and food was in short supply.

The delay in sending the army to the area, and its lack of training in counter-insurgency operations, meant that Museveni's forces were able to establish a firm foothold in the northern part of the district, mainly by means of coercion. Even when troops did arrive and opened their campaign confusion reigned among the people of Luwero as to which side they were dealing with at any one time, because both wore the same uniforms. Museveni's men did not hesitate to masquerade as UNLA troops when they raided villages to carry off children into captivity and to seize food supplies. There is no doubt that the indiscipline of the UNLA forces in the earlier stages of the campaign led to the harassment and even death of many innocent villagers. But to attribute all, or even a majority, of the atrocities in Luwero to the government's soldiers cannot be justified in view of the behaviour of Museveni's men before any UNLA soldiers reached the area, and of the evidence of some of those who were captured by the rebels and later escaped. Nevertheless, the propaganda launched against the government by those opposed to Obote was exceedingly effective, not least because it was masterminded by exiles in London who had the ear of influential people in Britain. Nor were foreign journalists ever admitted to the area under rebel control to see conditions there. By contrast, the problems in the refugee camps, exacerbated by the lack of resources at the government's disposal, provided ample material for Obote's critics.

It is particularly significant that, in spite of numerous acts of terrorism in and around Kampala and the often clumsy and heavy-handed response of the UNLA soldiery, there was never any full-scale rebellion in the rest of Buganda outside Luwero. Nor was there any evidence of the 'campaign of genocide' which the UNLA troops were said to have launched against the Baganda as a whole. The main reason for the relative peace in the former kingdom was that Obote's intensive campaign to sell coffee soon proved extremely profitable to a large section of the population. The added incentive of higher prices offered on 1 May 1981 further encouraged coffee growers to increase their output from the desperately low level to which it had sunk under Amin. Museveni's attempts to dissuade farmers from selling their produce to the coffee marketing board proved ineffective, and his appeals to international buyers to boycott Uganda coffee fell upon equally deaf ears.

In the early days of Museveni's campaign Obote approached Ssemogerere with a proposal for joint action by the two main political parties to combat the threat to peace. Ssemogerere said he was confident the rebels were supported by only a small section of the population and he offered the backing of the DP for Obote's efforts. This promising beginning was soon marred by the conditions Ssemogerere insisted upon as a prerequisite for his co-operation. The DP, he said, must have a majority on any body set up to co-ordinate the campaign and must be allowed to appoint the chairman. Obote could not concede those points and the plan came to nothing. Instead, as Museveni's rebellion continued the DP, far from helping to suppress it, itself became involved with the rebels.

The government was not helped by the continuing turmoil in the north-west. UNLA troops, struggling to deal with supporters of Amin from over the Sudanese and Zairean borders who struck unexpectedly against widely separated targets, pursued their vendetta against anyone they believed to be sympathetic to the exiled president, and in so doing ill-treated the guilty and innocent alike. Civilians caught in the crossfire between the contending parties fled to the Sudan, swelling the numbers of refugees camping north of the border. In spite of appeals from Obote, who visited both Zaire and the Sudan early in the year, they refused to return, preferring the bare subsistence provided in the camps to the uncertainty of life in West Nile District. Nor were they encouraged to return by the Sudanese government, which was receiving generous aid from the Western Powers to maintain them.

In the vicinity of Kampala itself rebel groups made a number of forays throughout 1981. In March a military convoy was ambushed seven miles north of the capital and a number of soldiers were killed. A few days later the main electricity line from the Owen Falls Dam was damaged and all buildings in Western Uganda dependent upon power from that source were plunged into darkness. The broadcasting station on Bugolobi Hill outside Kampala was also sabotaged, and even the UPC headquarters in the city were attacked. In April, a warehouse belonging to the coffee marketing board was set on fire, and three shops in Kampala, one of them belonging to Lieut.-Colonel Basilio Okello, commander of the Kampala garrison, were damaged by explosions. At Kakiri, eighteen miles north of Kampala, an army post was attacked by a rebel group which claimed to have killed a number of soldiers. While those activities may have demonstrated the inability of the government to maintain law and order they were even stronger proof of the rebels' disregard for the safety and well-being of people and property.

The Uganda Patriotic Movement unashamedly claimed that its military wing, the People's Resistance Army, had played a prominent role in most of the actions, although the Uganda Freedom Movement may also have been involved. Not surprisingly, the government concluded that the rebels were being harboured by some of the civilian population in the neighbourhood of the capital and, when not engaged in military operations, were posing as civilians themselves. Numbers of people were arrested, including some opposition politicians, which led to an outcry from critics of the government. Nor did Obote's threat of action against the people of Southern Uganda if they allowed their country to become destabilized do anything to enhance his popularity among the Bugandan leaders, who did their utmost to publicize the reprisals taken by the army against anyone suspected of assisting the rebels. False rumours of official acts of cruelty circulated freely among the more accurate accounts of army violence. George Bakulumpagi Wamala, publicity secretary of the UPM, was reported to have died of injuries received in prison after being arrested in Kampala. Twenty-five days later he escaped unharmed, but claimed that prisoners were beaten with barbed wire and clubbed to death.

Still gravely concerned by the problems arising from the indiscipline of the army, Obote initiated a plan to pension off the many soldiers who were unsuited to the requirements of the armed forces. He did not propose simply to disband them. His plan was to place them in camps where they would receive training in farming before being sent home. In the meantime he set about recruiting and training younger and better-educated men. As an interim measure he asked Nyerere not to withdraw the 10,000 Tanzanian troops who still remained in Uganda in June, as had been planned, but his request was rejected. In May he also applied to the British government for assistance in training his new recruits. The Ugandan high commissioner in London, Shafiq Arain, presented the request to the British foreign secretary, Lord Carrington. After a careful inquiry, Carrington concluded that the plan could best be carried out on a commonwealth basis, although Britain would be prepared to finance the undertaking and to provide a core of instructors. Sonnie Ramphal, the commonwealth secretary-general, learning of Britain's support for the scheme and of the British government's willingness to foot the bill, also gave his backing, and a small commonwealth team was duly despatched to Uganda. But the negotiations took time, and when the team arrived the army had already become involved in another campaign for which it was, as yet, ill prepared.

The government watched with dismay as the last of the Tanzanian troops began a two-months' phased withdrawal. Although the Tanzanians themselves had not always behaved with the restraint expected of trained soldiers it was clear that the ill-disciplined UNLA forces were far from ready to take responsibility for the security of the country. It would be some time before the team of commonwealth military instructors could begin their work, so that little could be expected of the rabble collected and armed in the wake of Amin's retreat or, given the example they offered, of the younger recruits Obote was beginning to enlist into the army. There can be little doubt, too, that the anger of many of the soldiers was further inflamed by the fact that the rebel attacks all took place in Buganda, among the people who had so warmly welcomed Amin's seizure of power and his destruction of the army which had supported Obote's first government. This in no way justified the army's excesses, and its activities were a serious challenge to the success Obote was beginning to have among the Baganda by his revival of the trade in coffee. On the soldiers' behalf, however, it must be said that false accusations were constantly made against them.

When some twenty civilians were killed and many others assaulted, and houses and shops were looted and burned by uniformed men at Mukono, twelve miles east of Kampala, a number of stories were quickly circulated. Some claimed that when three soldiers had been killed in an ambush their comrades had lost control of themselves and had run amok. Others said that the violence was the work of disaffected Acholi soldiers. There was, however, no disaffection of an ethnic character among the UNLA troops, and neither at that time nor later, when the charge was repeated to justify the break-up of the army, were any units composed exclusively of one ethnic group once Museveni had removed his predominantly Banyarwandan soldiers. The attack at Mukono was carried out by rebels, located in the vicinity, who, to the chagrin of the security forces, were quickly swallowed up among the civilian population.

In May, Otema Allimadi claimed that the government had the power to crush the rebels and would do so. A few days later, and equally optimistically, Obote himself announced at a press conference that the departure of the Tanzanian troops would in no way affect Uganda's ability to deal with its own security problems. It was sheer bravado, aimed at building up public confidence. Both statements had a hollow ring in the light of a recent attack on a police station in Rubaga, a suburb of Kampala, and the putting out of action by gunfire of the main water tower at Makerere University on the outskirts of the city. Even the presence of one thousand Tanzanian police, whom Nyerere had permitted to stay behind in Uganda in response to an impassioned plea from the vice-president, Muwanga, could make little impression on the security situation in the capital. There were repeated rebel attacks on police stations in the neighbourhood, when arms and ammunition, together with the uniforms which helped to confuse the identity of the combatants in the eyes of the civilian population, were captured to replenish dwindling supplies. In West Nile District, too, there were further outbreaks of violence, and on 24 June some sixty civilians were killed and one hundred wounded at a Verona Fathers' mission station at Ombaci when troops clashed with former supporters of Amin.

Although faced with so many demands upon his energy and ingenuity, Obote still strove to follow a policy of reconciliation. Criticism of conditions in the prisons led him to announce on 27 May that 3,000 detainees, most of them former supporters of Amin who had been arrested by Lule's government at the time of Amin's overthrow, would be released. But it was the economy which lay at the root of all his problems. If that could be restored, the dishonesty which had become a norm in Amin's day, and which for many was still the only means of survival, might persist for a time, but its *raison d'être* would gradually be removed, and the leaders of the opposition to the government would find it more difficult to arouse support for their campaign. In due course, the restoration of the trade in coffee would, no doubt, make its impact felt, but there was need for more immediate remedies. A number of countries came forward with offers of help, foremost among them the United Kingdom which made a grant of £10 million and promised more. Italy, too, was helpful and, to a lesser extent, the US. Mrs Indira Gandhi had always liked Obote, not least because he had made a favourable impression on her father, so that, within its limited means, India also gave assistance.

Obote was aware, however, that there was a need to restructure the economy more fundamentally than could be done even with those offers of help. It was on that account he turned to the IMF. The latter body proposed that, as a condition of its giving assistance, the currency should be allowed to float. Obote, who was his own finance minister, was deeply worried by the suggestion, fully appreciating the hardship it would cause. Some of his most senior advisers even recommended that he should reject the proposal, but he reluctantly, though firmly, insisted that there was no alternative. Gone was any idea of nationalizing the economy, because there was no economy to nationalize, and Obote had never been ideologically committed to nationalization as the best means of running the country. At that stage it clearly could not have offered the incentives needed to encourage farmers to produce the crops required to reestablish the economy on a sound footing.

The immediate result of adopting the IMF's recommendation was a fall in the value of the Ugandan shilling to 10 per cent of its former official exchange rate. For most people this was a disaster, although most of the population had enough land to supply the food they needed. Savings vanished overnight and wages became inadequate to meet even the most modest requirements. Obote responded by doubling the wages of the lowest-paid workers, but that was a feeble palliative. More positively, he forecast that, despite the unsettled state of the country, Uganda would meet the quota allocated to it under the international coffee agreement. Salt, sugar, soap and cigarettes, for months in short supply, now reappeared on the Kampala market, but at prices far beyond the means of the poorer people. Nevertheless, the World Bank, the EEC and other Western donors showed their confidence in the steps taken by the government by gradually increasing the allocation of aid to sectors vital to the country's recovery. The rehabilitation of agriculture and of some basic industries, as well as communications, all benefited accordingly. Later in the year, after Obote had reaffirmed his government's commitment to a mixed economy in a speech at his reinstallation as chancellor of Makerere University, representatives of Britain, the US, France, West Germany, Italy and Japan acknowledged his efforts by agreeing to reschedule Uganda's debt repayments.

These promising developments took place against a background of unremitting violence in some parts of the country, the results of rebel operations and the reaction to them of the UNLA. The village of Mutaga to the north of Kampala and near the military barracks at Bombo was the scene of a number of raids. At the end of August 1981 a landmine exploded in the village killing four soldiers. Not far away, in September, an army tank was destroyed, and in another attack in the same area a bus was wrecked. Civilians fled from their homes and took refuge in the bush. A further attack on a police station at Mukono, the scene of an earlier rebel operation, resulted in the death of five policemen. Again attempts were made to lay the blame on the army. Another landmine blew up a bus and killed twenty civilians on a road five miles east of Kampala. Far away to the north-east, in Karamoja, a region threatened almost continuously by famine, the activities of relief organizations were disrupted by armed men who tried to seize their goods. The army responded with its customarily clumsy vigour, and under cover of an operation to track down the raiders troops looted houses in the district headquarters in the town of Moroto. Thus violence bred violence, and frequently it was impossible to determine who was the guilty party. Not surprisingly, with all those pressing problems to be faced, Obote decided not to attend the Commonwealth Conference which was held in Melbourne in October 1981. Instead, he sent Prime Minister Otema Allimadi to represent Uganda at what proved to be a fairly uncontentious meeting.

In spite of Uganda's difficulties, an impartial observer, Charles Harrison, writing in *The Times* at the end of 1981, was prepared to take a reasonably sanguine view of the situation. While admitting that a number of areas outside Kampala were still being subjected to rebel attacks, he maintained that the inhabitants of the capital itself were experiencing a growing sense of security and that troops had been withdrawn to their barracks. This was indeed the case, for both Obote and Ojok were determined that the army should be kept under control in so far as their powers would allow. Moreover, Harrison went on, prices for some goods had fallen since the middle of the year and everyday items of food were readily available in the markets, but at a high price. Salaries generally lasted for only two weeks of the month, but most people were able to augment their cash income by growing food for themselves. Obote's forecast that the coffee quota would be met had been fulfilled, and the quota for 1981–2 had been raised by international agreement. The productivity of the tea estates was being gradually raised, and prospects for the cotton crop were good. Agricultural implements were in short supply, but conditions in most parts of the country, with the exception of West Nile, Karamoja and the Luwero region, were reasonably stable.[27] Even in Karamoja, the situation had improved as a result of heavy rains which had enabled a formerly pastoral people to begin to plant crops. There was still a lingering threat of famine, however, and news of the murder of a number of elders who had protested about the excesses of the army cast a shadow over any rejoicing at the prospect of better conditions in the north-east.

The new year began auspiciously when Obote announced that in a spirit of reconciliation he proposed to begin releasing the men arrested after the shootings and rebel activities early in 1981. Before the end of January nearly two hundred had been set free and in response, seven opposition MPs joined the government side while several hundred members of opposition parties transferred their allegiance to the UPC. The DP leader, Ssemogerere, remarked sourly that more innocent people had been killed in 1981 than in any year he could remember since independence. It was a claim he would have been hard pressed to substantiate, but there is no doubt that the Amin years had left people callous and self-seeking. In January 1982, George Bamuturaki, a prominent member of the DP, and Z. Okao, general manager of the Uganda National Housing and Construction Corporation, were shot dead in Kampala and six other persons were injured. In February, some 300 rebels attacked an army barracks on the outskirts of the capital in a bid to overthrow the government. The confinement of troops to barracks became difficult to enforce and indiscipline remained a serious problem. Assistance had been given by Kenya, the Sudan and Tanzania in an attempt to provide better training for the army, but it had been an uphill task. The long-awaited announcement that an advance party of the commonwealth military training team had left London early in March came as some relief, but only the most optimistic observer held out any hope of a marked improvement in the behaviour of the army so long as provocation remained an almost daily occurence.

A clear illustration of the difficulties faced by the government in its drive to maintain order was provided almost at once. It was reported that, during the rebel attack on the army barracks near Kampala, mortar bombs had been fired from the steps of the Roman Catholic cathedral on Rubaga Hill. Spokesmen for the Catholic Church insisted that the bombs had been fired without their knowledge, but, acting on information that arms and ammunition were still concealed in the vicinity, troops scoured the area and arrested a number of people in whose houses arms were found. In keeping with the anti-government propaganda waged by Obote's opponents, it was stated in the British press, on the strength of news received from Kampala, that soldiers had entered the cathedral during a service and had taken away some of the male worshippers.[28] Ssemogerere, for his part, claimed that 2,000 people had been arrested in the aftermath of the rebel attack, due to the overreaction of the security forces.[29] Under the evocative headline 'Obote says sorry to cardinal' it was then announced in *The Times* that the president had apologized to Cardinal Nsubuga for the troops' behaviour and had promised to investigate complaints of harassment by security forces.[30] Obote did indeed send for Cardinal Nsubuga and asked for information about what had taken place at Rubaga. Eventually the cardinal admitted that the troops had not entered the cathedral, but insisted that they had arrested some children who were themselves on the point of entering the building. Obote expressed surprise that children had been singled out for attention by the soldiers, but asked Nsubuga to let him have the names of the missing children and the schools they attended, together with the names of their parents, so that he could make enquiries. No names were ever forthcoming, in spite of several reminders, but the accusation had been made in the British press and was never corrected.

In the same way, Amnesty International's report in April of widespread torture and killings, and of the murder of people held in detention, was clearly not without foundation. But it seemed to assume that atrocities carried out by men in uniform were to be attributed only to members of the security forces, when blame might equally have been laid at the feet of the rebels who had openly set out to disrupt the life of the country. For *The Times* to comment that, in the light of the report, the only hope for Uganda was to discipline the armed forces and ensure economic progress, was a statement of the obvious.[31] It might have added that it would have been helpful if the rebels had ceased their operations.

The same editorial expressed the unhelpful view that 'it is now clear that Dr Obote, mainly because of his past, is not a leader capable of unifying the nation and governing by consent, yet it is not at all certain that anyone else could do better.' Immediately, Yusufu Lule took up his pen to congratulate the editor upon his assessment of Obote's position and for drawing attention to 'the deteriorating human rights situation in my unhappy country'. He disagreed, however, with the suggestion that discipling the army would produce good results, and that the violence in Uganda was largely anarchic and criminal rather than political. Once again he advanced the view that resistance to the regime had arisen because of the dubious elections of 1980 and their 'total negation of a carefully defined and organised democratic process'. It was equally the result, he claimed, of an army built purely on tribal lines and composed of Langi and Acholi from the north. To discipline such a force would simply make it a more efficient instrument of Obote's repression and entrench still further his dictatorship.[32] What he did not mention was that Obote had inherited the army, created in part at least under Lule's own presidency, that there had never been any bar to the recruitment of southerners and that Museveni had enlisted thousands of men from the south-west who were, at that very time, engaged in a guerrilla campaign which was ruining the country.

Obote himself was deeply aware of the difficulties he had to face. He did not relish the accusations of cruelty and torture levelled against the security forces and he constantly intervened to try to put an end to them. But he was involved in so many important issues that his attention was frequently diverted from the activities of the army and police. Moreover, to check the excesses of a frustrated military was not easy in face of the increasing activities of the rebels, who had been encouraged by assistance from Libya after a visit to Colonel Gaddafi by Museveni earlier in the year. It is not without significance that, although the visit was widely known, it aroused little adverse comment in the Western press, which was normally so critical of the Libyan leader.

In the last week of April five policemen were shot in an ambush, and within days another was shot at a roadblock set up near Kampala. In May, gunmen killed two chiefs and a local chairman of the UPC near Mpigi, to the sough-west of the capital. To preach restraint in those circumstances was difficult, but on 27 May, Obote ordered the army to refrain at all times from robbing or in any other way molesting civilians. It would be easier to fight the rebels, he said, if the troops had the sympathy and support of the civilian population.

Most of the complaints against the security forces still came from Baganda living in the vicinity of Kampala, and were faithfully relayed to the British press by the leaders of the opposition as an indication of the government's incompetence. It was even alleged that life for the average person was more dangerous than it had been under President Amin. If that were so, it was due primarily to rebel activity, since most of the incidents about which complaints were made were engineered by supporters of Museveni or his Baganda allies, who were uniformed terrorists by night and civilians by day, blending easily into their surroundings because they were local people. Later, Museveni himself was to congratulate those men for the support they had given to the rebel movement, but when their actions were given their correct attribution in 1982 they were simply reported as news items, without the undertones of moral condemnation that accompanied any criticism of the government. Meanwhile, the rest of the country, with the exception of West Nile District in the extreme north-west and Karamoja in the north-east, both areas still suffering the after effects of Amin's misrule, continued to be reasonably stable. In Karamoja law and order had once again broken down completely, and there was little that an army untrained for such delicate operations could do about it.

Obote felt he was beginning to make progress when the first sixteen officers and seventy-two NCOs trained by the commonwealth team passed out at a ceremony in Jinja early in June. It was only a tentative start to a Herculean task, but at least those men, by acting as instructors to others, would be increasing the impact of the new training methods Obote had sought to introduce. Perhaps a little prematurely from a security point of view, but widely from the standpoint of public relations, he accepted the advice of his senior security officers and withdrew all soldiers who were manning roadblocks, except for those on duty at the international airport in Entebbe. On 30 May, too, the *Sunday Times* carried a report commending Obote's achievements on the economic front. For the first time in the three turbulent years following Idi Amin's overthrow, it stated, Uganda looked like a country with a chance to rise from the ruins. Obote, it said, had achieved a near-miracle of stabilization. Consumer prices had fallen in the previous twelve months; exports were rising, and government revenue was rising faster than its spending. Already half the finance needed to launch 140 key projects aimed at boosting agriculture and industry had been raised, and Obote had despatched a team of senior people to London to try to encourage foreign investors to provide the rest of the money by offering them a range of incentives such as exemption from import duties and the freedom to repatriate profits.

This rosy picture must be qualified by a number of other factors. Prices had indeed fallen, but they still remained high in comparison with wages. Everything, from transport to technical skills, was still in short supply, and the absence of an effective infrastructure was making the implementation of many of the development schemes both slow and difficult. Nevertheless, thanks to Obote's urgent insistence upon reviving the country's exports of coffee, and thanks, too, to the assistance provided by Britain and the EC in the rehabilitation of the processing side of the industry, Uganda was once again the commonwealth's largest producer of that crop. Moreover, although the country still relied heavily upon coffee as the almost exclusive earner of foreign exchange, there was hope that that was only a temporary state of affairs. The year's cotton crop promised to be five times greater than that of the previous year, although still only a third of the crop of 1970, the last year of Obote's first presidency. The output of tea and tobacco was also rising, and the gift of $4 million by the US in August to help in the restoration of agriculture in general, together with the revival of the farmers' co-operative movement, gave further hope of economic improvement.

In spite of those successes, the political scene remained clouded by the continuation of terrorism. Libya was supplying arms and providing training for the rebels, and in July Museveni boasted that his forces had killed 118 Ugandan troops in the last two weeks. As if to justify those acts of violence, he then accused the army of slaughtering twenty-five older civilians who had been too slow to make their escape when government forces sought to trap the rebels. Binaisa, in the meantime, lamented that an invasion by British mercenaries, which he had planned, had failed to get off the ground because his American backers had been unable to raise the money to finance the enterprise. In a new report Amnesty International again accused the government of responsibility for the torture and killing of civilians by the army. The report admitted that the government was acting to prevent the ill treatment of civilians, but said that the attempt had met with little success. Angrily the government retorted that it had been given no opportunity to hear or to refute the allegations before their publication, and accused Amnesty International of being misled by a carefully orchestrated campaign of denigration by opponents of Obote's leadership.

It is easy to accept the government's response as the natural reaction of a repressive regime to criticism. Nor is it unlikely that the sort of army Obote had inherited was wholly blameless. Yet little effort was made by the government's accusers to substantiate their allegations by means of personal, on-the-spot, investigations. Obote imposed no restrictions on the movements of would-be observers in at least some of the areas where atrocities were alleged to have taken place, although they were denied access by the rebels to their own centres of operation. It seems strange that a ruler as oppressive as Obote's critics claimed him to be should have allowed those critics to make their accusations with apparent impunity. It is difficult, too, to equate the immunity which seems to have been accorded to prominent figures in the Democratic Party and the Roman Catholic Church, as well as to those of the former Bugandan leaders who had chosen to remain in Uganda, with the reputation for tyrannical behaviour ascribed to the president.

There remained, it is true, the problem of identifying armed men in uniform, but Obote himself consistently maintained that many of the charges made against the security forces were either false or exaggerated, or could be more accurately attributed to rebels masquerading as government troops. Certainly the rebels showed little compunction over blowing up buses or threatening civilian targets whenever they felt such actions might promote their campaign of terror. It is interesting to note that, after Obote's overthrow, the new government's zeal to condemn the excesses of its predecessor by setting up commissions of inquiry produced little in the way of testimony from those alleged to have suffered at Obote's hands. Sadly, the grisly piles of anonymous skulls subsequently paraded in Luwero as evidence of Obote's tyranny could testify neither for nor against him.

Chapter 11

Into exile once more

A long-standing problem suddenly reached its crisis during Obote's absence in Italy where he had medical treatment in September 1982. Tens of thousands of refugees had sought asylum in Uganda hard on the heels of the achievement of independence by neighbouring Rwanda in the 1960s. Obote was always sympathetic towards refugees, and these people had been housed by his government in camps, mainly in Ankole, where they had ethnic links with some of the population of that district. Some, however, had been located in what was to become Rakai District, near the town of Masaka in Buganda. That district, which did not exist as a local government unit at the time of the refugees' arrival, was later created by President Binaisa during his efforts to restructure the local authorities of Uganda, which had been destroyed by Amin. That task, and especially the creation of new districts, had imposed additional burdens upon a government which had difficulty in recruiting enough people competent to function as local officials, and even more difficulty in paying those it managed to employ. As a result, in the early years of Obote's second presidency the area was not well administered.

When Amin was in power some of the refugees had left the camps and had approached him seeking help. The president had responded by arresting and executing a number of Banyankole landowners whom he deemed to be hostile to his rule and had given their land to the suppliants. He was well-disposed towards the refugees because he had enrolled numbers of them in his armed forces, hoping that as aliens they could be relied upon to carry out his orders to deal with any Ugandans who aroused his displeasure. Seeing the strength of their position, some of the refugees brought false charges against the Banyankole in order to acquire still more of their land, but when Amin was overthrown most of them returned to their camps, leaving seething resentment among their Banyankole neighbours. Those feelings were strengthened by cases of cattle-rustling in the district which the inhabitants attributed to the Banyarwanda. The Roman Catholic Bishop of Mbarara, the leading town in Ankole, protested in person to Obote about stock theft by the refugees.

Before Obote left for Italy he appointed a minister to go to Mbarara with a letter to the district council urging the members to travel round the district in an attempt to sort out the problem. In Obote's absence, some Banyarwanda were arrested in the act of cattle-rustling. This provided the Banyankole with the ammunition they needed to strengthen their demand that the refugees should be forced to leave their country. Taking the law into their own hands they set about driving the refugees back to Rwanda. This was a spontaneous act by disgruntled members of the local population and was not in any way inspired by the chiefs or by the UPC youth wing as stated in the English press.[33] Paulo Muwanga, who was acting as president while Obote was away, took no action against the Banyankole. Instead, he showed his approval by stating that Banyarwandan refugees living in Buganda should also be ejected. The government of Rwanda demanded that those refugees who had managed to cross the border should be re-admitted to Uganda and called for urgent action to improve the conditions of all the Banyarwandan refugees. On his return from Italy, Obote immediately ordered that no further pressure should be put on the Banyarwanda to leave. He agreed that those who were still in Uganda should be free to remain, but they must be prepared to live in clearly defined areas. In March 1983, talks began to determine who was responsible for the wellbeing of all the refugees. Muwanga's behaviour during the troubles reflected little credit either upon himself or upon the government of which he was acting head, but Obote's swift intervention was noted with approval, even by some of those whose general attitude towards him was one of scepticism if not of open hostility.

The combination of pragmatism and compassion which was an important component of Obote's character was evident in connection with two other issues in 1983. In the first case Bugandan villagers were tiring of the rebels' terrorist tactics, which were having such a disruptive effect on their lives, and Obote learned that they were reluctantly beginning to look to the government to restore order. He responded quickly by announcing in January that if he heard of harassment or violence by the army against civilians the offenders would be dismissed or sent to prison. He hoped by this measure to divert the public anger aroused by the continued violence away from the security forces and towards the rebels whom he believed to be the true cause of Uganda's troubles. Already, in October of the previous year, thirty-two policemen had been dismissed for firing off their rifles without permission and thereby creating a minor panic in Kampala. Six weeks later, a number of commanders of army units had been arrested and tried by civilian courts for a range of offences. It was only a small step, but it was a move in the right direction and reflected the president's growing confidence in his ability to bring the security forces under control. Tragically, in April, the bullet-riddled body of Rajab Lutaaya, a DP official, was found at the roadside, three days after he had been taken away by men wearing police uniforms, and early in May, security forces seized hundreds of civilians for questioning from a number of Kampala suburbs. This latter action may have been deemed essential to crack down on terrorist activities, but it did not endear the troops to the inhabitants of the capital and it highlighted the problem Obote faced in controlling his armed forces while at the same time curbing the violent acts of the rebels.

Obote's second measure did not concern the rebels and their activities. In February, his personal campaign to enable non-Ugandans expelled by Amin to return and reclaim their confiscated property bore fruit when a law was passed, in the face of strong opposition from some members of the assembly, making that possible. The powerful Madhvani and Mehta families, who controlled international industrial empires and between them owned the bulk of Uganda's sugar estates, did not even wait for the bill to become law before recommencing their business activities. Other Asians, with less resources at their disposal, were more cautious, partly because they were uncertain of their future in a country that had treated them so harshly and partly because the new legislation stipulated that any property reclaimed could not be resold for five years. Disconcerting though this provision might be, Obote was anxious not only to right an injustice but also to make use of Asian expertise. He did not want the Asians to return solely to dispose of their possessions and then to quit Uganda for ever.

There were, however, other provisions which made the offer less than tempting to the exiled Asians. The Expropriation Act required all those who wished to repossess their property to make their applications before 22 May by sending £50. The claims would then be examined individually by a committee set up for the task and if they were approved the claimants must return to Uganda within 120 days. Property not so claimed would be auctioned to Ugandans and the proceeds sent to the former owners. In the circumstances of the time, the proceeds were unlikely to be generous. Spokesmen for the Asians pointed out that the requirements were far more onerous than those demanded of expropriated European property owners, whose claims were to be handled collectively by means of negotiations between their governments and the Ugandan government. Anxious to maintain good external relations, Obote waived the time limit for submitting claims, and the Ugandan high commissioner in London, himself an Asian, gave an assurance that in handling the claims no distinction would be made between Asians and Europeans.

Museveni could not witness even those tenuous signs of a return to normality without trying to undermine them. In January rebels had attacked a bus travelling along a main road north of Kampala, killing more than thirty passengers and wounding a further fourteen. In March, attempting to carry his campaign of disruption still further, Museveni called upon all foreign diplomats to leave the country before his rebel forces, describing themselves as the National Resistance Army (NRA), launched a new offensive. He went on to claim that his troops controlled hundreds of square miles of territory and had closed the main roads linking Kampala with Hoima, Masindi and Mubende, the leading towns to the north and west of the capital.[34] It was a wildly exaggerated statement. The rebels' activities emanated from a number of separate strongpoints only, but their propaganda was seized upon by Obote's opponents and disseminated wherever a credulous journalist could be found to pen a report favourable to their cause.

The rebels continued to make political capital from the serious damage they caused in the Kampala area by launching their operations, in uniform, from the security of friendly localities and then returning to the anonymity of civilian dress. In June 1983, uniformed men attacked Gayaza High School for Girls, twelve miles north of the capital, and the nearby Makerere University farm school. In both institutions casualties were inflicted, and the customary charges were made against the army by opponents of the government. The attacks were, however, carried out by rebels led by a man named Kaligonza, who later admitted that he and his men had been responsible for those and for many other operations in and around Kampala. In the Luwero District, the government was now trying to assist twenty thousand refugees, displaced as a result of the rebels' activities, by giving them clothes and farm implements. One of their camps was attacked and casualty figures varied, according to the source of the information, between eighty and two hundred. Again there were allegations and counter allegations, but there is little justification for the automatic assumption that this must have been part of a government policy of genocide against the Baganda. Many of the refugees were not Baganda, or even originally Banyoro, but immigrants from neighbouring districts who, attracted by the already mixed population of the district, had moved into what had previously been a fertile and underpopulated region. The vast relief operation launched in the Luwero District in July with the support of UNICEF, Save the Children, the Salvation Army, the British government and the European Community, also seems at odds with the policy of extermination which critics, both at the time and subsequently, have claimed the government was pursuing.

It was, for Obote, deeply disturbing that rebels should be determined to try to wreck the country and disseminate what were often false charges against his government at a time when as shrewd an observer as Ernest Stern, a vice-president of the World Bank who visited Uganda in July, fully endorsed the government's economic policies and promised the bank would continue to provide substantial aid. The offer to farmers of still higher prices for coffee, tea, cocoa and tobacco was not the mark of a government intent upon destroying the population of the country's richest agricultural region. It was greatly to the credit of the main body of Baganda, as well as of the government, that in spite of the rebels' activities the economic life of the region prospered as it did. But the good news on the economic front was constantly overshadowed by security problems. Malcolm Rifkind, the newly-appointed British minister of state for African affairs, who also visited Uganda in July, voiced his country's concern about the numbers of people who were said to have fled from their homes as a result of the security forces activities against the rebels. The Australian and Canadian high commissioners made similar representations to the president and vice-president. All three were allowed to visit parts of Luwero District to let them see the nature of the problems the government was facing.

It could not pass unnoticed, too, that criticism of the government persisted with a degree of freedom rarely encountered in other African countries. The government's relations with the press were damaged in June, however, when Muwanga precipitately banned two vernacular newspapers which had been pursuing a particularly virulent campaign against the regime. On learning of his vice-president's action Obote immediately tried to intervene, arguing that legal proceedings for libel would have been the appropriate way to handle the case. The attorney-general thought that such a plan would have had little hope of success and Obote, accepting that no-one had been arrested, again demonstrated what may have been a misguided loyalty to those who professed to be his friends by deciding not to revoke Muwanga's decision.

There were still a dozen other newspapers that regularly carried accounts of killings, which they attributed, as they saw fit, to the security forces or to the rebels. The daily newspaper *Munno*, the organ of the Roman Catholic Church in Uganda and a constant critic of the government, reported on 24 May 1983 that men in army uniforms had dumped fifty bodies, many of them bound and with bullet wounds, in the village of Masuliita, north of Kampala. The report did not specify who the men were, but the use of the expression 'army uniforms', rather than the less emotive 'uniforms', pointed the way in which readers might look, even though it was well known that army and police uniforms were worn by scores of people who had no connection with the security forces. The Democratic Party, some of whose members had defected to the UPC, also continued to attack the government freely in parliament, openly accusing Obote of being unable to control the security forces and of being indifferent to the harassment and even the murder of his political opponents. The DP was later to maintain that it was prohibited from holding public meetings until October 1984, but there is no substance to that claim. Nevertheless, the fact that, since February, the party had persistently urged the government to seek a reconciliation with the wholly uncompromising rebel leadership might have provided some justification for Obote to take a stern line against it.

Introducing his budget for 1983–4, Obote said that the black market, which had grown to such serious proportions under Amin, was at last being brought under control. For the first time in ten years, he went on, people could obtain everyday commodities freely. He was not exaggerating. Food supplies were now reasonably plentiful in most areas, even including Karamoja, which had suffered so severely from famine in previous years. This was a tribute to the efforts of the government and to the support it had received from a large proportion of the population. It owed a lot, too, to Uganda's good fortune in escaping the drought which had sorely afflicted most of its neighbours.

Obote freely admitted that there was still a long way to go to make up the ground lost by his predecessors. The basic necessities of life might now be available and the vast majority of the people could grow enough food to meet their own needs, but anything beyond that was still outside the reach of all but a few. There was a particular problem in relation to salaried officials, whose incomes, even after the 50 per cent increase announced in the budget, bore little relation to the prices of goods in the shops. As the civil servants themselves were quick to point out, prices had been raised immediately by the shopkeepers to match the salary increases. A senior civil servant earning 6,000 shillings a month could buy with that sum only eight gallons of petrol or twenty bottles of beer. This meant that wage-earners or salaried personnel must have a second source of income – to the obvious detriment of their main employment – if they wished to buy anything more than the essentials of life. Farming was the most popular alternative, but corruption ran it a close second. Bribery had become, and remained, the only means of obtaining any form of permit or service from anyone in a position to exercise authority. To eradicate such a mentality would take far longer than had been needed to inculcate it.

The best way to achieve that desirable end was, without doubt, to restore the economy to the comfortable level it had reached during Obote's first presidency and to ensure an equitable distribution of wealth. It was reassuring, therefore, that the coffee growers continued to meet their target, and it was hoped that other farmers would be encouraged to follow their example. The British government had shown its confidence in the government's economic programme by providing substantial aid to help in the rehabilitation of cotton growing. With the greater availability of insecticides, together with new facilities for the repair and maintenance of farm machinery, it was hoped to bring production to something near the level at which it had stood before Amin seized power. Britain had also assisted in the restoration of the turbines at the Owen Falls Dam, Uganda's largest producer of electricity, and the USSR had promised credits of $5 million to build up the textile mill started with Soviet help in the 1960s, and to found a school for agricultural technicians. At the same time, although the rate of inflation remained desperately high, as a legacy of the Amin era, it was steadily brought down, year by year, during Obote's second term of office, in spite of the floating of the shilling. But the continuing demoralization of some of the intelligentsia, encouraged by the anti-government propaganda of Obote's critics, resulted in the decision of twenty-four out of fifty-three graduates from Makerere University's medical school in 1983 to seek their fortunes in other countries.

Every improvement seemed to be shadowed by reports of setbacks. In the Luwero District refugees were reluctant to leave the austerity, but relative security, of their camps to return to their former homes because of their fear of the rebels. It was an opposition MP, not a supporter of the government, who informed the national assembly in July that thirty people, including seventeen soldiers, had been killed by dissidents in the very centre of the district. A few days later, thirty-five passengers were killed and a similar number wounded when armed men, most of them in civilian clothes, attacked a bus in the same area. Even in Kampala, although the atmosphere had become more relaxed, a strong security presence had to be maintained, and the newspapers frequently carried reports of the discovery of the bodies of people who had been murdered. Rebels attacked four lorries near Kabaze village, forty miles south-east of Kampala, and when surrounded by troops in a forest near the capital refused to surrender. Twenty-three of them were killed. In August three UPC youth wing members were killed by gunmen at Bukasa near Kampala, and not far away a policeman was shot dead. Early in September, the bullet-riddled bodies of three men were found at a village seventy miles south-west of Kampala and a government official who had been travelling in a car with them was presumed to have been kidnapped. In October, a DP member of the national assembly, Africanus Sembatya, was shot dead at his home in Kampala by gunmen who stole £35 and a tape recorder. Whether this was the work of government supporters or whether the murderers had a grudge against the dead man, or whether they were simply robbers, or a combination of any of these, it was impossible to prove.

Not without justification, Obote claimed, in the course of an address to mark the twenty-first anniversary of independence, that the government could not be held responsible for the plight of the inhabitants of the Luwero District. It was not the government that had started the troubles there, nor had it resisted all attempts at rehabilitation. Indeed, every effort had been made, within the limits imposed by conditions in the area, to keep the peace. If it had not been for the actions of Museveni there would have been no reason why the people of Luwero should not have made a valuable contribution to the gradual restoration of the country's economy. The same might equally well have been said about the effect on the inhabitants of Kampala of the sporadic violence in and around the capital. Continuing with his address, Obote went on to invite both Lule and Binaisa to return to Uganda. His government had not sent them into exile, he insisted, and if they wished to return to make their views known to the people of Uganda they would not be prevented from doing so. His policy was one of reconciliation, not revenge. His opponents were unreceptive to his offer. The Democratic Party decided to boycott the elections to eight parliamentary seats which had fallen vacant, on the grounds that conditions were insufficiently secure for voting to take place. It was ironic, in the circumstances, that it was a local chairman of the UPC who, along with seven others, was killed by gunmen in Masaka District in the week preceding the elections for the only two seats which were contested.

In spite of these many distractions Obote felt it right to attend the Conference of Commonwealth Heads of State which was held in New Delhi in November 1983. He was deeply gratified by the reception given him and much was made of the measure of democracy his government had been able to restore in Uganda. He was particularly impressed by the British prime minister, Margaret Thatcher, for whom he developed both a deep respect and a lasting friendship which were in no way undermined by his subsequent disapproval of Mrs Thatcher's resistance to the imposition of sanctions upon South Africa. Obote always distinguished between differences of opinion over specific issues and underlying feelings of respect and friendship or of dislike and animosity.

In December 1983 Obote suffered a severe personal blow which was to have serious repercussions upon his government. By that time, fighting in Luwero District was virtually at an end, and although the refugees were still reluctant to leave the relative security of their camps the rebels had withdrawn westward and northward with a view to trying to renew their struggle elsewhere. This success on the part of the government's forces reflected the increasing efficiency of the army under its newly trained officers, and the greater discipline which, under their more professional leadership, could be enforced by Major-General Ojok. Several officers had been punished for the misbehaviour of troops under their command, and Ojok had ordered that any soldiers found loitering off duty in Kampala should be subjected to disciplinary proceedings. Now, pursuing his operations against the rebels, Ojok boarded a helicopter which had recently landed to refuel. The fuel was in some way faulty, and the aircraft crashed near Masindi, killing Ojok, Lieut.-Colonel Alfred Otoo, commander of the airforce, and seven others.

There was no suggestion of sabotage, but the loss to Obote was incalculable, because although General Tito Okello was in nominal overall command, Ojok had been running the army almost single-handedly at the higher levels. He had escaped from Amin's Uganda and had subsequently held almost daily conversations with Obote while the two had lived in exile in Dar es Salaam. He was utterly loyal to Obote's government, but above all he was an outstandingly able commander in an army which was woefully deficient in well-trained senior officers, and he had won and maintained the respect of all the soldiers, no matter to which ethnic group they belonged. To replace him was impossible. The new generation of officers up to the rank of major were a great improvement upon their immediate predecessors but they were too young and inexperienced to hold such high office. The most senior officers, most of them still former NCOs promoted to fill the vacancies created by the rapid expansion of the army in the closing stages of the campaign against Amin, lacked virtually every quality needed for the post. Many of this latter group nevertheless aspired to promotion, and their ambition contributed greatly to Obote's undoing. He was aware that Ojok had thought highly of a Langi officer, Brigadier Smith Opon Acak, but hesitated to make an appointment until the procedure appropriate to promotions of such importance had been followed.

That procedure was slow to unfold. The ministry of defence spent several months considering the claims of the three brigadiers in the army and of several colonels and lieutenant colonels. Finally it presented a shortlist to General Okello and asked him to submit two names to them from the list. Okello put forward the names of Brigadier Smith Opon Acak and of Brigadier Basilio Okello. The latter was the general's own choice, both as a fellow Acholi and also as belonging to the old guard of promoted NCOs, as was the general himself. He did not, however, present the curriculum vitae of either of the men as was required by the regulations governing promotions. After he had given an oral account of the two candidates, which was notable only for its incoherence, he said he had no preference. The defence council, which was ultimately responsible for making the appointment, had to have recourse to the written reports on the two men which had been presented at the time they had both been promoted to the rank of brigadier.

The report on Basilio Okello made it clear that he had never been qualified for senior commissioned rank. He was one of those who had taken advantage of the arrangements made in 1967 under which senior NCOs were permitted to take a short course leading to a commission, on the understanding that they would retire in the rank of captain. It had been an interim measure to make use of the experience of some senior NCOs pending the emergence of a new generation of qualified young officers, and Okello himself would normally have retired in 1972. Amin's coup, and the need for officers to lead the Ugandan forces in exile when they invaded Uganda, had given him a respite, and the rapid expansion of the UNLA during and following upon the pursuit of Amin had led to his promotion beyond what had originally been intended. His further promotion to brigadier had been approved only in the absence of other qualified candidates, and was made on the understanding that he would retire after a further two years' service. Opon, by contrast, appeared to have taken the courses needed for promotion, and consequently it was he who became chief of staff. This lengthy description of Basilio Okello's career is necessary to understand subsequent events.

Opon was not a popular choice among senior officers, all of whom suffered from disabilities similar to those of the unsuccessful candidate. Moreover, the delay in making the appointment only served to enhance the struggle for power within the senior ranks which the elderly General Tito Okello was incapable of keeping under control, even had he wished to do so. By the time Obote appointed Opon on the advice of the defence council feelings were running high, and his action was immediately condemned in some quarters. The disaffection was to be compounded when Opon proved to be an unsuitable man for the job. He was not one of the old guard of NCOs and his paper qualifications were good, but it was soon clear that he lacked the qualities of leadership needed for the post of chief of staff. When Obote was later confronted by the disloyalty of some of his senior officers Opon proved he was not the man to handle the situation. The loss of Ojok had left Obote with a great feeling of loneliness and some of his own fire and drive seemed to die with his chief of staff.

Meanwhile, Obote was finding his hopes of crushing the rebels in the vicinity of Kampala impossible to realise. Intent upon blackening the reputation of the government in the eyes of the international community, attacks were increasingly concentrated upon targets which would attract attention. In January 1984, a French doctor, three Swiss women and a number of Ugandans, all Red Cross workers, were captured while making their way to a refugee camp forty miles from the capital. Most of them were released almost at once and it was clear that the rebels merely wished to demonstrate that they were still active in spite of the government's counter measures. In the same way the shooting of three Swiss engineers and a British accountant in two separate incidents on the road from Kampala to Kazi, the home of the Victoria Nyanza Sailing Club, was primarily aimed at embarrassing the government while its representatives were taking part in a conference of aid donors in Paris. The accountant's car was subsequently discovered in the garage of a DP member of the national assembly and some of his other possessions were found in the member's house, although how they came to be there was not clear. As one government minister remarked, 'We were just beginning to get some favourable comments from abroad about progress in our economy and an improved, though still difficult, security situation. It takes only a few determined men with guns, choosing the right time and place, to undo what we have achieved.'

Later in the month a gang killed more than thirty women and children in Muduuma, a village twenty-five miles from Kampala, to coincide with visits to Uganda by The Most Revd. Robert Runcie, Archbishop of Canterbury, and Timothy Raison, the British minister for overseas development. It had been hoped that these visits would engender the sort of goodwill which might strengthen Uganda's appeal to the World Bank and to Britain for further aid. Instead, news of the massacre on the eve of the archbishop's departure from Britain led Uganda's high commissioner in London to seek an urgent audience with Runcie to assure him that strong representations had been made to Obote about the need to reassure the world that Uganda was not collapsing into anarchy. Nevertheless, the archbishop expressed his concern to the president when they met, and Obote was forced to admit that he still faced many problems, particularly in dealing with the thousands of refugees created by the rebel campaign in Luwero. But he insisted that things were improving, and that in spite of an acute shortage of qualified staff the government was doing whatever it could to encourage the people to return to their homes. That they were slow to respond was due not only to fear but also to the devastation of their land resulting from what had virtually amounted to a civil war.

The rebels opened their campaign to the north-west of their previous area of operations by attacking the prison and army and police barracks in Masindi. This region had hitherto been peaceful and prosperous. There had at no time been any suggestion of attempted genocide there by the government. Yet the rebels had no compunction about carrying the war into that part of the country in the full knowledge that fighting must bring suffering to the civilian population. A spokesman for the NRA unhesitatingly claimed that 178 soldiers, 27 police and 18 prison warders had been killed and that large quantities of arms and ammunition had been captured. Lacking the controlling hand of Ojok, the security forces responded swiftly and violently to the new provocation. Thousands of civilians were rounded up and it was said that some were shot.

Emerging from the anonymity in which he had previously sheltered, General Tito Okello attempted to give the lead formerly presented by his chief of staff and announced that considerable public discontent had been aroused by the behaviour of some army officers. The civilians, he said, were the masters and the soldiers were their servants. An undisciplined officer was a danger to the army. His sentiments, though sound, produced little effect. Two months later, after a rebel attack aimed at destroying a telecommunications centre, a small body of troops under the command of a junior officer was despatched to the scene of the attack near Namugongo, a village which was the home of a theological college and which had not witnessed any rebel activity for some time. The troops were ambushed and suffered a number of casualties. The rebels then withdrew, whereupon the soldiers took their revenge upon the villagers, killing a number of them, including the principal of the college, and then set fire to houses after pillaging them. A larger body of troops, sent to reinforce the advance guard, met the looters returning with their spoils and placed them under arrest. The soldiers were subsequently dismissed from the service, while the officer and two sergeants, after trial by a civilian court, were imprisoned. The government acted promptly, but this well-publicized act of terrorism by the army served to discredit Obote and helped to justify the claims of those who maintained that the security forces were not only incapable of maintaining order but were themselves the source of much of Uganda's suffering.

In spite of such setbacks, Obote was able to announce in his budget speech in June that Uganda had achieved a balance of payments surplus for the first time in ten years. This was a personal triumph for the president. As his own finance minister he was mainly responsible for this success. He had followed carefully the advice of the World Bank and he had relied heavily upon E. Kamuntu, an able economist who virtually controlled the day to day running of the ministry of finance. He also had considerable confidence in the civil servants in the ministry. But the decision as to which policies were to be pursued was his own, and in spite of the heavy demands from other quarters he had worked ceaselessly at the task of restoring the economy, frequently sleeping in his office after working late at night and returning to his task as soon as he awoke. His prodigious application to the work in hand was a characteristic which only those in regular contact with him could appreciate. He did not have any close associates, believing that democratic government meant working with the people elected to office rather than creating a circle of his own friends. In principle this was to be commended, but it frequently left him isolated when his decisions, however sound, proved unpopular because they placed heavy demands upon those affected by them.

One important result of Obote's strict regulation of the economy was that, in spite of the immorality which marked most business transactions in the country, there was little evidence of the large-scale corruption among senior government officials which was common in most parts of Africa. Because Obote worked so closely with the World Bank, virtually all aid was handled externally by bank officials who, having been informed of Uganda's requirements, made their own purchases on behalf of the government. Consequently, little money reached Uganda and opportunities for corruption were reduced. The charge that money obtained from the sale of coffee did not reach the growers is difficult either to prove or to disprove. The growers were certainly paid at whatever price had been agreed when they handed over their crop to the coffee marketing board and there was little evidence of discontent over those payments. If further proof be required that senior officials did not make untoward profits it might be deduced from the fact that many of them are now living in exile and are showing few signs of having access to vast sources of wealth.

The overall success of Obote's economic policies, reinforced by the news in August that the country's largest tea growers, the Mityana and Toro Company, had produced 50 percent more tea between April and June than in the corresponding period in 1983, was recognized in a statement in London by Cole Dodge, the Kampala representative of UNICEF. Although the world's press concentrated largely upon Uganda's security problems, he said, it must be borne in mind that they affected only about 10 per cent of the country's area. Not only was there now a favourable balance of payments but for the past two years there had been an annual growth rate of 5 per cent. His comments did not add up to an undiluted eulogy of what was happening in Uganda because he went on to point out a number of areas where, in his view, there was an urgent need for remedial action. Clean water supplies, he said, were inadequate, with five thousand pumps in need of repair. The infant mortality rate was one in ten, due at least in part to the lack of immunization facilities. In view of the years of devastation parts of Uganda had suffered these figures were not surprising. He did the government less than justice, however, when he suggested that primary education had been starved of the money it urgently required. He based this assumption on the fact that only 27 per cent of boys and 12.5 per cent of girls were completing primary school, compared with 95 per cent in Kenya and Tanzania. What he overlooked was the fact that the primary course was of seven years' duration, and that Obote had not then been in office for seven years. Consequently, the children who had entered school since he came to power had not yet completed their courses, and during Amin's time schools had been almost entirely neglected. Considerable money had been made available for both primary and secondary education since Obote's return to power because he himself had always been deeply conscious of their importance.

Once again, however, acts of terrorism in the neighbourhood of the capital began to cloud the scene after a period of relative quiet. Thirteen people were hacked to death by unknown assailants in two separate incidents in July 1984. A fortnight later, five people including two policemen, were shot dead when gunmen opened fire on a taxi fourteen miles from Kampala. In August, rebels blew up a power station, causing a five-day blackout in the capital and the surrounding region, and in September, Colonel Alexander Trentyef, a Soviet military attaché, was shot and wounded while travelling in his car. Two months later, the NRA claimed to have killed eight Korean and twenty Ugandan soldiers. The Koreans, along with a detachment of British soldiers, had taken responsibility for training the Ugandan army after the withdrawal of the commonwealth team. To demonstrate that the government was taking seriously the task of punishing members of the security forces who were guilty of gross misbehaviour, four soldiers were sentenced to death for the murder of a Kampala businessman and the rape of his daughter, and three policemen also received the death sentence for the murder of a man who died in police custody on the Sesse Islands. Not as an act of leniency, for he deeply deplored such brutality, Obote commuted all these sentences to life imprisonment because he loathed the death penalty.

He was less certain in his handling of the not so clearly defined world of sedition and subversion. Early in November a number of journalists working for three newspapers were detained. Drake Ssekkebe, editor of the English-language daily, the *Star*, and Sam Katwere, the chief sub-editor, were arrested without charge, although their paper was known to have called for an inquiry into the wealth of certain ministers. They were released in January 1985. Others had been accused of reporting that the chief justice had colluded with the police and the executive in an attempt to arrest all the leading members of the Democratic Party. Two journalists, Sam Kiwanuka and Francis Kanyeihamba, who worked for the *Pilot*, a newspaper which supported the Roman Catholic Church, were acquitted of 'false and malicious publication' but were immediately re-arrested. In similar fashion, Balaki Kirya, a former minister who had been arrested, was discharged by the high court but was also re-arrested. In Kirya's case Obote maintained that he may not have been guilty of the charges brought against him, but he was known to be a prominent member of the Ugandan Freedom Movement which had been responsible for many of the acts of terrorism in and around Kampala.

It was an unconvincing and unjustifiable argument, produced by a situation in which the security forces were unable to overcome by lawful means people who were committed to violence and who were, moreover, sheltered by a population which, partly from fear of the terrorists and partly from mistrust of the government, was not prepared to co-operate by denouncing them. British troops and police in Northern Ireland face the same problem, but arrest on suspicion alone is not an option open to a democratic government, however frustrating the alternative may be. The conflict in Obote's own mind between the need for decisive action and his deep-seated respect for the law was reflected in the case of Dr Yoweri Kyesimira. Kyesimira, a professor of economics at Makerere University and, like Kirya, a member of the UFM, was acquitted in March of a treason charge but was detained in custody in spite of the issue of a writ of habeas corpus by a high court judge which declared his continued detention illegal. The Law Society of Uganda said its members would refuse to handle political cases unless the judge's ruling was respected.

So, in spite of misgivings on the part of the government, Kyesimira was released.

While the inflation rate had dropped from 100 per cent in 1980 to something between 25 and 30 per cent by 1985, the failure to maintain law and order by legal means bedevilled any attempt by the government to make the progress needed to convince its less committed opponents that co-operation against the rebels would bring them the peaceful conditions which they earnestly desired. Although Museveni's forces had virtually abandoned Luwero, the region remained depopulated, with coffee bushes neglected and the inhabitants still afraid to quit the camps for fear of a rebel return. In the neighbourhood of Kampala there were frequent acts of terrorism by undercover rebel units. Nevertheless, it was announced in April that elections would be held in December. Obote was not unmindful of the criticisms levelled against him for his failure, whatever justification there may have been for it, to hold elections in the later years of his first presidency. He was concerned to observe the requirements of the constitution and he as anxious to demonstrate that, in spite of the claims of opposition groups, the UPC still had the support of the majority of the electorate, a state of affairs about which he had no doubt. Ssemogerere responded by flying to England to ask for British assistance to ensure that the elections were fairly conducted. It was an action which would have had Obote's support if it had not, because of Ssemogerere's unilateral request, carried with it the implication that the government was not equally concerned about the matter. Although Obote was unaware at the time, Ssemogerere's action later appeared to have been intended to bring Obote and his UPC into disrepute as part of a wider plan to encompass their overthrow.

The pressure on Obote was building up. Twenty-seven DP members of the national assembly walked out as he began his budget speech in June, in protest, they said, at the deaths of 'hundreds of thousands' of people since 1980. These figures were readily quoted by journalists who made no effort to verify them or even to try to establish who was guilty of whatever number of deaths had occurred. More seriously, Amnesty International claimed on 18 June that 'many thousands' of Ugandans had been tortured by the army since Obote took office. Obote responded by inviting Amnesty International to send delegates unconditionally to Uganda to see the situation for themselves, but his offer was not taken up. That the government had failed to maintain law and order over the preceding four and a half years there can be no doubt, and Obote admitted that some of the killings must be attributed to the security forces. He pointed out, however, that whenever such actions came to his attention he had instituted inquiries, and since the improved training of the officers had made discipline more readily enforceable, many soldiers who had been found guilty of atrocities had been severely punished. He had had no evidence that Museveni, in spite of the much-vaunted discipline of his rebel supporters, had acted in the same way. Moreover the Democratic Party itself had done nothing to ease the government's task. One of its spokesmen was later to claim that the party had co-operated fully with the rebels – although that was after Museveni had seized power and so may have been aimed at winning the approval of those in office. The DP did, however, play an important role in the overthrow of Obote's government by means of a military cup.

Three factions played their part. First, the Democratic Party leaders were determined to put an end to UPC rule but either had little confidence in their party's prospects of defeating its opponents in the elections due to be held at the end of 1985 or else genuinely believed it was unlikely that the elections would be free and fair. Their immediate aim, therefore, was to circulate propaganda critical of the government. One of their acts was to demand equal representation on the electoral commission appointed by Obote to oversee the forthcoming elections and to insist that the chairmanship of the commission should rotate between the two parties. When Obote refused, the DP claimed that the commission would inevitably be biased. Next, in the course of debates in the national assembly in the middle of the year, DP representatives who had previously denounced the activities of the UNLA on every possible occasion began to speak well of the army, reserving their criticisms for the UPC government.

The second faction came from within the UPC itself, where there were a few members of a radical group who had always been at odds with Obote's more moderate outlook and who feared they would not be named as candidates in the forthcoming elections. In their own interests they were prepared to betray their colleagues, and they made it their task to subvert the party from within. It is possible that Paulo Muwanga, vice-president and hitherto an apparently loyal supporter of the UPC, was in some way associated with these people, although his part in the plot, if he really had one, is unclear. He was certainly at odds with Obote over the payment demanded by the Tanzanian government for the part its troops had played in the overthrow of Amin and in maintaining order in Uganda. While Obote argued that the claim was excessive, Muwanga insisted that it was reasonable. This dispute led to a measure of estrangement between the president and the vice-president and the latter became concerned that his chief no longer trusted him.

The third group was led by Museveni, whose campaign in Luwero had petered out under pressure from government forces and whose troops had withdrawn westward to begin harassing parts of the Western Province. He now saw an opportunity to revive his flagging fortunes by co-operating with any other party which was opposing the government. He, too, had no desire to see early elections, but he was at one with the others in wishing to oust the UPC. He concluded that his most promising role was to make himself responsible for keeping up the campaign of terrorism in the vicinity of Kampala, in association with other, smaller, dissident groups which were supported by the DP and the renegade UPC members.

All these conspirators recognized they could achieve nothing without the support of the army. They therefore set out to subborn General Tito Okello and Brigadier Basilio Okello. The latter they flattered by claiming that he and not Opon should have been chief of staff, and by promising that that would be his role when a new government was in power. They were particularly anxious that he, rather than the inert General Tito Okello, should be in command of any operations to overthrow the government by force. Tito Okello's loyalty was undermined by the offer of full overall control of the army and of the purchase of military supplies.

The two Okellos were simple men, easily beguiled by smooth-tongued politicians. But the politicians themselves, although united in their hostility to Obote's government, did not necessarily trust, or work in close collusion with, each other. This was illustrated when the coup was launched while Museveni was away in Sweden, trying to acquire arms and other supplies to revive his dispirited forces. In mid-July, troops seized strategic buildings in the centre of Kampala and set up roadblocks where they held up civilians whom they robbed of jewellery and clothing. Tito Okello fled to Acholi and would not return to the capital. In a pastoral letter Cardinal Nsubuga, at one with the Democratic Party, urged Obote to postpone the elections until 'peace and tranquility had been restored'. Obote, unwilling to lay himself open once again to the charge of witholding elections, refused, and insisted that the registration of voters should start immediately. If the DP and the NRM (National Resistance Movement, the political wing of what Museveni now called his National Resistance Army) feared the ballot box, he did not.

Too late, Obote began to get an inkling of the plotting that had been going on. While working in his office at 1 a.m. he was informed by a close associate, Dr Opiote, that the army in Gulu was marching on Kampala under the leadership of Basilio Okello. Obote at once attempted to contact some of the senior army officers who should have been available in the vicinity of Kampala. None was there except Brigadier Opon, who was in no condition to help. Obote then tried to speak to the commander of the battalion stationed in Kampala, but was told he was away. The man who was temporarily in charge said he had been appointed personally by Paulo Muwanga and was answerable only to him. It was then that Obote's doubts about his vice-president's loyalty began to revive. The acting commander of the battalion went on to say that all the men under his command had fled. This proved to be incorrect, but Obote did not discover the deception until too late. The commander himself fled that same day, but the troops, under their more junior leaders, put up a staunch resistance to Okello's forces when they came to seize the capital.

Obote then tried unsuccessfully to get in touch with Muwanga. Convinced that the infrastructure of his government had been undermined, he next summoned such cabinet ministers as he could contact and told them he did not want bloodshed and so proposed to leave the country. His aim was to remove the main object of the mutineers' hatred from the scene and by so doing to reduce the tension which had built up. He was driven, without encountering any difficulty, through Jinja to the eastern frontier and to Kenya. One minister who tried to follow him was intercepted and arrested. The others went to ground and eventually made their escape to Tanzania.

Mrs Obote was already in Kenya, attending a women's conference. Two of their sons were also in Kenya, in boarding schools. Characteristically, Obote had refused the offer of places for the boys in government schools in Uganda when he returned there in 1980, because he feared that they would be usurping the places of other boys who needed the education. His eldest son he sent to a private school in Busoga and the youngest to a primary school in Kampala. When the coup took place the youngest boy was spending the night with the parents of a friend. Obote tried to contact them but was unable to do so. He assumed that they must be away from home and that they would soon learn what had happened and take precautions to protect the boy. That is what happened, although only belatedly. When Basilio Okello reached Kampala he learned of the whereabouts of Obote's son and immediately sent for the man who was caring for him. The man's wife took the boy and fled with him to Kenya. Her husband was imprisoned, but was soon released when it was discovered that he was an Acholi because it would have been bad propaganda for the conquerors to be seen to harm one of their own people. The eldest son was hidden by the headmaster of his school, and when troops arrived to search for him the headmaster said their prey had already fled. He then took the boy to Kampala and got in touch with Muwanga who, to his credit, enabled the boy to escape to Kenya.

The family was safe, but Obote was penniless. Never one to concern himself greatly about his personal needs, or to give any thought for his own future, he had made no provision for a situation such as the one in which he now found himself, in spite of his experiences at the hands of Amin. He could not afford to pay the school fees of any of his children, but generous friends in Nairobi came to his rescue. They agreed to look after his wife and family, but Obote was anxious to distance himself further from Uganda, both for his own safety and to avoid embarrassing his friends in Kenya or endangering his supporters in Uganda by appearing to be planning to return. He accepted the offer of his friend, Kenneth Kaunda, to provide a refuge for him in Zambia. There he made his way, an exile for a second time, to ponder on the fate of the country for which he cared so deeply.

Uganda's future looked bleak. Many of the younger officers in the army had demanded an explanation as to why they had been called upon to take part in a coup. The appointment of Opon as chief of staff, rather than Basilio Okello, may have provided adequate grounds for Okello himself to lead a mutiny, but it scarcely seemed to provide an adequate justification for overthrowing the government for younger men who had been better prepared for responsible positions in the armed forces. To allay their doubts, a rumour was circulated accusing Obote of having planned to massacre all the Acholi soldiers in the army. As proof of that assertion, it was argued that the Acholi had borne the brunt of the fighting against the rebels and had suffered the heaviest casualties. Since the Acholi were by far the largest contingent in the army their participation in the fighting was bound to be extensive and their casualties proportionately high, but they had never suffered from discrimination of the sort that was now claimed. The argument failed to impress the young officers. As to the plot against the government, they asked why it was known only to DP politicians and to a mere handful of UPC men. The plotters shifted their ground uneasily and it was not until some months later that they proferred what they claimed to be the true reason for their action.

The doubts of the young officers were strengthened by wrangles over the appointment of a cabinet. The Okellos were not happy to take subordinate places, and the DP leaders, together with the renegade UPC members, felt their grip on the situation was being loosened by the military. Museveni, taken by surprise by the timing of the coup, tried to salvage his future by sending messages from Sweden approving what had taken place, but rejecting any proposal that the Okellos should set up their own military government. The NRA, he insisted, must be represented equally with the UNLA on any governing body.

Museveni's fears were sharpened when Okello was appointed head of state and Paulo Muwanga became prime minister, more especially because Muwanga was still widely held to have been the agent of Obote throughout all that had taken place over the last six years. Museveni hurried back to East Africa, but not to Uganda because the situation there appeared to have developed beyond his control. His hopes of playing a part in shaping Uganda's future revived, however, when the Okellos quickly demonstrated their inability to cope with the administrative and organizational problems with which they were faced. The new government could not handle the purchase and export of coffee with sufficient expertise to ensure that the country's main source of income was protected. Nor did it have the widespread confidence of the population. UPC supporters remained loyal to their party although there was little they could do against the military strength of the UNLA. So the Okello's turned to Museveni, seeking his assistance, but as a prerequisite of his co-operation Museveni insisted that Muwanga be removed from office. This was agreed, and talks then began in Nairobi in August 1985. It was a measure of the Okellos' ineptitude, and of their distrust of their political allies, that they were willing to accede to Museveni's demands to the extent, not only of giving him a free hand in the west of Uganda, but also of handing over to him control of the UNLA forces in that area. Thus, suddenly, Museveni's position was transformed from one of weakness to potential strength.

To give time for that strength to build up, Museveni prolonged the talks for several months, meanwhile increasing his demands and threatening action against the government if the demands were not met. The Okellos soon recognized that they were in no position to refuse. Their army had begun to disintegrate under their incompetent leadership and was in no mood to challenge the growing power of Museveni. An agreement seemed to have been reached in December 1985, but it quickly collapsed and open military conflict broke out between Museveni's NRA and the Okellos' UNLA. The latter proved no match for the revived rebel forces, and Museveni entered Kampala in January 1986. Okello fled and Museveni took his place as head of state. Much capital has since been made of the immediate return to peace in and around Kampala as a result of Museveni's seizure of power. Not least, it has been taken as evidence of the discipline he had inculcated into his troops. But it had been supporters of Museveni, and allies of his cause, who had been the perpetrators of the terrorist acts which had troubled the capital and its neighbourhood for so long. It was not surprising those acts now ceased. Moreover, Museveni had given strict orders that the Baganda were to be wooed, not threatened. He needed their support if he were to have any claim to govern the country.

The east and the north could hope for no such gentle treatment. Those had been, and still were, the areas where support for Obote and the UPC was strongest. The retreating UNLA did not endear itself to the inhabitants of those regions, because of the acts of pillage it perpetrated. To Museveni's surprise, the UNLA put up no resistance to his pursuit, and his own forces quickly swept through the eastern districts and round to the north, while other elements of his army approached from Western Uganda with the same objective. It was now that the vaunted discipline of the NRA was put to the test. In what was deemed to be hostile country heavy-handed methods were widely employed. Sympathizers have suggested that the brutality displayed towards the people of Northern Uganda was either in response to attacks by remnants of Okello supporters or was the work of troops who were not really members of the NRA. Neither argument can stand up to even the most superficial scrutiny. Acholi civilians were grievously ill-treated before any attempt was made to muster the broken UNLA forces for a counter-attack, and civilians who had little sympathy for the Okellos, but who were prepared to defend their homes against the ravages of Museveni's troops, were rounded up and massacred, actions which Museveni himself commended on the score that he was dealing with rebels.

If claims can be made that Acholi was the stronghold of the Okellos and of UNLA, the same could not be said of Lango and Teso Districts. Yet there, too, acts of cruelty and vandalism were widespread. Excuses were made, particularly in Teso, that the actions were the work of Karamojong cattle raiders, and that the only role of the NRA was to take counter action and to protect the citizens of the afflicted areas. But the tactics employed by the raiders were quite unlike those of the unsophisticated Karamojong, and the protection afforded to the people of Teso by the NRA resembled closely the horror tactics attributed by Museveni's supporters to the UNLA in Luwero. Amnesty International, which had previously been prepared to give Museveni's troops the benefit of any doubt which may have existed, and had even commented in an earlier report upon their excellent discipline, now became critical of what was going on. In September 1992, one of its reports claimed that the NRA was behaving as if it was above the law.

Visitors to Uganda who have seen only Buganda and the south-west have been favourably impressed by the general absence of danger and disturbances, but the picture has been different in the east and north. Since most visitors go to Buganda, it is the situation they encounter there that is transmitted as representative of the whole country. By contrast, anyone who had visited Northern and Eastern Uganda, or even the south-west, at the height of the struggles in Luwero and of terrorist activity in and around Kampala, would have found a peaceful and prosperous country. But few observers did that. There is another important difference between the two situations. Obote's government was elected, whatever criticisms there may have been about the conduct of those elections, and he was preparing to hold new elections at the time of his overthrow. Museveni achieved power by military means. Moreover, Museveni's rebel campaign was initially launched with no support from the electorate and gained the backing only of those who had failed to dethrone Obote by political means. The resistance subsequently offered by the people of Acholi, Lango and Teso, was not rebellion against a lawful government but a fight against conquest. Meanwhile, the other inhabitants of the Eastern Province were reluctantly compelled to resign themselves to defeat.

The prospect of a return to democratic government is, as yet, uncertain. So far, genuine elections, as opposed to the limited, indirect selection of representatives who were not permitted to campaign on behalf of any party or political programme, have been firmly postponed. To date, too, military rule has shown few signs of restoring prosperity, nor is security uniformly guaranteed through the country. Museveni may, however, benefit from following the British pattern of using Buganda as a power base from which to extend his authority outwards. Some of the Bugandan politicians active during Obote's first presidency who eventually found themselves at odds with his government, men like Mayanja-Nkangi or Abu Mayanja, or who had all along been opposed to him, like Ssemogerere, have found a niche in the new government. But if Museveni is to profit from this situation there must be tangible advantages for the Baganda generally, as well as for the rest of the country. It might, indeed, be argued, as Museveni has done, that military rule is now the only instrument capable of dealing with the economic and moral collapse of the country, the only means to guarantee unity in a society which, having started out without any powerful cohesive force, has torn itself apart completely. If this is true, it is a tragic outcome for a people who have endured so much while living in a country so well endowed by nature, one of the few in Africa where a rich soil and an equable climate seem to offer the prospect of a solid if not spectacular prosperity for the whole population.

Chapter 12

Reprise

Was Obote the ogre he has so often been represented as having been? Certainly there were some British civil servants who saw him in that light before independence. During his first period in office most Baganda regarded him as the villain who at first threatened and then overthrew their kingdom, and there were some expatriates who looked upon the closing years of his first presidency as a time, if not of tyranny, at least of oppression. It was, however, Obote's second term as president which brought more widespread obloquy upon his head. Yet, responding to Amnesty International's condemnatory report in June 1985, Malcolm Rifkind, Britain's minister of state at the foreign office, was more cautious, commenting that there had undoubtedly been atrocities and abuse of power during the Obote years, but that to compare them unfavourably with the excesses of Idi Amin was unreasonable. It was not exactly an encomium, but it at least suggested that the more outlandish accusations levelled against Obote might be looked at more carefully.

That the high hopes many had entertained for the future of an independent Uganda were not realized is beyond doubt. Yet it might reasonably be argued that those hopes were based upon insecure foundations from the beginning. Unquestionably Uganda was one of the best endowed countries in Africa from the standpoint of climate and natural resources. But it suffered to an excessive degree from the bane of all African countries – ethnic diversity. It was not simply that the population consisted of a variety of ethnic groups. The problem, as in other countries, was that Britain's policy of indirect administration had emphasized the ethnic identity of each group at the expense of any loyalty to a central authority. But, uniquely in Uganda, one of those groups had become, through the accident of history and to some extent by design on the part of Britain, not only preponderant in size and population but also central geographically and economically to Britain's administrative policy in the region. For anyone to expect that group to settle comfortably into a position of mere equality with the rest of the country, or even worse, to a position of potential inferiority, was indeed optimistic.

The independence constitution, which established Buganda in a federal relationship with the rest of Uganda, created more problems than it set out to solve. The description of Uganda simply as an 'independent state' is adequate testimony to the inability of the constitution-makers to define their creation. Obote, it is true, accepted that constitution. He even hoped it would work. After all, he had faced up to the problem of the differences between Buganda and the rest of the country with a measure of understanding and tolerance which had not been greatly in evidence among other political figures at the time. He had established a working relationship and a measure of trust with the *Kabaka* of Buganda and as a result had achieved what seemed like an impossible rapprochement between the UPC and *Kabaka Yekka*. Nevertheless, the position of Buganda meant that Obote could never enjoy the role of unchallenged leader of his country, which gave so many other African heads of state a honeymoon period after the achievement of independence. If this was true of Obote it would have been even more so of any other aspiring leader in Uganda. Certainly a Democratic Party led by a Mugandan commoner could never have hoped to win widespread support in Buganda at that time, while the *kabaka* would have been unacceptable as anything more than a figurehead to the rest of the country.

The break between the UPC and *Kabaka Yekka*, although possibly unavoidable, was actually occasioned by Obote's insistence upon honouring the terms of the independence agreement by holding a referendum in the Lost Counties. After that, his political rivals found it easy to enlist the aid of some of the Bugandan leaders in a series of manoeuvres intended to engineer his overthrow. For Obote to survive he was forced into open confrontation with his opponents, and although he was victorious, and carried with him a majority of the population of Uganda, he was compelled to revise the constitution and so expose himself to a charge of acting autocratically. Any prospect of seeking electoral support for his action was rendered null and void by the challenge thrown out to the central government by the Bugandan *lukiiko*, a gage which any government intent upon maintaining its authority would have been bound to take up. That this resulted in a military clash was regretted by no-one more than Obote himself, but on the basis of the information at his disposal at the time, and in the light of the military machinations which had taken place in the preceding months, the action is at least understandable and was possibly unavoidable.

From that time, any sort of accord between the government and the Bugandan leadership was out of the question, and the ensuing state of emergency arising from attempts on the life of Obote delayed the prospect of elections in spite of the president's desire to go ahead with them. That the security forces were heavy-handed in maintaining law and order inside Buganda was deplored by those who suffered from their attentions, but was not wholly surprising. Yet, even in those adverse circumstances, Obote was determined to hold elections in 1971 and made preparations accordingly.

Throughout the whole period, and in spite of fluctuations on the world market, Obote contrived to keep the economy on a sound and expanding basis. Exports of coffee and cotton rose well beyond the levels achieved during the British Protectorate, and the restrictions imposed by international coffee agreements in the West were circumvented by arrangements to sell to the Eastern Bloc. Negotiations with a number of countries on either side of the iron curtain brought technical and financial assistance where it was most needed, and the impartiality with which those arrangements were made gave the lie to accusations of pro-communist sympathies on the part of the government. Although Obote had been interested in socialism before independence, and maintained his interest afterwards, he was never dogmatic in either his economic or political outlook. The manner in which his *Common Man's Charter* was criticized by both left and right, was an indication of the moderate line he was attempting to pursue. Moreover, the money accruing from his policies benefited education, and particularly the hitherto rather neglected secondary education, as well as the country's medical services, in a manner to be envied by other emergent nations.

Perhaps the clearest evidence of Obote's pragmatic approach to the problems he encountered was to be seen in his relations with the leaders of other African and commonwealth countries. He respected men of such divergent outlook as Presidents Nkrumah and Banda, while he held in deep respect President Nyerere of Tanzania and Prime Minister Sir Abubakar Tafawa Balewa of Nigeria, both men of wisdom and restraint. He enjoyed the friendship of Harold Wilson and Margaret Thatcher, and while disagreeing with the former over his policy towards Rhodesia and with the latter over the imposition of sanctions upon South Africa, he was prepared to acknowledge the difficulties they faced and to offer whatever assistance lay within his power to find a way forward. He recognized the shrewdness of Premier Chou En-lai and warmed to the enthusiasm of President Kennedy. In all his international contacts he admired those who were prepared to negotiate in order to reach a conclusion acceptable to all parties.

His overthrow by Amin could not be compared with the military coups in, for example, Ghana or Nigeria. Here was no professional officer corps intervening to rid the country of a tyrant or to put an end to consummate political corruption, however much some Baganda might, in retrospect, have wished to describe it in that way. A tiny group of men, threatened with discovery in the act of deflecting public funds into the wrong channels, decided to stage a coup to save themselves. Amin himself probably bore no animosity towards Obote and totally failed to foresee the consequences of his action. That he and his fellow conspirators were able to succeed was due, in the first instance, to the support of the private army Idi Amin had almost incidentally created for himself within the national army, to the skill with which defence minister Onama was able to deprive the rest of the army of leadership at the crucial moment, and to the delighted acquiescence of the Baganda who surrounded Kampala.

In exile Obote remained the key figure in the campaign to rid the contry of Amin. After the abortive attempt at an invasion in 1972, Nyerere's agreement with Amin meant that little could be done from Tanzania. However, Amin's misrule only served to enhance the happier memories of Obote's regime, even among many of those who had rejoiced to see him go. The fact was that there was no obvious alternative leader to whom the people of Uganda could turn, and most expected that if Amin were ever to go Obote would return to office. The intervention of David Owen, which led to the appointment of Yusufu Lule as President of Uganda after Amin's overthrow, was the result of a total misapprehension on the British foreign secretary's part. For most of the Baganda, Lule was acceptable not so much for his abilities as for the fact that he was a Muganda. His appointment held out the hope that the Baganda would be able to play the leading role in the country's affairs which they had always regarded as their rightful inheritance. The rest of the population looked to him with hope rather than with conviction. He seemed a decent man, and his record, in so far as they knew it, was unimpeachable. But he soon proved his inability to master the unhelpful political situation with which he had been presented. Godfrey Binaisa, although a much tougher politician, lacked the breadth of support needed to counter the hostility of his fellow Baganda, who regarded him as a renegade and who hated him for supplanting Lule.

Obote's return to Uganda was widely welcomed, but the delay occasioned by Owen proved to have had dangerous consequences. A year of failure to promote economic recovery, coupled with the disappointed hopes of the Baganda resulting from Lule's overthrow, meant, on the one hand, that corruption had become even more deeply seated and, on the other, that the Baganda's grievance against Obote had had time to fester all over again. The alliance of convenience between the Bugandan leadership and the once-hated Democratic Party was a measure of the hostility which had had time to build up in the wake of the unrealized hopes of a return to peace and prosperity. Thus, suspicions about the trustworthiness of the election held in December 1980 developed in fertile soil, and were strengthened by the idiosyncratic if not actually questionable conduct of Muwanga.

Even though Obote's victory was vigorously questioned by his opponents, all was not wholly lost. The Democratic Party did not pursue the court actions it had initiated to challenge some of the election results and seemed prepared to act as a constitutional opposition. The action which destroyed all hope of a peaceful outcome was Museveni's decision to launch a campaign of terrorism. He may well have believed that the elections had demonstrated the complete futility of relying upon any political party to act firmly and honourably. He might have drawn parallels with events in Ghana and Nigeria, where efforts to return to civilian rule after a military coup had proved unsuccessful because of the self-seeking or incompetence of the politicians. But such comparisons were unsound. No election-rigging could account for the complete failure of Museveni's party to attract support at the polling stations. Like Amin, he had only limited support within the army, and even that came from men whom he had himself recruited, mainly from his own ethnic group. Yet he was prepared to attack both military and civilian targets indiscriminately, to threaten coffee growers and even to urge foreign diplomats to leave the country for their own safety.

The great complaint about Obote's second presidency, and the one upon which the accusations of tyranny are mainly based, is that he failed to restore order, and that his security forces reacted with such cruelty and violence to the acts of terrorism perpetrated by the rebels that the sufferings endured by the population at large were greater than those to which they had been subjected by Amin. That the security forces were violent and undisciplined there can be no doubt. On Obote's behalf it can only be said that he inherited them from his predecessors and that they had been recruited haphazardly and too precipitately to help in the overthrow of Amin. Moreover, he introduced a scheme whereby unsuitable men were discharged and retrained for civilian life, and began to replace them with better educated persons. The officer corps, however, lacked the training and ability to control the men under their nominal command. Yet here again Obote acted, managing to get a commonwealth training team to try to instill order in their midst, after which there was some improvement, at least among the junior ranks of officers. At that stage he was able, for the first time, to launch a campaign of action against officers and other ranks charged with offences against civilians. It was an immense task, often frustrated by the anger of the soldiery at the apparent impunity with which the rebels attacked all and sundry, then sought refuge and anonymity among the civilian population of Buganda. Nor must it be forgotten that acts of violence and indiscriminate cruelty were not restricted to the security forces. The rebels themselves were not averse from using coercion when hatred of Obote proved inadequate to inspire civilians to give their support to the rebels' cause, but they never gave an opportunity to outside observers to view the areas said to be under their control.

What was very striking was that so much of the country remained peaceful during Obote's second term in office, and there were high hopes of a return to material prosperity. Even external critics of the security scene gave full credit to the economic recovery which gained momentum with each succeeding year, in spite of the troubles in some parts of the country. The suggestion that only military rule could revitalize a Ugandan population whose morale had been shattered by war and uncertainty seems ironical in view of the fact that it was unjustified and unjustifiable military action which, after the elections of December 1980, destroyed all immediate hope of a peaceful settlement and stirred up once again interneccine strife and endemic fear.

Obote's second term of office was not a time of triumph and he himself was far from being indifferent to the sufferings of the people he and his party were attempting to govern. His whole upbringing had taught him endurance, but above all it had taught him the virtue of discussion rather than violence. To see violence all around, and to have to rely on force to try to contain it, was foreign to his entire concept of government. He had never been more than superficially attracted by the pan-African dreams of Nkrumah and others. Uganda had seemed to him an adequate unit for administrative purposes, and he inherited a workable administrative structure and a sound economy, both of which by his nature, he preferred to adapt slowly to the needs of his people rather than imposing some ideological conceit of his own creation or borrowed from others. It could be claimed that by retaining both an economy and a system of government laid down by Britain, Obote perpetuated an alien lifestyle inappropriate to the needs of an African country and at odds with the thinking of the masses of the people. While this may be true in so far as the government of Buganda was concerned, it could not apply to Buganda's economy which, more than in any other part of the country, had responded eagerly to the lead given by Britain.

Outside the kingdom, too, it is easy to underestimate the change which was unobtrusively taking place in the outlook of the people in general. While neither British administration nor Obote's government had changed the fundamental pattern of daily life in the villages there had been a change in people's aspirations. Education for the children was a widespread concern, with the consequent need for money to pay for it. This had already led to greater mobility among the male population in particular as the men sought employment, even if only of a temporary character, in other parts of the country, and from that sprang a deeper understanding of the world outside the villages. Education, too, brought new hopes of, and opportunities for, alternative types of employment. At the same time, participation in elections to district councils and more recently to the national assembly, although it may not initially have opened people's minds to wider issues, offered them new channels through which to express themselves without destroying a sense of responsibility to traditional institutions of family and clan. Above all, the potential leaders of the future had, like Obote himself, grown up in the traditions of their families while absorbing and assimilating the new ideas introduced by the colonial power. For Obote to have ignored these developments would have been disastrous. Uganda's way ahead, like that of the other former colonial dependencies, was already a mixture of old and new and could not readily be changed.

Obote's aim was a united Uganda, and he was prepared to make many concessions to achieve it. After a promising start, he ultimately failed to achieve that objective for reasons which would have severely taxed the abilities of any other post-independence leader. He had, indeed, an astonishing measure of success, particularly in the economic sphere, and Uganda's partial descent into civil strife was due, not to tyranny on Obote's part, but to the complex composition of the country and to those, some of them sincere, some self-seeking, who were prepared to use force, or to benefit from the use of force by others, to promote local or individual interests to the detriment of a united country.

That Obote made mistakes there is no doubt, especially in his assessment of character. His only justification was that without trust government was impossible. If he had possessed the personality of Nkrumah would he have had greater hope of success? Nkrumah had traditionalists to deal with just as Obote had, and for a time he triumphed over them. But the traditionalists in Ghana had neither the geographically central position which the Baganda enjoyed nor their special historical relationship with the colonial power which set Buganda so firmly apart from the rest of the country. And Nkrumah's dominating character, which endeared him to the people of Ghana when he challenged their British overlords, became oppressive after independence when local identities and local privileges felt stifled by the unifying power of the state. In so many ways Obote's more accommodating, less assertive manner was better suited to mollify the prickly self awareness of the country's different communities, while his commitment to unity meant that the concept of a united Uganda would not be lost sight of.

Faced by equally powerful divisive forces both of history and religion the people of Nigeria have also suffered the disastrous effects of civil war and have been subjected to long periods of military rule, although not of the tyrannical sort imposed by Amin upon Uganda. They, too, experimented with a federal constitution, albeit of a less complicated nature than that with which Uganda began its career of independence. And they, too, have yet to find a practical means of reintroducing a civilian government strong enough to contain the conflicting elements within their society and to create a unified state.

Obote himself was often slow to act because he found important decisions hard to take. But when he reached a decision he did so in the light of what he believed to be the best information available to him, and he accepted responsibility for the consequences. His attempt to insist that all significant business should be discussed by the full cabinet before any decision was taken about the policy to be adopted had to be modified when the sheer weight of government business threatened to hold up essential action. This meant he was not always aware in advance of what was to be done in his name and in the name of his government. This was certainly true in the case of the excesses of the security forces both in action and in their treatment of prisoners. Yet when misdeeds were brought to his attention he tried to rectify them and to punish the offenders. Where he was most open to criticism, however, was in his failure to dismiss the ministers or the senior military men ultimately responsible to him for what had gone wrong. Too often they were given the benefit of the doubt. Not one of his ministers was dropped from the cabinet throughout the whole of his second presidency, which betokens a measure of trust his critics might, if kindly disposed, attribute to inertia but would be more inclined to describe as irresponsible.

It should not be forgotten that talent was not so plentiful that it would have been easy to find replacements for any who were demoted. Obote had to work without the support which could have been supplied by the hundreds of educated people who had died at the hands of Amin and his followers or who had fled the country and were unwilling to abandon the security which some of them had found elsewhere to return to an uncertain future in Uganda. Nevertheless, when he became president for the second time Obote was convinced that even a devastated country which, in spite of everything, had experienced a population explosion beyond the resources of most other African countries to sustain, could still recover if the people were prepared to talk to each other and work together. He persisted in that conviction despite the many difficulties he encountered, and he went into exile for the second time, firmly believing in the virtues of pragmatic discussion and in the importance of sounding out the opinions of the electorate.

He still reads widely, as he always tried to do even when the pressure of responsibility was at its height. He is fascinated most of all by the works of Shakespeare, and he is moved to admiration by the poet's wisdom as much as by the astonishing range of subject matter to be found in his plays. The Bible is also a favourite, with the Gospels his first choice, although he has a profound admiration for St Paul. Political autobiography he finds engrossing, but he reads almost anything that comes his way, including books on geography, which at Makerere he had found less than appealing, and also biology, which he sees as the key to many of Africa's problems. And he continues to hope for the return of peace and prosperity to Uganda.

Notes

1 Kabaka of Buganda (Sir Edward Mutesa) (1967) *Desecration of my Kingdom*, p. 160, London: Constable.
2 G. S. K. Ibingira (1973) *The Forging of an African Nation*, pp. 200–9, New York: Viking Press, and Kampala: Uganda Publishing house.
3 Kabaka of Buganda (Sir Edward Mutesa) (1967) *Desecration of my Kingdom*, passim.
4 Harold Macmillan (1973) *At the End of the Day, 1961–1963*, pp. 292–3, London, Basingstoke: Macmillan.
5 D. Wadada Nabudere (1980) *Imperialism and Revolution in Uganda*, p. 260, London: Onyx Press, and Dar es Salaam: Tanganyika Publishing House.
6 Kabaka of Buganda (Sir Edward Mutesa) (1967) *Desecration of my Kingdom*, pp. 183–4.
7 Akiiki B. Mujaju (1987), 'The Gold Allegations and Political Developments in Uganda', *African Affairs*, 345, October 1987, pp. 479–504.
8 Kabaka of Buganda (Sir Edward Mutesa) (1967) *Desecration of my Kingdom*, p. 183.
9 Harold Wilson (1971) *The Labour Government, 1964–1979: a personal record*, pp. 276–87, London: Weidenfeld & Nicolson and Michael Joseph.
10 G. S. K. Ibingira (1973) *The Forging of an African Nation*, p. 289.
11 Kabaka of Buganda (Sir Edward Mutesa) (1967) *Desecration of my Kingdom*, p. 174.
12 ibid., pp. 594–8.
13 *Le Monde*, 5 August 1969.
14 Mahmood Mamdani (1976) *Politics and Class Formation in Uganda*, pp. 266–81, London: Heinemann.
15 Gerald Murphy (1984) *Copper Mandarin*, pp. 108–9, London, New York, Regency Press.
16 *The Times*, 19 May 1971.
17 Brian Tetley in the *Observer*, 14 March 1971.
18 *The Times*, 9 June 1971.
19 *The Times*, 26 August 1971.
20 David Owen (1991) *Time to Declare*, p. 274, London: Michael Joseph.
21 Cherry Gertzel (1980) 'Uganda after Amin: the continuing search for leadership and control', *African Affairs*, 317, October 1980, pp. 461–89.
22 Bruce Loudon in the *Daily Telegraph*, 19 July 1979.
23 ibid.
24 Cherry Gertzel (1980) 'Uganda after Amin: the continuing search for leadership and control', *African Affairs*, 317, October 1980, p. 476.

25 ibid., pp. 478–81.
26 *The Times*, 15 November 1979.
27 *The Times*, 22 December 1981.
28 *The Times*, 25 February 1982.
29 *Guardian*, 17 March 1982.
30 *The Times*, 19 March 1982.
31 *The Times*, 8 July 1982.
32 *The Times*, 12 July 1982.
33 *The Times*, 9 & 16 October 1982.
34 *The Times*, 5 March 1983.

Index